WITHDRAWN
UTSA Libraries

Planning the Post-Industrial City

"I may be a tad early, but my instinct is the future is coming back."

Drawing by Wm. Hamilton; © 1979 The New Yorker Magazine, Inc.

Planning the Post-Industrial City

By Harvey S. Perloff

Planners Press
American Planning Association
Washington, D.C.   Chicago, Illinois

Planners Press, Chicago 60637

©1980 by the American Planning Association.
All rights reserved. ISBN 0-918286-21-2

Library of Congress Catalog Card Number 80-67753

To Mimi, Jeff, and Gregg
Key to my past, present, and future.

Table Of Contents

Acknowledgments xi

PART 1.   MAJOR CHARACTERISTICS OF CURRENT PLANNING PRACTICE

Chapter 1   Introduction 3

Chapter 2   Planning in Los Angeles: Maintaining the Single-Family Neighborhood 21

Chapter 3   Planning in San Francisco: A Focus on Preservation 35

Chapter 4   Planning in Boston: The Economic Development Game 43

Chapter 5   Planning in Cleveland: A Unique Social Concern 53

Chapter 6   Planning in Phoenix: Land-Use Basics 65

Chapter 7   Planning in the Atlanta Region: A Serious Attempt at Alternatives 73

Chapter 8   Lessons to be Drawn from a Review of Current Planning 81

PART 2. PRINCIPLES OF TIME-CONSCIOUS PLANNING

Chapter 9   Recent Progress in Theory and Practice 91

Chapter 10   Contributing to Societal Learning 95

Chapter 11   The Use of Images of the Future 101

Chapter 12   The Need to Develop Knowledge for Action 107

Chapter 13   Determining the Appropriate Sources of Knowledge and Political Power 111

PART 3. THE PAST COMPONENT OF THE FUTURE

Chapter 14   The Future as Containing Elements of the Past, Present, and Future 119

Chapter 15   Inheritance as an Aspect of Planning 123

Chapter 16   The Inheritance Component: Asset Accounting 133

Chapter 17   Governmental Decisions on Capital Maintenance and New Construction 145

PART 4. THE PRESENT COMPONENT OF THE FUTURE

Chapter 18   The Emerging Planning Paradigm 157

Chapter 19   Information Needed for Time-Oriented Planning 163

PART 5. THE FUTURE ASPECTS OF THE FUTURE

Chapter 20   Reaching for Future Possibilities 181

Chapter 21   Approaches to Forecasting in Time-Conscious Planning 189

Chapter 22   Forecasting Accuracy 199

Chapter 23   The Time Horizon in Forecasting 207

PART 6. BOLSTERING THE PLANNING PROCESS

Chapter 24   Introduction to Planning-Process Considerations ... 215

Chapter 25   The Definition and Establishment of Goals 219

Chapter 26   Development of "Strategies-and-Policies" General Plans 233

Chapter 27   The Art of Creating Policies, Plans, and Programs .. 243

Chapter 28   Requirements of Implementation: Working with Many Actors 253

Chapter 29   Implementation: Organization of Planning and the Recruitment and Education of Planners 263

Chapter 30   Summing Up 271

References 299

Index 319

Acknowledgements

This book has been six years in the making.

Contacts with several city planning operations across the country made me aware of the fact that urban planning was caught in an uncomfortable and largely ineffectual transitional stage. The traditional physical master plan approach (with much of the planning dependent on land-use designations and zoning) was being gradually abandoned as its shortcomings were increasingly publicized, but this was being done reluctantly because of the obvious value of some aspects of the approach and because it was an old, well-understood friend. The policies general plan approach (which emphasizes proposals of strategies and policies over a range of matters with which city planning is concerned) was evolving in different cities in a variety of forms, with few agreed upon principles. In this transitional stage, the long-range concerns, which were dominant in the physical master plan approach, were not always being attended to, since the newer policies planning approach is drawn to more immediate, transient matters. But in the newer approach, planning was not yet equipped to deal with the short-range issues either. The nonphysical concerns (social, economic, fiscal, administrative) were beginning to be addressed more seriously than in the past, but in quite idiosyncratic fashion. Thus, there was much confusion.

When I began to realize that city planning was going through an important experimental phase and that there was much to be learned from what was going on, I set out to record the lessons that could be learned.

I organized a seminar within the planning program at UCLA (University of California at Los Angeles) on approaches to the future in urban planning where the issues of a new paradigm for urban planning (to use Thomas Kuhn's term for a conceptual framework within which research or action is carried out) could be addressed in depth. Over the six-year period, the strengths and weaknesses of actual planning practices were closely observed. Attention was given to the planning problems involved in the transformation through which American cities were passing towards a postindustrial society (together with cities in other economically advanced countries) and to the issues involved in dealing with the long-run future. The students brought many fresh insights to the task and often challenged certain of my hypotheses successfully.

In addition, several of my students worked with me as research assistants outside of the classroom, and I owe a great deal to them. Tim Regan provided substantial materials on current planning practice and did a very thoughtful job of helping me to edit the final version of this volume. Joseph Beaton provided excellent editorial assistance in an earlier version of the book, helpfully pointing to some gaps in information or logic. Others provided valuable "raw materials" for various subjects covered in the study: Frank Klett on planning documents in several of the cities, on population projections, and on Delphi (a case study of the use of the Delphi technique in the California Department of Transportation); Robert Kraushaar on futures literature and on asset management practices in Los Angeles; Diodoro Acosta on some administrative issues; Cindy Felice on time horizons in various planning operations; Lillian Barros on asset accounting; Lee Lashway and Leif Regvall on planning practice in several cities; and Jennifer Spiegel on capital budgeting.

I received a grant from the Charles F. Kettering Foundation to cover some of the cost of research assistance. The foundation also sponsored a review session of an earlier version of the book at the Academy of Contemporary Problems in Columbus, Ohio, in April 1979. I am very grateful to James Kunde, then director of the urban affairs program of the Charles F. Kettering Foundation, for his generous support of the study. The book owes a great deal to his imaginative support. I received extremely valuable suggestions from those who attended the review session which provided the base for a substantial revision of the book. I want to thank those who took part (none of whom is in the slightest degree to blame for the shortcomings that remain in the book): Edmund Bacon, vice president, Mondev International, Ltd.; Richard Damm, chief, governor's office of planning and research, state of California (who provided a thoughtful and detailed written review of the manuscript); Councilman Sidney Gardner of Hartford, Connecticut; Denton U. Kent, executive director, Columbia Region Association of Governments, Portland,

Oregon; Norman Krumholz, then director, Cleveland City Planning Commission; John P. Robin, professor of public affairs, University of Pittsburgh; Jerrold R. Voss, chairman, Department of City and Regional Planning, Ohio State University. Also I wish to thank from the Academy for Contemporary Problems, Herrington J. Bryce, James G. Coke, Patrick J. Henry, Kenneth D. Rainey, Gail G. Schwartz, and Ralph R. Widner (Widner not only served as a gracious host, but provided many valuable insights on how the book might be improved); from the Charles F. Kettering Foundation, Dan Berry, James E. Kunde, and James L. Shanahan. Berry, Shanahan, and Bryce provided written follow-up suggestions.

Some of the most valuable suggestions were received from individuals associated with the APA—Israel Stollman, Michael J. Meshenberg, and Frank So. So gave me a detailed commentary on an earlier version of my book which substantially influenced the revised version.

It seemed important to relate what was happening in American city planning to developments in urban planning in other economically advanced parts of the world, and the Ford Foundation provided financial assistance for visits to a number of European countries and to Japan during a sabbatical year. During these visits, I not only had a close look at the urban planning underway, but I could visit and spend time with European and Japanese scholars concerned with planning issues close to those I was pursuing. A number of these scholars decided to launch planning studies parallel to mine, including Peter Hall of Great Britain, Leo H. Klaassen of the Netherlands, Gabriele Scimemi of Italy, Arie Shachar of Israel, and Hidehiko Sazanami of Japan. The study by Peter Hall is complete; the others are in various stages of preparation. I received extremely valuable suggestions on my work from this very able group.

Finally, I received thoughtful comments from Wayne F. Anderson, executive director, Advisory Commission on Intergovernmental Relations Washington, D.C., and from John Friedmann, my inventive colleague at UCLA. My special thanks are due to the various planning directors (and former planning directors) and members of planning staffs who both provided information and reviewed the chapters on their cities and made many suggestions. This group includes Calvin Hamilton, Hethie Parmesano, Jon Perica, and Glenn Johnson of Los Angeles; Allan Jacobs of San Francisco; Alexander Ganz of Boston; Norman Krumholz of Cleveland; Thomas H. Roberts and Paul Kelman of Altanta; and John W. Beatty and Richard F. Counts of Phoenix. A disclaimer of responsibility for anything that appears in the book on the part of this group is particularly important since in two cases there was substantial disagreement with my interpretation of what was going on in the given city.

The description of planning practice in various cities (presented in Part 1 of this volume) covers the situation during the 1970s. While changes in planning in these cities by the time of publication can be anticipated, the lessons to be learned from the experience of the 1970s should remain pertinent.

Thanks are also due to Jean King and Diane Baldwin, who typed the various versions of the volume with intelligence and good humor; to Roxie Harris, a proficient proofreader; and to Sylvia Lewis and Sandra Schroeder, who prepared the manuscript for publication.

My wife, Mimi, was a close companion throughout giving me wise advice and sound editorial judgment.

Harvey S. Perloff
University of California at
Los Angeles

PART 1
MAJOR CHARACTERISTICS OF CURRENT PLANNING PRACTICE

Chapter 1
Introduction

American cities face enormous problems, and their difficulties seem to be intensifying. It does not help to realize that they are sharing such problems with cities throughout the industrialized world and, to some extent, with urban communities in developing countries as well. The future seems uncertain and threatening. It is not surprising then that urban planning, which evolved as a mechanism for coping with urban problems and creating guidelines for the future, has increasingly come under questioning from the outside and under even more intensive questioning from within the planning profession itself.

The questions being raised are basic and far-reaching:

● Should urban planning concentrate on the pressing immediate problems or be more concerned with the long-run issues?

● Should it function mainly as a *technical* operation or as a *political* set of activities? Should it emphasize research or political action?

● Should its approach be largely *normative*, seeking to define and seek a better future? Or should it emphasize the *positive* aspects, such as empirically detailed policy analyses to meet the decision needs of the mayor and city council?

● Should it emphasize the traditional physical issues, mainly land use, housing, and environment? Or should it encompass the broad range of urban issues, including those with a social, economic, and fiscal dimension?

● Is a single agency, such as a city planning department and commission, responsible for urban planning? Or is it a given set of activities of municipal government as a whole?

The very form of the questions being raised, and their basic nature, reflect the uncertain status of urban planning in the United States, as well as its special history. Much of the content and style of urban planning today reflects *departures from* unsuccessful practices in the past—particularly reliance on a relatively rigid physical master plan to guide urban development and a largely intuitive and centralized approach to its creation—rather than *movement toward* any agreed upon new principles or practices. In part, this is a reasonable pulling away from old paradigms[1] suggesting a sensible instinct for experimentation. However, it also reflects inadequate learning from past experience, a lag in practicing concepts that have already been well developed in theory, as well as an inadequate effort to create the new paradigms that hold promise for the future.

The most striking feature of this rejection-of-the-past phenomenon is the fact that, while urban planning was mainly created to guide urban development into the future, there is presently relatively little future in planning. This explains why there should be an issue today about concentrating on immediate problems *versus* concern with the long-range future. Something important was lost in learning to come to grips with issues of immediate political concern. The other issues mentioned earlier, which create so much uncertainty in the present practice of urban planning, similarly are the result of an unresolved development of urban planning activities. A glance at the history of city planning and at some general tendencies of humankind is suggestive in learning how this came about.

SOME LEADS FROM HISTORY

Throughout history, people have regarded the future with both fear and hope. They have sought continuity and stability while at the same time wanting change or something better. People may differ in the amounts of each they seek and may do so in a conservative or a liberal posture, but they are still subject to conflicting emotions (Marris, 1974). This dichotomy has had a significant impact on activities relating specifically to the future.

Individuals learned early that they would have to join with others in trying to cope with an uncertain future, and planning became one of the instrumen-

[1]Thomas S. Kuhn's book (1964) popularized this term to describe frameworks within which research—or other activities—are carried out. This concept will be discussed further in Chapter 10.

talities for collectively addressing the future. When people began to build and live in cities, city planning evolved as a tool for stamping a desired urban form on the landscape as the general context for urban living patterns. Throughout most of recorded history, the desired forms were those of the ruler or ruling class and were based on political, military, and economic considerations. In more democratic times, hopes associated with planning as a mechanism for achieving a better future have been tempered by fears associated with controls on the freedom of individual action. Thus the ambivalence about the future itself was combined with uncertainty about the planning instrumentality. This compounded ambivalence has colored everything associated with urban planning.

The modern city planning movement in the United States came into being at the turn of the 20th century. In the early decades, planning had a very forceful, if totally static, relationship to the future. The early leaders of the city planning movement, who came largely from the fields of architecture, landscape architecture, and engineering, were principally concerned with the design and appearance of American cities. These planners were the direct heirs of the leaders of the colonial period who had sought to build American cities along lines that would provide order, beauty, and pride in community. They were the successors of William Penn, Thomas Jefferson, and the others who had brought the concepts of city planning to the American shores. They were the heirs of a city planning tradition going back thousands of years to the great periods of Egyptian, Greek, and Roman building. Consequently, it is not surprising that the patrons of early 20th-century plans would have been the most prominent leaders of the business community.

These early planners and their backers were confronting cities that were growing at a fantastically rapid pace and were deeply disturbed by the haphazard manner in which this growth was taking place. They bemoaned the problems of a jumbled pattern of land use which provided practically no open space or land for recreation. Traffic was rapidly becoming a nightmare. Abominable crowding was found in the poorer sections of the cities, and disease was a serious problem. There was little beauty anywhere. These planners hoped to introduce order and amenity and, in the process, to increase property values.

The major plans of the early decades of the 20th century projected grand designs for city redevelopment and growth. There seemed to be a particular concern for boulevards, roadways, parks, open space, lakes and river fronts, and public structures and plazas along with some controls on building. These plans, soon to be called *master plans,* were intended to guide the future development of the cities and to provide end states that would be satisfying to residents and conducive to industrial and commercial expansion.

The tone and the aspirations of this early strategy has endowed urban planning with special characteristics. This feeling was best expressed by Daniel Burnham, whose plan for Chicago was probably the outstanding example of this period, when he said:

> Make no little plans, they have no magic to stir men's blood and probably themselves will not be realized. Make big plans; aim high in hope and work, remembering that a noble, logical diagram once recorded will never die (Hines, 1974: xvii; xxiii; 401, footnote 8).

Coming as they did from the design professions and acceding to the influences of business sponsors, these early planners gave little thought to the public regulation of land use as an aid in preventing blight and achieving development goals. Public controls were of concern only to those directly involved with the problems that unregulated growth precipitates. As Mel Scott (1971: 75) points out in his comprehensive history of the city planning movement:

> The steps taken by cities to restrict the uses of private property came almost exclusively in response to the demands of housing reformers and municipal fire and health departments.

The achievements of the far more advanced European city planning, particularly in cities such as Frankfurt, were greatly admired by American planners. The Americans were, however, far from ready to follow the European lead in proposing control of future growth through municipal ownership of land around the city.

There were periods in the early part of the century when the city planners and social reformers joined forces to press for urgently needed urban improvements and to generate a greater concern for the people who lived in the cities. Unfortunately, most of these coalitions soon dissolved, leaving city planning as an endeavor with a predominantly physical orientation.

Among those planner-reformer coalitions that did persevere, *zoning* became a positive area of concentration, beginning around the time of World War I. Only gradually were public controls on development accepted as a component of urban planning. Public regulation of building and land use did not become commonplace until the trauma of the Great Depression of the 1930s.

The images and the language of this early period of American urban planning were oriented toward the future—probably more so than at any time since. The purpose of planning was to imprint a consciously designed physical image on the future. The image was invariably the **present** translated into a more orderly and beautiful picture of the future. The master plan was appropriately named as it was to provide a physical framework for the entire developing urban plant. Through the plan, one could readily visualize the future city with its broad avenues, generous open space and waterfronts, beautiful buildings and plazas, and decent homes for all. However, little, if any, thought was given to what the economy of the future might require or to the impact of technology. Planners failed to consider the possibility of changing lifestyles—what people would want and could actually afford.

Whether more than a small group of individuals could have been greatly moved by the projection of an orderly design for city growth or a future picture of grand public places is doubtful. Neither could one expect the average urbanite to overlook the implications of the close tie of the city planning effort to the elite commerce clubs and other business sponsors of the proposed master plans. With the benefit of hindsight, one can understand why only very limited elements of these plans were ever carried out and why city planning was essentially peripheral to the major forces and events of the day.

Still, the long-run future had reality for early planners. They wanted to create something totally satisfying and to guide city development along predetermined lines. This thrust toward the future was soon to be minimized as the nation was caught up in more overriding concerns—first with the Great Depression and then with three wars.

The extended depression of the 30s was to have a profound effect on all thinking about collective action, including city planning. Economic and social concerns came to the fore. The building of houses, roads, and other capital items began to be related to the provision of jobs and incomes for those in need and to the phases of the business cycle. The terrible housing conditions of the poorer families were increasingly viewed as of major public concern and were to be overcome by programs of public housing and slum clearance. The federal government needed to take a leadership role to help the cities overcome the dire social and economic problems they were facing.

City planning agencies were ill equipped to cope with the newer social concerns and had neither concepts, methods, nor the personnel to make much of a contribution. The planners could and did collect data about economic and social conditions in their communities. They developed public works programs which were at times related to the long-range city plan. Many planning agencies were forced to curtail their activities while others were abolished entirely because of the fiscal difficulties of city governments. In this atmosphere, preoccupation with the more pressing problems was inevitable. Few long-range city plans, created in and for a different set of conditions, provided the kind of framework that could have permitted planning agencies to constructively attack such depression-related problems. Contingency planning was not part of the planning repertoire.

Conditions during World War II brought even greater stress on the more immediate problems of housing, transportation, civil defense, and the urban issues that related to the war effort. The long-range planning of the war period was limited largely to postwar planning. Much of this work focused on the kinds of problems that had dominated the 30s—including concerns about full employment, social security, slum clearance, and the provision of better housing.

After World War II, federal leadership became more evident in urban development. This was particularly so in the tremendous economic and urban growth that followed World War II and the Korean conflict. The dominant features were the government programs of mortgage insurance, highway building, and grants for public facilities that fostered the rapid expansion of the suburbs. All this hectic federal activity was carried out without any national planning. The federal government's planning arm, the National Resources Planning Board, born during the depression, had been abolished by Congress in 1943. The form and character of urban development throughout the country were strongly impacted by the federal programs, but no mechanisms existed to guide development or even to monitor the impacts. The subsequent decline of many central cities seemed to come as a surprise to many federal officials. Urban planning agencies were left with the task of loosely guiding developments locally under the pressure of the forces underway as pushed along by the federal government programs.

Despite the fact that, in the postwar period, planning increasingly encompassed more social and economic elements and focused more on current growth and problems of the city, the physical master plan approach continued to dominate. Urban planning methodology experienced little change in substance even when the name was switched from *master plan* to *general plan* during the 50s and 60s.

The use of the basic approach was effectively symbolized in the general plan prepared for Philadelphia in the late 50s. Long-range, comprehensive urban planning had become a key feature of the civic renaissance of Philadelphia's experience in the 50s under the administrations of Joseph Clark and Richard Dilworth. Probably the outstanding effort of the period, the Philadelphia plan encompassed governmental reorganization, physical rejuvenation of historical parts of the city, and industrial promotion.

Essentially, the Philadelphia plan was concerned with a strategy of development aimed at bolstering the economic position of the central city vis-à-vis the suburbs. It concentrated both on physical public improvements designed to increase the vitality of the city economy and the development of a transportation system linking the center easily and quickly with its metropolitan market. Expressway construction was coordinated with redevelopment to provide access to newly cleared industrial sites. Furthermore, the strategy called for improvements in central city residential areas that would prevent further flight to the suburbs by the higher-income families.

Execution of the comprehensive plan was to be accomplished by capital improvement programming and budgeting. Of additional significance was the fact that the Philadelphia planners developed new devices to measure progress toward achievement of the plan.

Unfortunately, the entire plan and financial strategy were based on assumptions about a future of an extremely questionable nature, particularly in the face of the powerful decentralizing forces as fueled by the federal government programs. Scott (1971: 535) summarizes the weaknesses:

> In addition to the primary assumption that Philadelphia would remain the dominant regional center, there was an especially risky second assumption postulating that economic growth would proceed with sufficient rapidity to enable the city to invest in the public facilities called for. Least tenable of all was the third assumption that the city would maintain "a balanced population, including middle and high as well as low income families." In the next five or six years the city lost 150,000 or more of its long-time residents, saw its low income population increase (mostly by immigration of poor Negroes from the South), and watched the number of unemployed rise above 100,000.

The planners confused hopes for the future and future images with unfolding reality. Little attention was given to the fact that local efforts were often incompatible with the national policies and programs. The hold of the physical master plan approach was apparent even as the nature of the goals and planning techniques changed significantly. With so little capacity for dealing with the long-run future and the great social transformation already well underway, even the most highly regarded and strongly backed planning in the nation—Philadelphia's—could not transcend its role as a reference point for carrying out individual projects and programs such as Penn Center, Independence Mall, a transformed Society Hill, the Food Distribution Center, the Schuylkill Expressway, a new housing code, and a limited industrial development program.

The lessons of the Philadelphia planning experience were not lost on municipal officials. It highlighted the difficulty, even under relatively favorable political conditions, of trying to achieve long-range goals and to sustain long-range development efforts. In the face of continuous frustration, urban planners turned to the more limited and more urgent problems of the day. A new realism took hold in urban planning in the middle and late 60s, as substantial federal funds in the form of categorical grants became available to cities. These grants were to be used for such projects as housing and renewal efforts and for education, health, and other public services and facilities. At the same time, new concepts and tools of policy analysis and plan formulation were coming into use from the fields of economics, systems analysis, program budgeting, and the fledgling policy sciences.

Planning theorists increasingly pointed to the weaknesses of the general physical (comprehensive) plan as traditionally formulated. Some urged that the logical framework for individual planning and action decision should be a medium-term policies plan rather than a physically oriented, long-range master or general plan (Meyerson, 1956).

This logic was appealing to planners in this period of the new realism because it met the need to combine the social and economic concerns of urban planning with the physical concerns and provided the flexibility required by a rapidly changing urban environment. However, by the 70s, the appropriate form and content of a municipal policies plan had not yet become apparent. Urban planning was left dangling between two worlds: the world of the physical master plan which was understood but which had readily acknowledged weaknesses, and the world of flexible policies planning which could address the urgent problems but would do so at the expense of both the long-run future and a framework for physical development. In a sense, the real work-a-day **present** was discovered by urban planning while in the process much of its concern for the long-run **future** was lost.

The increasing emphasis on the immediate issues of the day has not been a matter of professional preference alone, a simple reflection of professional discouragement with the usefulness of the physical master plan approach. A review of city planning in the United States today, as sampled in the remainder of Part 1 of this volume, suggests that there cannot be much political capital in concern for long-range matters. It is hard to imagine that intelligent politicians and bureaucrats all around the country are permitting good opportunities to pass them by. Long-range planning is simply not seen as significantly protecting or advancing the interests of important groups in the community as was the case in the earlier part of the century. Moreover, during the 1970s, America's traditional belief in the powers of the market economy reasserted itself after the great expansion of governmental activities in the 1960s. The absence of long-range thinking and coordinated action at the federal level was even more an element of discouragement for future-oriented planning at the local level. All this is particularly striking considering the importance of the long-run future for just about everyone.

AN INTEREST IN THE LONG RUN

An individual who is now approaching a 50th birthday has, on the average, something like 20 or 25 years of life to look forward to. A younger person just finishing college or graduate school probably has something like 50 years of life to be concerned with—a life spanning two generations. Given the anticipated improvements in medicine and other factors influencing longevity, a baby born today may live to be 75 or 100 years old. This new life expectancy of three or four generations is truly long range.

In another significant realm, most present-day structures will probably last 40 to 50 years and some possibly over 100 years. The urban patterns, the roadways, and the relationships of work places to home and to major public facilities may well last as long or longer. Most urbanities are living in cities developed well over a generation ago; some are living in cities that have changed little for over a century. While the process of change in urban cities can certainly be quickened, a high cost is attached. Such transitions cannot be lightly undertaken. Our institutions often outlast our buildings and urban patterns. Whether in governing, regulating, supplying services and facilities, or providing amusements for our leisure time, the longevity of these institutions has much to do with our capacity to deal with events as they unfold.

Today's decisions, whether personal or collective, clearly reach into the future and often into the distant future. Individuals are not unaware of this fact. They take a wide variety of measures to deal with this reality and the uncertainties it inevitably entails. They buy insurance (on life, health, cars, and many other items of concern) and/or pay taxes for social insurance. If they can afford it, people save. And it is of no small importance that for very many people, over 90 percent of total savings are tied up for decades in the equity of a home. Many others, of course, cannot save, and they turn to other forms of providing for the future. People from all walks of life join political parties and other similar groups that promise to look out for their welfare. Many join economic groups, such as labor unions, chambers of commerce, and property owners associations, organized to protect their welfare. Since parents see education as a key factor in providing for the future of their children, they often do everything possible to provide for the education of their children, including moving to communities that have a reputation for good schools.

Businesses, particularly the larger ones, make even more elaborate provisions for the future. Concern for the preservation of assets over time is a key to the accounting system employed. Concern for the organization's position in the competitive field often involves substantial and detailed planning. Expenditures for research and development (R&D) are for some businesses an important part of such planning and provision for the future (although not always consistently supported). Nonbusiness institutions make their own provisions for the future, often involving the accumulation of funds such as endowments and making plans to delineate a firm place for the institution in the scheme of things.

This practical system of providing for an uncertain future is reflected in and enhanced by the present organization of urban governments and activities and in the attitudes of politicians about what is good planning. Many politicians, reflecting the attitudes of constituents, see urban planning as essentially an instrumentality for the defense of property values.

Frequently the zoning component becomes totally dominant—the major tool for defense of neighborhood character and property values—leaving the planning framework of zoning well in the background. This phenomenon can be translated into the building of urban communities that, from the inception, are geared to providing the following: (1) a safe atmosphere for property values, (2) the provision of limited, high-level services, including education of children, without unusually high property tax rates (which often means keeping out poor people who require a wide range of public services not needed by the middle class), (3) substantial, protected areas for taxpaying industry and zoning to permit its continuing expansion, (4) a well-developed system of freeways and highways so that individuals may get to work with ease while maintaining a preferred home environment and (5) a local government that reflects all these interests. For very many people, it all adds up to **suburbia**.

When the older central city can no longer provide adequate protection into the long-run future for the property values of the middle- and upper-income groups, who comprise the largest part of urban society today, the quality of education they desire, and/or a secure home atmosphere, then those who can simply relocate to communities that do provide these things. To stay and work hard for the desired future requires patience and the acceptance of risks in the face of uncertainties. Everyone knows how rarely things are effectively turned around. People are intimidated by the possibility of losing the main part of their savings (tied up in their homes). To expect individuals who are not themselves poor to help the poor through substantial taxation and to effect socially decent behavior (such as willingness to live with one's neighbors no matter what the color of their skin or income) is not at all unreasonable. However, to expect people to jeopardize their provisions for the future and their children's future is much less realistic. Naturally, the governments of the central cities must weigh the interests of the large and powerful middle- and upper-income groups as well as those of the poorer groups in making their decisions. They literally cannot afford to have the wealthier families move to the suburbs.

The tendency of some wealthier individuals and families to return to the city (many of these are newly formed households), or what has come to be called *gentrification*, essentially reflects a new calculation of personal costs and benefits in the face of changing house prices and a new calculation of the risk factor. The importance of personal future-oriented calculations remains a major consideration for municipal government.

Since what is planned in municipal government is reflective of political will, planners must relate to the basic interests of individuals and of political and economic groups. That helps explain certain of the current characteristics of urban planning, such as the strong emphasis on zoning (which is the key to the protection of property values), on trying to maintain the economic importance of downtown, and on the extension of the transportation and utility systems. There are, however, different ways of reflecting political will and of reacting to the pressures of various interest groups. A narrowly conceived approach can make planning simply a tool of the strongest interests, viewing requirements only in myopic and immediate terms. Fortunately, there are also possibilities for a broader approach which seeks to reconcile differing interests by showing the way to a generally better future which can provide some improvement in the situation of all—or most—groups. (This issue will be discussed at later points in this volume.)

It was pointed out earlier that planning came into being to enhance the Janus-like desires of people for continuity and security on the one hand and for change and something better over the long run on the other. In recent years, urban planning has given up the earlier thrust toward something better as characterized by the make-no-little-plans slogan of the physical master plan approach, but it has not yet evolved an approach which can concern itself with the long-run future while attending to current problems and current pressures. In the process, unfortunately, planning seems to have lost the capacity to do either very well and is substantially removed from doing both of them well simultaneously. Yet, that is precisely what urban planning should be trying to accomplish since, while other instrumentalities, particularly the local government administrative agencies, and other approaches, such as those of systems analysts and management analysts, can contribute in important ways to the current issues, only the planning approach has the potential to deal with both.

Yet another reason exists for evolving an approach which can encompass the present and the future simultaneously. Efforts to deal with current problems can only mitigate their impacts. They cannot undo the mistaken decisions of the past. Basic improvements in the urban system within a political jurisdiction can be achieved only by dealing with the long-run future. Such improvements require change in behavior patterns (as in the adoption of a conservation ethic) and in infrastructure which occur through gradual processes and are normally put in place sequentially.

In the search for basic improvements in the urban system lies the hope of resolving conflicting interests, since only such adjustments have the potential for bringing about gains for most groups. Planning must make the potential for improvement real enough. This potential must be stated in terms meaningful enough to the average resident to be politically effective.

Only if planning can develop the concepts and tools to carry out simultaneously both the immediate or short-run and the long-run tasks well, and if the general public and the political and economic leadership can be convinced that it can do these tasks well, will planning be in a position to make a substantial difference in urban human affairs. The remainder of this volume is devoted to rounding out suggestions of principles, approaches, and tools that promise usefulness in guiding current urban decisions toward a desired future. These suggestions emerge out of a concern for the logic of passage through time whenever value is placed on minimizing uncertainty in urban life and maximizing the probabilities of achieving desired future conditions.

Before embarking on these tasks, the particular importance of concern should be noted for the long-range future under the urban conditions faced today, conditions so powerfully impacted by a national and international transformation.

DEALING WITH A MAJOR NATIONAL TRANSFORMATION

Cities and metropolitan regions in the United States (and other industrialized nations) are in the forefront of a major transformation that scholars have variously labeled the postindustrial society, the services age, or the communications age. This transformation is more than a matter of rapid social change; it involves *an interrelated set of changes* that are giving new structure to the society. Capturing the essence of a societal transformation in a label is not easy nor, in fact, is it a simple task to distinguish the essence from the derived characteristics. This phenomenon involves the way people make a living and use technology, the way they live and relate to each other and—even more important for cities—where they live and work.

The Changing Urban Economy

There is a continuing reduction in the proportion of workers in manufacturing and all other goods-producing activities, accompanied by an increase in employment in service activities. Manufacturing employees as a percentage of employees in nonagricultural establishments in the United States fell from 34 percent in 1950 to 24 percent in 1978, while service employment rose from 59 percent to 70 percent. Manufacturing and processing industries have also relaxed their locational requirements with advances in and growth of trucking, automation, miniaturization, and related developments that have provided a more footloose character to location decisions. With far fewer ties to the location of natural resources, waterways, or rail centers, these industries have responded to other locational advantages, such as the availability of natural or man-made amenities, space for parking, and a high-level work force. Over time, manufacturing has become more and more market oriented. Thus, manufacturing firms can be expected to continue to move to where clusters of people have located because of residential preferences.

All of these developments have had a regional impact—relocation away from the older industrial regions—as well as a deconcentration impact, relocation away from the central cities. Mature urbanization has spread out (speeded by the improvements in methods of communication) and developed into many clusters of activities across the national landscape. The move of manufacturing firms from the cities has restricted the job opportunities of both unskilled and semiskilled workers, whose unemployment rate is high even in prosperity. Cities are loaded with severe problems of poverty and dependency, and economic development has become a political imperative. We can look ahead to a highly mixed urban situation, with some communities impacted by very rapid growth and others impacted by substantial declines. National laws and standards for grants will have to be more sensitive than ever to great differences among urban places. General rules may be hard to establish and carry out.

The increasing importance of service industries and service employment has been accompanied by the striking rise in importance of the professional and technical sector, or what sociologist Daniel Bell (1973) calls the "knowledge class." This has been closely tied to a remarkable development of communications and information handling technology. These developments have added to locational footlooseness. However, significant problems are connected with service activities. One is the problem of little, if any, increases in productivity in many of the service industries. This could have a negative impact on standards of living over time. Another problem is that some of the most important service activities—such as health, education, and the arts—involve complex issues of public and private support beyond normal market arrangements. Since our communities have not been very ingenious in dealing with not-for-profit financing, some major problems of services financing lie ahead. Yet another problem is that the development of some of these services, such as the important tourist industry, requires the creation of special urban infrastructure far different than that put into place during the previous industrial age. Also, many of the promising newer service activities—for example, nutrition and other new health activities, conferencing and other educational activities, protective services, and psychological services—require infant industry assistance if they are to develop soundly and well. Urban economic development efforts have not yet come to grips with the cities' dependence on service industries and the special treatment they require (Perloff, 1978).

The Changing Population Structure

Significant changes in population and labor force are underway which promise to have a profound impact on urban development in the decades to come. These include the low birthrates of the native population accompanied by the increase of foreign worker in-migration, both legal and illegal. Ethnic tensions are resulting and can be expected to intensify as the numbers of immigrants increase and unless effective means are found for dealing with the problems involved. A high and possibly increasing proportion of women will enter the labor market, in part at least because of the desire to increase standards of living or just to maintain them. Many small and nontraditional households are being formed. The speed and scale of changes in lifestyle is intensifying. A wide variety of housing types and neighborhood arrangements are likely to be in demand. A greater proportion of jobs, in both services and goods production, require high levels of skill. There is increasing danger of the formation of a permanent underclass of those without the requisite skills.

The problems of urban planning and of national policy must encompass issues centering on human resources, including complex questions of skill requirements and highly delicate issues of intergroup relations. More than ever, planning and policy must be concerned with lifestyle groups and must be sensitive to lifestyle changes.

Pressure on Resources

As population and economic activities spread across the national landscape, pressure intensifies on natural resources, particularly the amenity resources, such as lakes, beaches, mountains, and deserts. Problems of air, water, visual, and noise pollution are intensifying within the built-up urban centers. As natural and man-made amenities continue to draw population—with industry often following—the problem of "not killing the thing we love" increases. But jobs and income also pose personal and societal problems. Thus planning can look ahead, as a characteristic of our postindustrial society, to continued and probably heightening struggle between those emphasizing protection of the environment, and the need for a national conservation ethic, and those emphasizing the need for economic development.

Energy shortages can be expected to have a profound impact on urban life in the next decades. The spread urbanism developed during the last three decades will pose enormous problems for individuals and urban communities alike in a period of high-cost and uncertain energy. Automobile-oriented lifestyles may have to be modified, and special efforts will have to be made to seek balance in given geographic areas between places of work and homes rather than continuing in energy-consuming locational patterns.

Net social benefit is difficult to calculate in all of these. Urban planning, as well as national policy, must be prepared to make such calculations. Resource shortages can seriously depress standards of living. The job ahead for planning is thus much more complex than ever before.

Fiscal Pressures

Many of the trends which have been identified result in financial difficulties for city governments. This is particularly true of the out-migration of industries and wealthier families from the older cities and the in-migration of poorer households. In such cases, costs often escalate well beyond the rise in the tax base. While national and state governments can compensate for differences in fiscal capacity between the wealthier and poorer municipalities, the political strength of the richer suburban areas can generally be expected to block more than token compensation, leaving older cities with heavy fiscal burdens. To add to their difficulties, such cities have to face the financial pressures associated with aging infrastructure. They can live off their capital only so long. The financial problems of older municipalities are greater in federal systems, as in the United States and Canada, than in unified national political systems. In each, however, the potentials of both physical and economic development can be realized only if fiscal planning is an integral part of urban planning and of budgeting. Municipal governments can no longer manage their complex developmental problems without sophisticated fiscal-conscious, and future-oriented, planning and management.

Our urban civilization is not coping as well as could be desired with the great transformation it is facing. All indicators suggest that the transformation is not close to completion, and that its effects will be experienced through the next generation and beyond. The elements of the societal transformation already experienced and those that are anticipated require that the politician, the administrator, and the urban planner consider the *long-range future* in making current decisions in a purposeful, well-planned way.

Comprehending the logic of the heavy emphasis in municipal governments on the severe urban problems of *today* is not difficult. The dilemma posed is that a community's capacity for coping with present-day problems and for achieving short-term goals is greatly limited if plans are not already underway for guiding developments toward a conscientiously conceived, desired long-run future.

Even the most dedicated efforts to overcome the pressing problems of the day can at best be expected to only partially succeed (and normally at great cost) because such efforts involve trying to undo the results of previous decisions. This becomes apparent when traffic congestion in our cities is studied. Congestion is the result of decisions made in the past, including decisions on city form, location incentives and disincentives, freeway and highway construction, and automobile and gasoline pricing policies. In the same light, the intensifying anger, alienation, and personal incapacity in the ghettoes are just as surely the result of inadequacies of past decisions or simply indecision. The solution or mitigation of deep-rooted urban problems calls for carefully selected investments in the future and often changes in behavior patterns, normally with expected payoff only in the long-run future.

Considering the societal transformation noted earlier, urban accommodation to the transformation can come only over the long run. The human, socioeconomic, and physical problems caused by the transformation can be mitigated only over the long run, and new opportunities provided by the transformations can only be realized over the long run.

To deal with both the problems and adjustments on the one side and with the new opportunities (the possibility of a better future) on the other, municipal and metropolitan-regional governments—as well as the national government—will need strong and sophisticated planning operations and strong management capabilities. This volume is concerned with the kind of urban planning that needs to be done given the situation faced by urban communities in the United States and other industrialized countries. While the focus is on American urban planning, most of what is said is directly applicable to planning in municipalities in other countries as well.

WHAT FOLLOWS NEXT

To work towards substantial improvements in urban planning over time, the realities of actual planning practice must be understood and its strengths and weaknesses must be appreciated. The next few chapters examine briefly the planning approach to the future as well as to the current situation being carried out in some of the nation's major cities. Cities of varying sizes have been chosen as representative of planning activities in the different parts of the country. The emphasis is on central cities, although the planning work of one regional agency (that of Atlanta) is also examined.

The actual plans examined do not fully reflect all of the planning that takes place in these cities—much less the actualization of such plans. Nevertheless, the plans can demonstrate how these planning agencies are *approaching* the long-run future. The lessons that may be drawn from this exploration of current urban planning practices—as a base for thinking about the needed improvements in planning—are summarized in Chapter 8.

Two important features of planning as a tool of decisionmaking can be found in a review of urban planning in various cities across the country. First, uncertainty is felt as to how to combine considerations of the future with the more immediate concerns. In some cities, the long-run future has more or less slipped from view, and where the long-run future does appear, the relationship to more immediate concerns is anything but apparent. And second, each city is going its own individual way.

More differences than similarities seem to exist in the content and form of planning in the various cities studied. Boston emphasizes economic development, relating proposals for physical development to the goals of increasing jobs and income. The middle-range programs (ten years) are dominant. Cleveland, with an emphasis on the short term, focuses mainly on the problems of the poor and disadvantaged. San Francisco stresses preservation of a city which its residents evidently find quite satisfactory. Phoenix is currently emphasizing the psychological well-being to be gained from a future urban form (the urban village) to replace the formlessness that rapid growth has caused. All these taken together provide a fascinating picture of a search for ways to deal effectively with the complex issues facing urban planning today.

Chapter 2
Planning in Los Angeles: Maintaining the Single-Family Neighborhood

BACKGROUND

City planning in Los Angeles is part of a complex governmental process which has developed nearly as intricately and as extensively in a political sense as the city has in a physical sense. Urban planning in Los Angeles focuses on land use and physical development of the city. Recently other dimensions of planning, such as community social service planning, have come to be shared with a growing number of federally funded agencies operating as part of the fabric of local government.

To comprehend planning in Los Angeles, the city itself must be understood. Los Angeles grew at a phenomenal pace. In 1870, the population was little more than 5,000, but by 1900, it had grown to 100,000. The city had over 1 million residents in 1930, nearly 2 million in 1950, and by the end of the 1970s, Los Angeles was the third largest city in the United States with a population of some 2.8 million in a five county area of over 11 million. Only in the last decade has the rate of population growth shown signs of significantly slowing down.

An important factor sustaining the growth of the city has been its ability to tap distant and abundant sources of water. Lying on a semiarid coastal plain between the Mojave Desert and the Pacific Ocean, Los Angeles' local water supply was too meager to adequately serve its residents by the early 1900s. The Department of Water and Power (DWP) was formed in 1902 and immediately began to reorganize the city's water supplies. In its search for supplemental sources, the DWP constructed aqueducts to tap the Owens Valley some 230 miles to the north and the Colorado River 300 miles to the east. During the past several years, the state of California has been working to complete a third aqueduct to bring water from the Feather River near Sacramento, some 450 miles north of Los Angeles. The actions of the DWP have in a very real sense been among the most powerful influences on the long-range growth and development of Los Angeles.

In sheer physical size, Los Angeles ranks second in the nation, extending over 464 square miles. It is approximately twice the size of Chicago. Los Angeles is comprised of 70 identifiable communities which, although lacking established boundaries and governmental operations, are nevertheless claimed by residents as their home communities.

The city has five major ethnic groups which are estimated to make up more than half of the 1980 population, according to precensus statistics. Mexican Americans are concentrated in the barrios and communities of East Los Angeles while blacks predominate in South Central Los Angeles. Chinese, Japanese, Koreans, and Filipinos are the largest segments of a growing Asian population, which has recently come to include many Vietnamese. Although Los Angeles is known for its Watts and East Side, its Chinatown and Little Tokyo, members of all major ethnic groups live in ethnically integrated districts in many parts of the city (Los Angeles Community Bureau Analysis, 1977).

No less than seven separate offices coordinate planning for the land-use and physical development of the city. These are the director of planning and the Department of City Planning, the zoning administrators, the Board of Zoning Appeals, the Environmental Review Board, the General Plan Advisory Board, the City Planning Commission, and the City Council.

The council's role is the most influential one. The powers granted it by the city charter are extensive and of such a nature that the distinction between administrative and legislative functions is often blurred. Los Angeles has 15 council members, which are elected from separate districts of approximately 180,000 persons each. The districts are individually larger than most U.S. cities—another indication of the scale of Los Angeles.

The council actively participates in land-use planning for the city. The Department of City Planning is technically staff to the council and cooperates closely with the representatives of any districts affected by its activities. The department assists the planning director in preparing, revising, and updating the many parts of the general plan which are then considered for adoption by the city planning commission and later by the council itself. The council has closely scrutinized planning documents, sometimes debating at considerable length and amending them before adopting them. A 1977 amendment to the city charter further strengthens the role of the council with regard to the general plan. "The Council may, on its own initiative, propose amendments to the General Plan and shall refer any such amendment to the Director of Planning, the City Planning Commission, and the Mayor for recommendation" (Los Angeles City Charter, Section 96.5(3)(f).

The director of planning heads the city planning department and is advised by both the city planning commission (composed of five citizens appointed by the mayor and approved by the council) and by the general plan advisory board (composed of the managers and directors of all city agencies at the planning policymaking level). The planning director also heads the general plan advisory board which confers regularly on all matters pertaining to the general plan and coordinates the efforts of the various city agencies.

The relationship of the planning commission to the director and the department is crucial. The completion of the community plans and other special plans has been a major goal of the planning commission. One of its continuing problems has been to thoroughly familiarize new commissioners with the meaning and application of the adopted plans and policies. The commission is responsible for interpreting those plans through its decisions on zoning and conditional use permits.

Planning in Los Angeles is also affected by two unique types of departments in the city government. Los Angeles has several proprietary (independent) departments, such as Department of Airports, the Harbor Department, and the Department of Water and Power. Neither the mayor nor the council controls the budgets of these departments, whose spending powers exceed those of many U.S. cities. These departments may contract with other governments, including foreign governments, for the "purchase or sale of properties, goods or services without the express consent of the City Council" (Howell, 1977:11). Coordination with city planning can only be accomplished through very good interdepartmental relations—an ingredient not always present.

A growing part of the fabric of city government are federally funded planning agencies such as the Community Development Department (CDD), the City Housing Authority (CHA), and Community Redevelopment Agency (CRA). The CDD, created in 1977 to consolidate the programs of five separate federally funded offices in Los Angeles government, is probably the planning department's most important rival. The duties of this department are:

> . . . to plan, develop, propose, carry out and/or cause to be carried out . . . agreements and policies for eliminating, reducing, and preventing obsolescence and blight in the City; providing for the rehabilitation of and for new community facilities and housing; conducting programs designed to improve the qualifications of disadvantaged and unskilled persons for regular employment in the public and private sectors; provide for community organization-operated programs in the various communities of the City; conducting programs designed to serve the aged and alleviate problems of the aged; and, in general, initiate and, with the Mayor's and Council's approval, implement remedial programs to enhance the physical and social conditions of the communities (Administrative Code for the City of Los Angeles, Div. 22, Ch. 19, Art. 1, Sec. 22.462).

Thus the CDD is responsible for a wide range of community improvements of a physical, social, and economic nature. While the planning department's comments on CDD programming and funding are part of the review process, coordination with such a superagency promises to be difficult at best. One wonders how the long-range plans for the city will be impacted by the availability of federal funding, that is, for the most part, tied to federal rather than local priorities.

A point that can easily be overlooked in examining urban planning in American cities is the official framework within which such planning takes place and the official constraints that sometimes are imposed on such planning. In the case of Los Angeles, the content of the general plan has been constrained by the city administrative officer (CAO) who evaluates budget requests of the Department of City Planning for the mayor. It has been the CAO's position for many years that *physical* planning is the only legitimate task of the planning department. For example, the positions of planning economist and urban sociologist were eliminated from the department's budget (and this in the city that was the scene of the Watts riots). At times, the city attorney has also ruled against moves by the planning department to incorporate innovative changes into the plans, particularly where new forms of property control were involved.

Planning in Los Angeles is thus highly defined and sharply limited in its ability to provide leadership toward the future. With this brief background of the governmental context for city planning in Los Angeles, the general plan itself can be considered.

THE GENERAL PLAN FORMAT

The Los Angeles current general plan is the result of a process begun in

1965 with a formation of a goals council. The organization of public and private citizens was charged with stimulating "citizen participation in developing the fundamental base for a comprehensive approach to planning the vast City of Los Angeles" (Los Angeles Department of City Planning, 1969b: 72). The goals eventually identified by the goals council reflected a strong distaste for smog and traffic congestion and a strong preference for the single-family home lifestyle, the development of a rapid transit system, the preservation of the city's open space, and improvement of recreation facilities.

The second step in the process was the development of four alternative design concepts for the future physical form of the city. While no time horizon was attached to any of these alternatives, the concepts did purport to represent differing values and policies. Each concept addressed the identified goals in a broad fashion while relying on a single future population level (of 5 million in Los Angeles and 10 million in the metropolitan area). None of the concepts treated the implications that the alternatives might have upon the poor, the aged, minorities, or those lacking employable skills.

In contrast to the widely publicized efforts of the goals council, relatively few residents ever heard about these alternatives. Despite "a lack of coordination and an inadequate understanding of Los Angeles' political complexities (which) bedeviled the project from the start" (Los Angeles Department of City Planning, 1969b: 76), these efforts were at least serious attempts to involve citizens and to plan for the future.

From the findings of the goals council and a consideration of the concepts, a single *concept* emerged intended to be "a continuous reference (for) the future form and long-range development of the City of Los Angeles" (Los Angeles Department of City Planning, 1970: 1). Known as the "centers concept," this reference envisions the future Los Angeles as containing many centers which "will be the dominant physical elements in the City due to their high development intensity and concentration of people and activities." Surrounding these centers will be low-density suburbs made up mostly of single-family residences. Connecting the centers will be a "comprehensive transportation system including: a fully developed highway and freeway system, a rapid transit network with feeder lines, and local bus transit." The major objective of the concept is to maintain the single-family home lifestyle of the city's population. Most new growth is to be channeled into the higher-density centers. The latter would feature high-rise residences and most major commercial activities.

The second portion of the general plan is the citywide plan which addresses the city as a whole and provides the framework for more detailed parts of the general plan. The citywide plan is directed toward longer range development (20 years) and represents an effort to coordinate decisions on land use, transportation, public facilities, and the environment to achieve the goals embodied in the concept. Associated with the plan are numerous technical subelements including a service system element, circulation element, and environmental element.

For more specific planning purposes, Los Angeles is divided into 35 subareas called communities or districts. Plans for these areas are targeted for 1990 and rely upon a single population projected based on the 1970 census. They contain both short-term (5 year) and long-range (20 year) features.

A community or district plan has three significant parts. The official plan is a policy and program document which addresses the land-use, transportation, and service system elements of the general plan as they will be implemented in the local community until 1990. An implementation report identifies these actions which the city must take during the first five years of the plan's life in order to accomplish the long-range objectives. The environmental impact report (EIR) details those implementation measures which the city council is to take and the alternative actions considered during the plan's development. The EIR also evaluates the environmental impacts of the plan in accordance with California state law.

CONCEPT LOS ANGELES

The concept is urban design or redesign on a grand scale. The underlying assumption seems to be that most of the city's problems stem from an inefficient and unwieldy structure of land uses and that the solution to the present problems would also serve to cope with the problems of the future.

> The Concept seeks to restructure the City in order to eliminate or alleviate current problems and to anticipate and deal with future issues before they become serious problems (Los Angeles Department of City Planning, 1970:1).

The main difficulty is seen as uncontrolled growth which can lead to the erosion of the Southern California single-family lifestyle. The concept (as well as the citywide plan) was originally drafted at the end of the 1960s when substantial growth in the city's population was not only expected but considered desirable. The original version of the concept indicated that the plan was to accommodate a population of 5 million persons (to be attained sometime after the year 2000) as compared to the 2.8 million population of 1970. In the progrowth language of the time, the concept stated:

One possible way of minimizing future problems would be to place a restraint upon the City's growth. However, it is not considered feasible to limit population within the foreseeable future; to attempt to do so would probably result in severe economic and social repercussions. Furthermore, the large physical size of Los Angeles is adequate to accommodate continued growth without detriment to the City's established lifestyle if such growth is guided by comprehensive planning (Los Angeles Department of City Planning, 1970:6).

While continued growth was considered desirable, a continuation of current land-use patterns was not. A serious effort was to be made to limit residential sprawl and to protect single-family residential areas from intrusion by "incompatible" land uses. New building activity was to be directed into high-density centers and their immediate surrounding areas.

By the time the city council adopted the concept and citywide plan in April 1974, population projections for the city had been drastically reduced, and no growth concepts had gained political currency. All statistics were removed from the documents and the following was inserted to a new version of the concept:

> Population growth is not necessary for the achievement of this Concept. In the long term, the future population growth of the City is uncertain. If this growth continues the rate may be substantially below rates of growth which have occurred in the past. The plan provides that such growth as does occur can be accommodated through proper land use control and other policy implementation techniques (Los Angeles Department of City Planning, 1974a:2).

The emergence of the centers described in the concept is a long-range event which will depend upon the construction of new public and private facilities and upon the provision of transportation systems capable of making the centers viable focal points on the landscape of the immensely sprawling city.

While the concept does not address the possibility that Los Angeles population may stabilize or even decline in the future, it nevertheless presents a solid image of what the city might be like in the decades to come.

THE CITYWIDE PLAN

The citywide plan is designed to be a framework for implementation during the first 20 years of the life of the concept. For this middle-range plan, the city planners felt that a specific population projection was needed—one that would enable them to specify housing needs, transportation, and public service and facilities requirements. The language also suggests that the population figure employed (3.2 million by 1990) is a combination of a forecast based on existing trends and a desirable future population total for the city. While the methodology is questionable, there is at least a clear appreciation of the political nature of population figures—they can serve to win or lose support for a plan.

The main concern of the citywide plan is to provide the base for a coherent set of location and timing decisions on land use, transportation, and public facilities. Toward this end, the plan was developed by involving many of the operating agencies in the hope that decisions on these key elements in the future would be worked out in a coordinated fashion. As in the concept, no provisions are made for a significantly lower population level or for other major changes such as the availability of federal or state financing.

COMMUNITY AND DISTRICT PLANS

Community and district plans in Los Angeles, like the concept and citywide plan, are essentially land-use planning documents. The description of these plans as community plans must be understood in the context of metropolitan Los Angeles. What is considered a community in Los Angeles is actually the equivalent of a medium-sized city. For example, Hollywood, one of the communities, covers nearly 28 square miles and has a population in excess of 200,000. The size of community planning study areas varies widely.

Citizen participation in community planning varies widely since the planning department is staff to the council and must cooperate with any council member whose district is part of the planning study area. Citizen advisory committees are council appointed, and community plans have been carefully scrutinized by the city council.

Some highlights from two of the community plans are presented here to indicate the manner in which the future has been addressed at that level. (As there is some variation among the community plans, these two cannot be considered representative of all such plans.)

Hollywood

Hollywood, apart from its fame as a center for the motion picture and television industry, is also the home of some of Los Angeles' important medical and educational institutions, thriving commercial enterprises, and many of its residents. An interesting feature of the Hollywood plan, developed in 1969, was the presentation of three alternative design concepts for guiding the future physical development of the Hollywood area. The design concepts were prepared primarily to stimulate community response, helping residents to imagine various future physical forms of Hollywood. The alternatives were discussed in terms of lifestyles.

The first concept introduced the prospect of developing a concentrated commercial core as the center around which relatively intensive new growth would occur:

> Highrise residential areas to be developed around the Hollywood business district (the commercial core) would take advantage of the expanded range of shopping, service, educational, cultural and entertainment activities within the urban center (Los Angeles Department of City Planning, 1969a:1).

This particular alternative most readily agreed with the concept.

The second alternative was openly oriented towards the automobile. The concept sought to retain the identities of existing neighborhoods, offering minimal change in the pattern of single-family homes. The commercial district would not expand but rather intensify to meet new demand. The bus system would continue as the only public form of transit.

The third concept was designed around a possible alternative rapid transit route which would have connected Hollywood's existing medical and educational institutions with its high-density residential corridor (along Hollywood and Sunset boulevards) and the Hollywood commercial district to form a linear community. This proposal called for the integration of commercial, residential, educational, and medical land uses while providing a wide range of housing choices and cultural and commercial activities.

The plan which was eventually adopted reflected some aspects of each of the design concepts. The political forces which shaped the official document were as complex and important to the outcome in Hollywood as the general plan for an entire city somewhere else might be. What is significant, in view of the changes which have occurred since the plan's adoption, is that a variety of lifestyles were at least considered. The popularity of Hollywood waned during the early 1970s, and private investment in housing and commercial development were below the levels anticipated by the plan. Recently, however, Hollywood has been making a comeback. And the ethnic composition has changed from predominantly white to one containing a greater percentage of minority ethnic groups.

Although the alternatives were mainly design oriented rather than fully developed alternative planning approaches, they hint at the importance of addressing alternative futures in planning for a subcity area.

Northeast Los Angeles

Unlike the Hollywood plan area, the Northeast Los Angeles district is a predominantly low density residential area made up of several small, ethnically distinct communities laced by hillsides and mountainous terrain. A unique community made up of Hispanic and Asian residents, it serves as an entry point for many South and Central Americans as well as Mexicans. The plan for this community is aimed at preserving both the single-family residential character of the various neighborhoods and the surrounding natural environment. In the short term, residents will probably continue to rely heavily upon the automobile, but the extension of existing bus service is encouraged.

Three alternative plans to the proposed Northeast Los Angeles district plan are cited in the environmental impact report. They are (1) no plan, (2) a no-growth plan, and (3) a projected growth plan (Los Angeles Department of City Planning, 1974c: 24-45). The first states what might happen if there were no controls on development in the area: excessive population growth, incompatible land uses, and a lack of adequate public facilities. The second or no-growth plan would, according to the EIR, cause a severe dislocation of the area economy since construction of new housing might be curtailed, rehabilitation of the community would dwindle or cease altogether, housing prices would rise and force out lower-income families, and public facilities would only be maintained at current levels. The projected growth plan assumes a maximum capacity population and would require upward adjustment of land use, transportation, and public facilities demands from those cited in the proposed plan.

Each alternative represents an extreme situation in contrast to the proposed plan. Only the projected growth plan is a probable outcome. The brevity of analysis given these alternatives leads one to suspect that they constitute a pro forma exercise rather than indicating viable alternative futures for the Northeast district.

The community plans are essentially extensions of the citywide plan, looking to the future largely in terms of land use, transportation, public facilities, and urban design. Change is viewed mainly in terms of a physical restructuring to eliminate a portion of the city's problems while programs that other city departments would implement are recommended.

PLANS OF OPERATING AGENCIES

The goals of a general plan can be realized only if the city operating agencies gear their own plans and programs to the guidelines set by the city planning department. It is, therefore, interesting to note the extent to which operating plans in Los Angeles do, as a matter of fact, follow the dictates of the general plan. A review of the plans of several operating agencies revealed that in all but one case, that of transportation, the objective of agency planning is simply to accommodate anticipated growth. A case in point is the plans of the powerful Los Angeles Department of Water and Power. Thus, while the general plan makes much of the need to contain development in the open mountainous areas of the city, the DWP plans make no judgments about future subdivision activity in these areas; rather, "the water systems must be prepared to construct the facilities as they are needed" (Los Angeles Department of Water and Power, 1972: 6). On the possible increases in density through changes from single-family dwelling, the department takes this position:

> As changes in population density and land use begin to materialize, plans begin for the reconstruction of the system, but actual reconstruction is begun only when the increased demand necessitates the change and the ultimate needs of the area are determinable (Los Angeles Department of Water and Power, 1972: 24).

Clearly, the water department's orientation is toward supplying "naturally," resulting demand rather than in trying to shape development and demand in line with the guidelines of the city's general plan.

The position of the water department would be reasonable if the remainder of the planning guidance system were working effectively. For example, a purely responsive posture vis-à-vis development in the mountainous areas would not be harmful if the planning department had already prevented such development. But if other tools are not available, the denial of water service may be the only "stick" stopping unwanted development.

Finding any references to the Los Angeles general plan is difficult in the planning documents of operating agencies in the fields of education, health, welfare, and police. Plans for these agencies are mainly of a short- and medium-term nature and touch on few matters which are central to the city's general plan. They simply are in different worlds.

Only the Southern California Rapid Transit District (SCRTD) seems at all wired in to the planning department's image of the future. Thus, the agency's plans refer specifically to the "centers concept" for future development and the important role assigned to rail mass transit in the concept and citywide plan. SCRTD also sees itself in an active role in achieving the projected future by influencing the pattern of land use.

> The recommended rapid transit system will provide Southern Californians the opportunity to focus growth in transit centers of accessibility and thus provide a greater variety of lifestyles (Southern California Rapid Transit District, 1973: 1).

Another indication of the closeness of SCRTD's planning with the "centers concept" of the general plan is the way the various transit corridors were evolved.

> The evaluative criteria . . . were developed by the study team to provide measurements that relate to broader goal statements of the City of Los Angeles, the County of Los Angeles, and the Southern California Association of Governments (Southern California Rapid Transit District, 1973: 54).

In general, a close correspondence exists between the plans of the transportation agency and those of the city's general plan, at least in part because both are based upon a common assessment of past trends and the changing nature of Los Angeles as a city. But as in the general plan, aside from the desire to bring about certain limited changes in land use, very little else in the transportation planning deals with the future. Problems addressed are the issues of the present, such as congestion, air pollution, mobility, energy use, and aesthetics. There is no reference to new problems that may develop or to contingency planning for new conditions. The latter has special relevance to transportation planning in Los Angeles. Each attempt in the 1960s and 1970s to gain voter support for the construction of a rail mass transit has been defeated. Yet, no plans have been developed for a substantial improvement in the existing system. Little attention has been devoted to the use of paratransit and substantial changes in the approach to transportation pricing.

Perhaps the most important correspondence between the plans of operating agencies and those of the city planning department will in the future be those of the community development department. Because the CDD is responsible for many short- and intermediate-range programs, such as housing and community facility rehabilitation, job training, and assistance to the aged, its activities will greatly influence the implementation of the general plan over time. The planning department does comment on community development block grant applications and in other ways expresses its opinion on CDD programming, but CDD is directly responsible for implementation. The interaction of these two agencies is too new to permit further comment, but it is certain to be an important one to watch in the 1980s.

CONCLUSION

The general plan framework for Los Angeles provides an important basis upon which to carry out long-range planning. The concept in particular has set forth a strong (physical) image for the future city. However, the success of implementation is likely to depend more heavily upon the actions of currently independent agencies and of federally funded agencies, operating incrementally, than upon the rather limited sphere of influence of the city planning department. In fact, the real work of planning in Los Angeles may need to focus more intensively than ever upon guiding and controlling programming of federal and state originated funds at the local level.

Chapter 3
Planning in San Francisco: A Focus on Preservation

BACKGROUND

San Francisco is, in many respects, the opposite of Los Angeles. Physically compact, the city covers a land area of less than 45 square miles and is situated at the tip of a peninsula which separates the Pacific Ocean from the southern part of San Francisco Bay. Many residents live in attractive row houses whose walls adjoin one another to give the city a uniquely European flavor and a density second only to that of New York City (Jacobs, 1978: 23).

San Franciscans take great pride in their environment with its many hills and beautiful views of the bay and the ocean. Twice during the 1960s, they thwarted the efforts of the state highway commission to build freeways through their city. In 1974, they voted in favor of a bond issue that would permit the city to purchase San Francisco's last remaining open spaces. And as Allan Jacobs (1978: 17) suggests, in perhaps no other major American city has urban design been as significant a political issue as it has been in San Francisco.

San Francisco is the hub of a large metropolitan area of more than 4.5 million people. It is a center for transportation, finance, industry, government, shipping (both national and international trade), and the arts and cultural life. Despite its system of cable cars, ferries, electric buses, trolleys and the Bay Area Rapid Transit (BART), congestion is a major problem as thousands of commuters and tourists flock to the city each day.

San Francisco was the scene of the "flower children" during the 1960s—a movement indicative of the range of lifestyles to be found in this very cosmopolitan town. The city is also home to many ethnic minorities including blacks, Chinese, Japanese, Filipinos, Mexicans, and Central Americans.

San Francisco is a charter city like Los Angeles. However, its mayor has somewhat stronger executive powers. Its board of 11 supervisors is the fundamental policymaking arm of government (Jacobs, 1978: 26). Citizen commissions set policy for many departments, agencies, and other governmental entities. San Franciscans are active and vocal in other ways as well: Meetings of the board of supervisors are often well attended and the debate is lively.

San Francisco has a chief administrative officer (CAO) who exercises considerable control over the day-to-day affairs of city government.

> At least nine large departments are under the direction of the CAO . . . over 7,000 of the city's employees were in agencies under the CAO in 1974 . . . [and] unlike any other officer of government, [the CAO] enjoys discretionary control over a large amount of money, namely that part of the city's hotel tax that is used to support cultural activities (Jacobs, 1978: 31).

The city planning department is responsible to the city planning commission and is under the leadership of the planning director.

> The responsibilities and powers of the planning department reflect a primary concern with the physical environment, particularly with the uses of land and buildings, and with transportation planning, zoning and public improvements . . . The major responsibility of the planning department is the preparation of the (physical) master plan for the city (Jacobs, 1978: 41).

The future as seen in planning in San Francisco (represented by the comprehensive plan for the city, 1971–74) is to be a preserved and improved present. The impression given in the various plans is one of general satisfaction with the way San Francisco looks and feels, but this satisfaction is further tempered by a desire to improve certain parts of the city and protect others from decline. Words such as "preservation," "protection," and "conservation" are sprinkled throughout the texts. The grand vision of what the city should become is essentially an assertion of how lovely it already is. The view of the future is skeptical and cautious.

GOALS, PLANNING ELEMENTS, AND ACTION AGENCIES

Three major goals surface in all the planning elements surveyed: preservation of the character of San Francisco, improvement of natural and neighborhood environments, and enhancement of the city's central economic role within the region.

Preservation

The urban design element is the most preservation oriented, although the preservation goal colors all the planning elements. Following is an illustrative sample of passages from that element:

> Certainly the old should not be replaced unless the new is better . . . As San Francisco grows and changes new development can and must be fitted in with the established city and neighborhood patterns in a complementary way . . . Historic buildings, and in fact nearly all older buildings regardless of their historic affiliations provide a richness of character, texture and human scale that is unlikely to be repeated in new development (San Francisco Department of City Planning, 1971b: 16, 17, 33).

This goal of preservation is also strongly reflected in the residence element and in its implementation strategy and programs (San Francisco Department of City Planning, 1973b: 12-14, 22-24, 29-34). The desire expressed therein is to restore and rehabilitate as much of the existing housing as possible. This is combined with a desire to add to the total number of housing opportunities available to current residents through in-filling and through the rehabilitation and redevelopment of blighted areas through the Federally Assisted Code Enforcement (FACE) program and limited local redevelopment authority (Jacobs, 1978: 132). A major objective is to fit new development comfortably into the existing residential environment. The basic housing strategy is to be revised every five years while the funding and implementation targets are to be prepared yearly.

The plan suggests certain criteria for public housing projects which are aimed at curtailing some of the redevelopment agency's activities. The redevelopment agency has had a great deal to do with shaping San Francisco and reshaping it in response to changing economic forces. The planning department has had difficulty restraining the heavily funded and politically influential agency when its actions did not align with the department's recommendations (Jacobs, 1978: 1, 20-21, 108). From the outside, it would seem that neither the redevelopment agency nor the planning department has a long-range vision for the future which could specifically guide the redevelopment activities. Neither the agency nor the department is considering the long-term causes of blight or those changes in San Francisco's economy which are significant for decisions on redevelopment. Nor are they considering the long-term effects of redevelopment itself. Thus local control over redevelopment by a federally funded agency is politically limited, and change is taking place without benefit of long-range local public guidance.

The community safety element would seem most accurately to characterize planning in San Francisco. It attempts both to stabilize the present character of the city and to retain the ability to react to any unmanageable but inevitable hazards. In this element, potential seismic and fire hazards are recognized, and steps are outlined to deal with those hazards. The emphasis in the plan is twofold: (1) to alter the built environment to meet safety requirements and (2) to improve the ability to respond to these hazards when they occur (San Francisco Department of City Planning, 1974: 36-37). Whatever is done for safety reasons should be compatible with what exists. The second emphasis reflects the inherent difficulty of foreseeing when seismic and fire hazards will occur, making imperative the ability to respond to them when they do occur. This is no doubt the most appropriate application of San Francisco's planning style—the preservation of the city's character in the face of inevitable changes and threats to that character.

Environment

The goal of *improving* the environment appears most forcefully in the recreation and open space element (1973) and its corresponding implementation programs (1974). The element and programs are divided into four sections: the regional system, the San Francisco shoreline, the citywide system, and the neighborhood level. The approach to guiding future development varies in each case, ranging from reliance on new institutions to quite specific physical plans.

The regional section calls for a new regional open space agency. The proposed organization would have taxing power and would, therefore, be in a position to acquire open space throughout the region as a way of shaping development and adding needed recreational facilities. The shoreline plan looks toward preserving and complementing San Francisco's shoreline by creating new parks and by making new development compatible with existing development. The methods suggested are the established ones—master plans, regulations, zoning, and some public ownership. The citywide section is oriented primarily toward the creation and maintenance of specialized recreational activities throughout the city. While many recreational and open spaces are designated and their funding and administration proposed, little discussion has occurred of how needs and use may change over time. The major emphasis is on improving the present situation through acquisition of desirable areas and intensifying the recreational use of existing facilities. The neighborhood section is concerned with "providing opportunities for recreation and enjoyment of open space in every San Francisco neighborhood" (San Francisco Department of City Planning, 1973a: 38). The emphasis is on improving the environmental quality of "high-need neighborhoods." These neighborhoods are specifically named and the character of their high need is described. However, any mention of how these needs may change over time or of how recreational investments will fit into the city's overall pattern of economic and social development is missing. For example, will increased amenities affect housing costs substantially?

The implementation programs for the recreation element attempt to establish the current need for open and recreational space in San Francisco and to determine the costs and funding sources to fill these needs. A November 1974 amendment has established an *ad valorem* property tax in order to operationalize the goals of the recreation element and to provide funds for the acquisition, maintenance, and administration of new open space (Spring, 1975). This will be in operation for 15 years although the planning department expresses a desire to complete acquisitions within 10 years or less to overcome rising land prices, inflation, and development pressures. While this charter amendment is not yet officially incorporated into the general plan, it was intended to implement the recreation and open space element. The question remains as to how this funding mechanism will affect, and be affected by, other city services and development in the future. The evaluation of its effects appears limited to its recreational impacts.

Neighborhood Planning

San Francisco's planning department has recognized the enthusiasm and concern of its residents for the conservation and improvement of their neighborhoods by sponsoring a number of neighborhood planning efforts. While these efforts are largely in the realm of physical improvements, the initiation of the planning effort at the local level is an important indicator of the issues that the residents wish to address. Such programs as tree planting and landscaping of neighborhoods, provision of play areas and community gardens, installation of corner traffic lights and other devices, or reducing the volume of traffic through residential areas reflect the desire of San Franciscans to maintain the quality of the residential environment.

Some neighborhoods have formed associations to plan for their changes and have enlisted the help of the planning department and the San Francisco Planning and Urban Renewal Association (SPUR), a private organization, in accomplishing their goals. The planning department has also published a series of tabloids briefly describing examples of neighborhood projects. These tabloids outline the procedural steps which resident groups must follow to comply with laws and ordinances in the planning process and identify sources of financial and technical assistance.

Transportation

The goal of maintaining San Francisco as the dominant city in the bay area appears most powerfully in the transportation element. The major objective of this plan is to "use the transportation system as a means for guiding development and improving the environment" (San Francisco Department of City Planning, 1972: 10) while meeting the mobility needs of the city's residents and visitors. Policies have been developed to:

1. Support and strengthen efforts toward a city-centered region through the development of the regional rapid transit system.
2. Provide for the role of downtown as the primary financial and administrative center for the region.
3. Build and maintain rapid transit lines from downtown to all suburban corridors and major activity centers in San Francisco.
4. Intensify overall transit service in the "central area" (San Francisco Department of City Planning, 1972: 9-13).

The notion of guiding development is eventually defined by the desire to enhance the city's central role in the region through improving the accessibility of its downtown with rapid transit. Improving the environment is defined as encouraging the use and improvement of transit while trying to minimize the negative impacts of automobile usage—congestion, pollution, visual degradation and land-use dominance—particularly in protected residential areas. Both of these objectives should serve to improve the economic position of San Francisco in the region.

Rapid transit is the main transportation tool for improving the accessibility of the downtown area. This consists mostly of the commuter rail service operated by BART which services most of the bay area region. Although there is cross-bay commuter bus service offered by the AC Transit Company, the most significant form of regional transit is, and will be in the future, BART. The hope was that BART would make San Francisco's downtown more accessible to suburban commuters who work in the city's concentrated service economy (finance, insurance, real estate, government, and so on) and to regional shoppers and visitors (Webber, 1976: 81-85). This was to induce economic growth and serve to reshape at least part of San Francisco's physical appearance. Whether BART can have this kind of impact while carrying as small a portion of the commuters as it does is doubtful. And just how compatible are the twin objectives of strengthening the downtown area and preserving it? Various groups in the community have expressed concern over the "Manhattanization" of San Francisco.

The San Francisco Municipal Railway (Muni) is the agency responsible for the second part of San Francisco's transportation objectives—the reduction of automobile use while transit use is increased. Communication and cooperation between the city's planning department and the transit agency appear to be quite good. While the planning department is to develop general transportation goals, the Muni is responsible for operational matters. Not only is it responsible for the provision of transit service in the city, but it also sees itself as a transit advocacy agency (Matoff, 1977). It wants aggressively to seek increased transit usage within the city by improving the system's efficiency. To this end, the Muni has two objectives: (1) to better coordinate local transit systems (mainly its own bus and light rail systems) with the regional network transit (AC cross-bay commuter buses and BART) and (2) to improve the local citywide transit service.

The first of these objectives, the coordination of local and regional transit service, involves the rearrangement of fares, schedules and service connections between systems for a more effective total service level. This will require certain new institutional arrangements which are currently being developed to make such coordinated planning possible.

The second objective, improved intracity downtown access and service, will require changes in Muni's institutional situation. Muni is currently operating in precarious fiscal and administrative conditions. Its share of the city's tightening budget is subject to periodic reductions because of the fluctuating political popularity of transit in the city administration. Attempts at managerial and service improvements are hampered by dated administrative procedures which require approval from outside the transit agency itself. Efforts are being made toward greater institutional autonomy. The ability of the city to accommodate the economic growth will have some bearing on the success of these efforts.

Water

Planning in the water department seems to proceed apart from any communication with the central planning agency (except insofar as the planning department fulfills its EIR duties). While the water department countenances a 20-30 year horizon, the future is seen essentially as an extended present, a projection of current trends. Changes in social, environmental, or technological realities have not been considered, even though there is evidence of such change. People are beginning to value conservation more highly, resource shortages are becoming more frequent, and water recycling technology is advancing. Yet, these factors are not within the planning purview of the water department. And the planning, although long range, is basically reactive. It tries to adjust growth, hazards, and changes to present conditions rather than adjusting present conditions to future goals and expectations.

CONCLUSION: THE QUESTION OF GROWTH

Some of the inherent contradictions in planning converge on the growth/no-growth issue. The San Francisco general plan assumes a stable population for the future (and clearly prefers the maintenance of the existing environment over increased population growth) but expects increased employment through continuing economic development in the bay region generally and in the San Francisco downtown area specifically. A desire is expressed for economic progress on the one hand and for preservation of the present character of San Francisco on the other. While the attractiveness of each is easy to understand, this probably implies the lack of an agreed upon image of the future. While the two can certainly be made compatible, they will not be so without quite substantial long-range planning and forethought.

There is something very attractive about the open recognition in San Francisco's planning that much of what is is good and should be an important part of the city's future. And one can readily admit the felicitous turn of phrase summing up much of the spirit of the planning: "Certainly the old should not be replaced unless the new is better." However, the desire for preservation is not related meaningfully to the powerful social and economic changes that are underway. It is wishful thinking to assume that all good things can be preserved and the undesirable elements changed or improved. One looks in vain in San Francisco planning for the logic of stability versus change in guiding development toward the future.

Chapter 4
Planning in Boston: The Economic Development Game

BACKGROUND

Boston, the capital of Massachusetts, has demonstrated unusual vigor in regaining its place among the top American cities during the last 15 years. In 1975, the city's population stabilized at approximately 637,000. It had peaked in 1950 at more than 800,000 and seen declines of 100,000 in the 1950s and of 60,000 in the 1960s. Planners in Boston attribute the stabilization to a "decade long neighborhood revitalization effort" (Boston Redevelopment Authority, 1977d: 7) as well as to the growing attractiveness of central cities due to the high cost of energy and suburban housing, to the rise of two-worker families, and to the preference of smaller households for central location (Boston Redevelopment Authority, 1977c: 16-17).

To understand the Boston of today, one must look back over a period of some 50 years:

> Central city Boston experienced a thirty-year depression following 1929 well into the post World War II years long after the nation as a whole and most of its large cities were well on the way to recovery. The Boston of the present is just now returning to market size of 1929 in terms of total personal income (measured in dollars of constant value) following a one-fourth loss in the thirty years after 1929. The broad decline in personal income levels reflected a major shift in population composition, whose magnitude is measured by the fall by one-fifth in per capita income over the 1929-59 period (measured in dollars of constant value) (Boston Redevelopment Authority, 1977b: 2).

After World War II, the substantial loss of middle-class families was nearly offset by an in-migration of poor families. The overall annual rate of population decline was −1.4 percent during 1950-60 and −0.8 percent during 1960-70. There was an outflow of manufacturing and of wholesale and retail trade to the suburbs and a fall in taxable property values, with accompanying neglect of public facilities.

Boston fought the decline with a large and sustained urban renewal program which emphasized the attraction of service jobs to the downtown area and the modernization of the city's public infrastructure. Federal and state financing as well as private investment were sought and obtained. An economic turnaround began in the late 1960s, reflecting the national trend of many central city downtown areas to become services-oriented economy centers.

During the 1970s, Boston's newly revitalized economy appeared to have weathered its major tests. As a result of two recessions (in 1971 and 1975), total jobs in Boston declined from a 1970 high of nearly 576,000 to a low of 514,000 in 1976. The services and manufacturing sectors both registered significant gains during 1977 and the following year (Boston Redevelopment Authority, 1978a, 1978b, and 1979). While the city's economy was surviving the impact of recession, its neighborhoods were suffering from a notable lack of private sector housing construction and a rise in housing demand. The previous decade of development left some of the city's neighborhoods in a state of social, economic, and/or physical decline. This fact has provided the focus for the city's current planning effort.

THE KEY ROLE OF THE BOSTON REDEVELOPMENT AUTHORITY

Before describing that effort, a word about the Boston Redevelopment Authority, the agency responsible for planning in Boston, is in order. In 1960, then Mayor John Collins announced the "90 Million Dollar Development Program for Boston." The urban renewal program was subsequently formalized in the 1965-75 general plan. To pave the way for badly needed federal financing and to consolidate the planning and development efforts of the city planning commission, the housing agency and the redevelopment agency, he created the Boston Redevelopment Authority. Its responsibilities include both planning/research functions and development authority. The BRA's planning focus encompasses physical, economic, and transportation planning, and its personnel serves as staff to the city's zoning board. The BRA also administers and makes recommendations (to the deputy mayor on fiscal affairs) on all property tax exemptions. Massachusetts Law 121A provides that new construction which eliminates blight may qualify for an exemption from one half of the property tax payment. Since Boston's city revenues derive exclusively from property taxes, planning's role is a very significant influence upon the fiscal affairs and the physical development of the city.

CHARACTER OF BOSTON'S PLANNING

Boston planning may be characterized as a highly conscious effort significantly to influence the middle-range future (the next ten years) in a clear-cut direction—the strengthening of the central city economy as the foundation for a better life for the residents of and workers in the city. It is an attempt to take advantage of social and economic trends which favor the city while using these strengths to improve and maintain its neighborhood areas. Evidently, the long-range future is thought to be a matter for later attention when the current situation is substantially improved.

Almost classic emphasis on economic development and investment in public facilities dominated the general plan for 1965–75 and even more so the succeeding plan for 1975–85. While the 1965–75 plan concentrated almost exclusively on economic development of the downtown, the 1975–85 plan is attempting to focus more on revitalization of the residential neighborhoods and their more decentralized economic activities.

The current plan has two major goals. The first is to continue to reinforce the development of the downtown services-oriented economy with public investment. This is to improve the job and income opportunities of residents and strengthen the revenue base of the city. The second goal is to improve the city as a place to live through housing construction and rehabilitation as well as public facilities and service improvements (Ganz, 1974: 3). Of the $12 billion combined public and private investment projected for the 1975-85 period, $4 billion is scheduled for the first goal of downtown development and $8 billion is scheduled for the second goal of investment in the neighborhoods other than downtown (White, 1975: Section IV, 5-7). Both of these goals are seen to be highly interdependent. Development of the downtown economy should stimulate investment in other parts of the city and will generate revenues to be used in neighborhood revitalization. Similarly, improvement of the city as a place to live is intended to make investment in downtown and other economic activities more desirable.

Boston's strategy for achieving these goals consists of (1) the use of local municipal investment in public facilities to leverage greater investment by the private sector and other public agencies, (2) fiscal policy and reform, and (3) planning which includes projections of social and economic trends and establishment of targets for public and private investment (White, 1975: Section III, 1-18).

Investment Leveraging

The first of these, *investment leveraging*, is based on the premise that the keys to the welfare of the city's residents are the jobs and income which private development produces. The public role is to provide "urban infrastructure and amenities which facilitate and make possible the private investment effort" in homes and businesses (White, 1975: Section IV, 3). Further, "the City investment commitment and the planning and development horizon to which it relates would be the fulcrum inducing and facilitating a much larger state and federal commitment of funds and an even larger private investment role encouraged by the combined city/state/federal public investment and what it would mean for expanding opportunities (for profitable private investment) in Boston" (White, 1975: Section IV, 16). Of the $12 billion combined public and private investment anticipated for Boston in the 1975-85 period, only 7 percent is expected to come directly from the city. This strategically key share would be used largely for schools and community facilities. It is this local 7 percent share which is seen as central to facilitating, guiding, and programming the combined public and private investment. The one fourth anticipated state share of the program would be directed mainly at higher education, public schools, and highway, port, and airport facilities. The one fifth anticipated federal share of the program would consist mostly of grants for public transit programs. The remaining one half of the anticipated investment would come from private sources directed primarily in office, retail, medical, housing, public utilities, and industrial development. Of this private investment, three fourths would come mainly from long-term loan and mortgage financing and one fourth from the direct investment and reinvestment of private earnings (White, 1975: Section IV, 17, 18).

Fiscal Policy and Reform

The second tool for achieving Boston's goals is seen to be fiscal policy and reform. This consists of three parts. First, the proportion of municipal expenditures invested in capital improvements and public facilities is to be marginally increased relative to expenditures in operating items. This is a fundamental theme in Boston's approach to and faith in the future: *investments now will pay off in the future*. The second part of fiscal policy is to limit the share of municipal expenditures, and increases thereof, to a certain proportion (5 to 6 percent) of the gross city product. Growth of municipal expenditures is then made possible only by an increase of the gross city product. Finally, Boston is seeking fiscal reform which would decrease its reliance on relatively inelastic property taxes and would give it "a larger share of the revenues the city raises for the state and federal government" (White, 1975: Section III, 3). In this respect, Boston sees the impediments to its development as being mainly fiscal rather than economic. The city's only operating revenue source is currently the property tax. The economic growth the city is generating is not being reflected in its property tax revenues but rather is being reflected in the payments of federal and state income taxes and in state sales taxes. Further, the services-oriented economic activity in the city has a low capital investment per worker as compared to that of manufacturing. Thus the growth in employment is not reflected well by the property tax. Compounding this fiscal problem, the city has a great deal of property which has been granted tax-exempt status through state legislation. Boston is seeking fiscal reform to reduce its reliance on the property tax and to get a revenue source which is more responsive to economic growth. The city is pushing for legislation which would require the state to reimburse localities for revenues lost due to tax-exempt status. It is also seeking to have certain service responsibilities taken over by the state. Boston is also endeavoring to gain an expansion of sales and income taxes, changes in property taxation, and perhaps the use of a statewide property tax (White, 1974: 40-44).

Planning Approach

A number of planning tools are directly involved in implementing the city's goals including a series of social and economic surveys and projections, investment targets, and specific plans for the downtown and for the neighborhoods.

Population and income estimates necessarily play a large role in a development program such as Boston's. These provide a base for projecting housing demand, for articulating goals for residential development and neighborhood revitalization, for projecting retail sales, and as an element in estimating tax yields. They also provide a base for describing the change in population composition (an anticipated reversal of the 1950-70 outflow of middle-class families, continued growth of middle-class unrelated individuals, modest growth in the more centrally located neighborhoods, and stabilization in the older ethnic neighborhoods). Similarly, a whole body of projections and forecasts deal with the future of the city's economy and with the downtown. These include projections to 1985 of production and employment by industry and comparisons with national, state, and metropolitan region projections. Finally, there are projections for public sector expenditures and revenues (property value base and yield) and for financing an indebtness-management strategy.

Investment targets are given central importance since investment—both public and private—is seen as the main vehicle for the implementation of goals and development plans. These targets are by economic sector, by public and private, by type, and by financial strategy involved. There is a downtown plan with targets aimed at strengthening economic activity and employment at the center where such activity is already concentrated. And there is a ten year program for neighborhood revitalization including long-term programs for community and home improvement as well as housing demolition. There are ten year targets for housing construction, investment targets for commercial construction and retail trade revival and growth. There are employment targets for various economic sectors. Finally, survey information is available on planned investments in medical facilities and institutions of higher learning, on public utilities investments, and the investment plans of the federal government, the state, and the semiautonomous state agencies operating in the fields of airports, seaports, public transit, water supply, and parks and recreation.

These investment targets and socioeconomic projections are made in terms of specific plans for the downtown as well as for the neighborhoods. The downtown plan has site-specific components designating areas for either conservation, development, or controlled growth:

> Boston's Downtown Plan is based on a strategy of concentrated growth of Downtown as the center of job-creating services activities, as the prime residential development area of the City, as a revived center for shopping . . . (and) . . . the Downtown will absorb most of the City's projected office development and hotel development, and the larger share of projected retail development, as well as the major part of anticipated investment in public utilities. For housing, fully one-half of projected new construction of dwelling units will be in the Downtown. In public improvements, however, the Downtown share is lesser (White, 1975: Section III, 7; Section IV, 6).

Along with this will be new facilities for medical and higher learning institutions, for cultural and arts activities, and for the promotion of tourism. These will be planned on the basis of the existing character of the downtown: conservation of desirable living environments, redevelopment of those areas which are beyond rehabilitation, and a mixture of both in some areas. This plan will be central to the city's targets for investment, jobs, and income.

The plan for neighborhood revitalization originally entailed investments in public facilities and improvements, transportation, and housing construction and rehabilitation. These investments were seen as central to making Boston a desirable place in which to live. They were tied to specific neighborhoods of Boston and reflected the different character and needs of the neighborhoods. Each of the city's 15 neighborhoods had a different investment profile which spanned ten years. These investment schedules included detailed projections of each neighborhood's population and characteristics, its income and distribution, and the productivity of different economic activities (office industry, retail trade, hotels, tourism, medical services, higher education, and manufacturing in the neighborhood). Targets were established for each neighborhood, and programs were developed to channel investments in that direction.

In 1977, the focus for neighborhood revitalization changed. Previously, public investment had been channeled into schools, libraries, police and fire stations, parks, community facilities, and housing rehabilitation. By 1977, high unemployment had become widespread in most of the older ethnic neighborhoods:

> (T)he fiscal crunch is limiting public investment, the growing property tax burden is threatening the viability of investor-owned multi-family housing, and inadequate income and opportunity are the main danger for neighborhood stability.

Therefore:

> The new generation of medium and long-term neighborhood planning and development programs is concerned with unemployment and jobs and income, expanding the economic base, private investment stimulation, matching job creation with skills development of the neighborhood labor force, providing the requisite public sector economic and social infrastructure, prospects for population and households, and the dynamics of housing markets and financing (Boston Redevelopment Authority, 1977a: 12-13).

Neighborhood revitalization strategy, while still concerned with encouraging new housing starts and continued rehabilitation of older dwellings, has shifted its attention. The current approach is an aggressive attack upon those forces seen as limiting investment in, and the stability of, the city's neighborhoods. It concentrates both on job development and the matching of those jobs with available skills at the neighborhood level.

THE BOSTON PLAN

Reflecting this new neighborhood revitalization strategy is the *Boston Plan*, a comprehensive proposal to the federal government which outlines the potentialities and needs of four Boston neighborhoods. Boston is seeking $122 million in federal funds in order to leverage an additional $470 million in private and other public monies to achieve its goals in each of these neighborhoods. The Boston plan is an ambitious proposal encompassing some 72 projects in Hyde Park, Blue Hill Avenue, The Harbor, and Columbia Point. The plan details separate approaches to each of these neighborhoods. In one case, the preservation of the existing neighborhood quality is central, while in another, the plan calls for a broad revitalization effort. In a third, the creation of an entirely new neighborhood is proposed.

An overriding concern is the creation of jobs and the training of Boston residents to fill those jobs. The plan recognizes that private investment in the city's housing and commercial sector (and, therefore, the vitality of the neighborhoods) is dependent upon the employment and income levels of the residents. The plan also addresses the important issues of expanding the municipal tax base, encouraging commercial and industrial development, improving the quality of housing and transportation, and increasing community confidence (that neighborhoods are a good investment).

What is significant about the Boston plan is its emphasis on reporting to the federal government its specific program needs in the context of its overall city planning effort and its attempt to coordinate federal funding.

SOME PROBLEMS

While Boston has greatly strengthened its economic base and vastly improved its public infrastructure, it has experienced an unequal development process. Private sector housing construction has been minimal, while housing demand has continued to climb. High unemployment has troubled the city's young and minority workers. Many low-skilled manufacturing jobs have left the city with most new jobs available in the higher-skilled services employment. Neighborhoods are just beginning to experience a shift from predominantly FHA financing to private bank mortgage financing (Boston Redevelopment Authority, 1979: 46, 72-73). The recent refocusing of neighborhood revitalization efforts is an attempt to respond to these shortfalls.

Boston's significant planning experimentation in the economic realm brings to the forefront how recent and limited is the experience of urban planners in this realm. There are clear operational advantages in Boston's focusing on the middle-range (ten year) horizon. But something is also lost in the lack of serious attention to the long-term transformations that Boston, together with other American cities, is experiencing. A major economic turnabout will almost certainly require decades and carefully planned long-term changes in physical, institutional, and behavioral elements. It would seem logical that the time concerns of planning match these change requirements.

Chapter 5
Planning in Cleveland:
A Unique Social Concern

BACKGROUND

Cleveland, an important port, is a major industrial center for Ohio and most of the United States. It is a leading producer of transportation equipment, machine tools, chemicals, petroleum products, paint, clothing, and electrical equipment. The decline in Cleveland's population indicates the socioeconomic troubles which have plagued her over the past 30 years. The population peaked in 1950 at 914,000, fell to 876,000 by 1960, to 751,000 by 1970, and to 560,000 at the end of the 1970s (roughly the same population as in 1910).

In common with other older central cities, Cleveland is suffering from substantial disinvestment. Developed nearly to its physical limits, private redevelopment is extremely limited. Many industries and middle- and upper-income residents have left or are leaving. During the 1950s, they were being replaced by a lower income, less skilled, and less mobile population. Since the early 1960s, these residents have not been replaced at all. The lowest spectrum of the housing market has been experiencing abandonment and complete collapse. The deterioration of many of Cleveland's neighborhoods has encouraged those who can to move to the suburbs.

During the 1960s, Cleveland mounted a major urban renewal program aimed at providing much needed public housing, new downtown office construction, and the expansion of the convention center. But none of these efforts has slowed the out-migration of the city's middle- and upper-income residents.

A serious problem in Cleveland is high unemployment, particularly among blacks who make up 40 percent of the population. Since the city economy is heavily geared toward manufacturing, the recessions of the 1970s were felt more keenly than in other cities whose economies have proportionately more services-oriented employment.

Air and water pollution are also major problems. Industrial waste and automobile emissions account for some of the poor environmental quality, but the city's sewage system (which for years could not prevent sewage from spilling over into storm drains during heavy runoffs) has also contributed to health hazards.

Most significant, however, is the poverty of many of the city's residents. In 1975, one out of every four Clevelanders "depend(ed) on some sort of public assistance as (his) primary source of income" (Krumholz, Cogger, and Linner, 1975: 299). This factor has provided the major focus for urban planning in Cleveland.

Urban planning in Cleveland focuses on the severe socioeconomic problems of the city and attempts to deal with these problems as directly as possible. (While the present tense is used throughout, the picture provided here of planning in Cleveland reflects the situation in the latter half of the 1970s.) As such, its thrust is not towards the future but rather towards the present—to the problems that currently press upon the city. Its orientation is not toward the environmental problems of the entire city as is usual in American city planning; rather, it is toward the welfare of a particular group, the city's poor and disadvantaged population. Planning undertakes a well-defined *advocacy approach,* which is openly political whereas most city planning tries to adopt a "politically neutral" stance. Cleveland's planning represents a significant break with the past and is an experiment of major importance.

BASIC ASSUMPTIONS

In these conditions, the planning commission makes at least four assumptions upon which to base its approach to the future (Krumholz and Cogger, 1977: 1-3). The first of these is that the trend of decreasing population and jobs will not be significantly reversed. The purpose of revitalization is to learn how to "grow old gracefully" rather than to "restore lost youth." This assumption implies the notion of broad structural social change that cities must accept and deal with. The second assumption is that local incentives to developers will have little effect in determining business and industrial locations. Such incentives tend to cancel each other out between and within jurisdictions, and their "only likely effect will be to increase the expected rate of return on private capital" (Krumholz and Cogger, 1977: 2).

The third assumption is that local fiscal crises are not brought about by cycles in the national economy. Improvement in the national economy will not automatically improve the economy of Cleveland. The last assumption is that, while federal money can be expected to help somewhat, it will not bail Cleveland out of her problems.

The crux of these assumptions seems to be that Cleveland is not in great demand as a place to invest in either by businesses or by individuals due to its diminishing importance in the regional and national economies. Since this situation is not likely to change in the near future, how can the city's "old age" and the poverty it engenders be approached? What kind of revitalization strategy is called for?

Approach

The main principle of Cleveland's approach to the future is to advocate the interests of Cleveland's present residents in all policy issues that come up. The planners advocate the interests of these residents who are hurt the most by the city's decline and who have the least power and resources:

> In the context of limited resources and pervasive inequalities, the Cleveland City Planning Commission will give first and priority attention to the task of promoting a wider range of choices for those individuals and groups who have few, if any, choices (Cleveland City Planning Commission, 1974: 72).

This has become the overriding goal of the commission—the ultimate measure of effectiveness. In order to achieve this goal, the commission has adopted an "income strategy" on the assumption that the major vehicle of choice is income. Poverty is the major indicator of limited choice.

Cleveland's revitalization strategy is designed to work from the bottom up. As Norman Krumholz, director of the city planning commission during the 1970s, states, it is based on "the fact that until the social and economic problems of the poor are abated, central cities are not going to attract much new investment or development" (Krumholz, Cogger, and Linner, 1976: 5). The basic principle is that it is best to start dealing with the problems at their worst rather than to place revitalization hopes on potential returns from possible investments.

Forms of Advocacy

The commission's advocacy effort has two levels of expression. The commission sees itself first as serving in an advisory capacity to both the local officials and to political decisionmakers at the state and federal levels. It seeks to provide information, constructive criticism, and advice to those who make decisions affecting the interests of Cleveland residents. The commission feels that its effectiveness should be judged by how well it represents the conditions in Cleveland, the effects of poverty, and the means for achieving greater equality.

The second level of Cleveland's advocacy approach is to take an openly political and activist role in public policy formulation and implementation. The commission recognizes the need to take on and often oppose other agencies and organizations in policy and fiscal matters. Implicit in this level of planning is the assumption that:

> Those planners who, in the tradition of our profession, look to political leaders for clear statements of goals or objectives will be eternally frustrated. The political process is a decision process, not a process of goal formulation. Elected officials usually avoid clearly identifying goals and objectives . . . While the political process demands that goals remain ambiguous, the planning process requires that they be clearly defined. Unless planners are prepared to select goals for themselves, they will flounder aimlessly in search for direction or serve as rationalizers and expeditors for the narrow and shifting interests of others (Krumholz, Cogger, and Linner, 1976: 16).

The planning commission actively advocates what it considers to be the interests of Cleveland residents in a shifting, transitory, and partisan political arena. In performing their advisory function, Cleveland planners have had to become "more innovative, more entrepreneurial and more aggressive."

The problems that face the aging city of Cleveland (and many central cities in general) are "poverty, unemployment, inadequate mobility, deteriorating neighborhoods, and declining municipal services." These problems are of the highest priority for the city. What kind of activities do Cleveland planners engage in, considering their basic redistributive goal and their activist stance? Krumholz and Cogger (1977: 4-10) have summarized the commission's activities into four categories. The key principle in all four categories is better management within the "real parameters" of the city.

"Quid Pro Quo"

The first activity is "the imposition of restraints." This involves "the notion that the city and its residents should expect something in return for granting subsidies, (which is) a startling concept to those who view public funds primarily as a way to take all the private risk out of what used to be called private enterprise" (Krumholz and Cogger, 1977: 4-5). This activity entails performing strict cost/benefit analyses on projects which involve public subsidy, authorization, or administration. Projects are then measured by how well they achieve the highest priority goals, namely, how much do low-income persons benefit and what kind of costs must they suffer? If a project benefits those with the fewest choices or if its benefits to other groups, such as developers or suburban dwellers, causes significant spillovers to higher priority groups, then the project is given approval and support by the commission. If it does not, the members actively oppose it. In this capacity, they perform the role of a watchdog on the "private use of the public interest." The commission's literature abounds with examples of this activity—both successful and unsuccessful.

Investments

The second activity is a corollary of the first. Krumholz and Cogger (1977: 5) call this the development of creative investment proposals. It involves two tasks. The first is to program the city's resources in such ways as to leverage private investment in meaningful ways. For the most part, these proposals are intended to be small-scale efforts at achieving real but unglamorous results. The second task under this rubric is to work with city operating departments to improve, reorient, and economize services in light of the commission's broader goals. In this vein, Krumholz and Cogger use the homely example of how the city's Division of Waste Collection and Disposal, after working with the planning staff, now "talks about picking up garbage heuristically!"

Shrinkage

The third type of activity involves "policies for constructive shrinkage." This entails reexamining the kinds of responsibilities for facilities and services that the city has and determining the kind they should have. The planning commission approaches fiscal policy with an emphasis on maintaining and improving existing capital resources rather than investing in new construction. It orients the city toward divesting itself of certain responsibilities, such as transit which can better be handled by an agency with a larger fiscal base. In searching for suitable transfers, the planning commission tries to insure that services either are improved or stay the same but never worsen. And it attempts to create new services which are needed locally due to the city's decline, but which are not provided by other regional, state, or federal agencies.

Community Organizations

The final category is that of "strengthening community organizations" (Krumholz and Cogger, 1977: 9). This involves cooperation with community groups, helping them to define their interests and learning from them what is going on in the neighborhoods. Such joint efforts create political allies which serve as a countervailing political force against the claims of downtown capital interests, suburban interests, and others who do not accept the validity of central-city residents' needs. They also reflect an unusual level of political activism on the part of the planning commission, an activism that is outside the normal confines of government protocol.

APPROACH TO THE FUTURE

Cleveland's approach to the future is largely politically and socially oriented. It assumes that revitalization involves drawing strict political lines around economic processes and defining new economic roles and activities for the city. Imposing restraints and strengthening community organization are seen as providing an environment in which both creative investment and constructive shrinkage can be applied. How is this approach reflected in specific fiscal strategies and programs?

POLICIES AND PROGRAMS

Income policy is seen as central to everything else. Poverty diminishes the freedom to choose housing, limits mobility, and engenders neighborhood deterioration. There is a reflexive quality to the relationship between income level and housing, mobility, and neighborhood quality. Consequently, the commission has designed all policies around improving incomes and increasing the choices that are created thereby. Vehicles for increasing incomes consist of federal transfers, local services and expenditures, and local development authority and planning.

Policies to directly affect income involve either improvement of employment opportunities or direct federal subsidization of local incomes. Employment improvement involves using locally controlled federal subsidies to create service employment which hires local low-income residents. It can also involve using subsidies, either local or federal, to stimulate employment in the private sector. In this case, the commission would weigh carefully the amount of a subsidy given against the number of jobs created. The commission has also made a point of evaluating the kinds of industry which might prosper in the city and which would, therefore, justify efforts to help keep them in the city (such as market advice and technical assistance). They want to avoid spending effort and money on businesses and industries which will probably leave the city anyway. Other steps toward improving the employment opportunities of residents are services such as skill-training, daycare centers, and even improved transit which would remove obstacles to employment. The commission also supports the proposed federal Family Assistance Plan which would provide direct income subsidies. This is perhaps the most radical method of subsidizing local incomes.

Since all these objectives require federal government assistance, the main tactic has become active lobbying. A major part of the commission's income strategy consists of garnering greater local income from federal sources.

Housing Subsidies

In assessing the housing market in Cleveland, the commission has determined that "there is an adequate supply of housing available for Cleveland households" (Wright, 1973: 24). There is also a substantial amount of housing which is filtering down. Therefore, the housing problem in Cleveland is centered around an "ineffective demand for housing, that is, the inability, due to low incomes, of a large segment of Cleveland's households to expend an amount for housing which is adequate to maintain a unit in standard condition." Although units are filtering down, new residents are not able to maintain them in standard condition or pay rents adequate for normal maintenance. Owners are thereby induced to let quality or "housing service delivery" decline in order to meet effective demand. The planning commission concludes that:

> (1) housing subsidies should be primarily directed at the basic problem—ineffective demand (low income)—which requires subsidies directed toward the demand side of the market rather than the supply side; (2) housing subsidies directed toward the supply side of the market should have as their objectives the preservation and maintenance of the existing housing stock . . . Given the definition of the housing market problem in Cleveland, it could be hypothesized that the impact of the federal programs has been injurious to the private housing market (Wright, 1973: 24).

Revitalization of the housing market in Cleveland thus is seen as requiring that the effective demand of residents be improved. For this, only minimal new construction is needed, while the existing housing stock needs to be maintained and rehabilitated through subsidies to either the resident or the owner. Success in achieving these objectives depends on the availability of federal funds which can be guided by the local advocacy effort. The thrust of the commission here again is on increased lobbying of the federal government.

Transportation

Similarly, the approach of the planning commission to transportation is based on promoting the interests of the lower-income residents of the city. The objective is primarily to enhance the mobility of the transit dependent and, if it does not conflict with the interests of the city or the commission's goal, to enhance the mobility of those not dependent on transit as well. The effect of the transportation objectives is to deemphasize middle- and upper-income and suburban needs and to draw attention to lower-income and central-city needs.

To achieve these objectives, the commission has involved itself in transit planning at local, state, and federal levels as a vocal advocate of the city residents' interests. The commission recognizes that Cleveland and central cities in general have suffered from past transportation policies which have favored highway construction for the suburbs and which have led to disinvestment in the city. As a result, the commission has blocked construction of highways which were deemed destructive of the city. It has done this with a hard line policy against further highway construction unless the city is shown to clearly benefit. This policy includes stipulations that the city's share of the costs should be waived, that compensation for lost tax revenues be made, and that any housing units removed be replaced.

The commission also opposes any large-scale, capital intensive rapid rail transit which might burden the city with high costs but would do little to serve the transportation needs of the city's low-income residents:

> When it became apparent that the Cleveland Transit System was doomed to chronic deficits and could only (offer) less and less service at higher and higher fares, (the Commission) worked hard for the regionalization of the system. But (its) work was focused on guaranteed service improvements to city residents (especially the transit-dependent) and fare cuts as the price of transfer of CTS to the Regional Transit Authority. The Commission has pledged to advocate the "mobility needs of the transit-dependent over those of highly mobile groups in the population."[1]

[1] Norman Krumnolz 1978: personal communication.

Finally, the commission supports efforts to improve local bus transit with increased service and subsidized fares. This kind of transportation is seen as most effective in enhancing the mobility of lower-income residents, since it will improve their ability to find employment and give them greater freedom to choose employment in different locations.

Prevention of Deterioration

Policies for community development are designed specifically to arrest the physical deterioration of the city. Although they are not directly income oriented, they do have effects on income. While the community development objectives of the commission resemble traditional physical general plans more than the other sections of the report, these physical objectives are to be achieved in a different way. The center of concern is not the general public interest but rather the interest of one group in the community. Cost/benefit analysis is directed at the interests of the city's low-income residents rather than land-use efficiency and urban design is seen in general interest terms. This objective is consistent with the other objectives and relates to a goal that serves to integrate all the policy proposals.

One major problem faced by Cleveland has been that of housing abandonment, which is caused by speculation on the declining real estate market. Owners have allowed property to deteriorate hoping that the land market would improve. Barring such improvement, they would allow the city to pay for clearing the land and then try to buy it back in public auction at reduced rates. This possibility encouraged tax delinquency and speculative abandonment. Thanks to recent state legislation, Cleveland now has the authority to counter this trend by taking title to land which has delinquent back taxes and/or other processing liens on it for which a buyer cannot be found. While the city's ownership of such land is not immediately valuable, it does serve three functions. (1) It takes low-valued land off the market, decreasing the likelihood that it will enter into a costly cycle of continual foreclosure and public auction which gives no guarantee that the land will ever be used productively. (2) It gives the city some control over future use of the land through either small- or large-scale redevelopment efforts. (3) And most important, it provides a disincentive to the abandonment of buildings. Although it is politically risky for the city to hold on to such land, especially for long periods of time, "analysis indicates that land banking will impose very few additional costs on government (while it) offers the potential for substantial benefits."

Urban Renewal

Cleveland's experience with urban renewal has suggested directions for its community development programs. The city's experience with urban renewal has been mixed. Only one project can be considered completely successful. Perhaps the major determining factor in the relative success of the city's renewal efforts has been demand for the type of development encompassed in a given project. In fact, the city's successful renewal project satisfied most of the demand for office space in the city (Susan Olson, 1973: 25-28; 1974: 13-15). Increases in property tax revenues are what make a renewal project pay for the land price write-downs and increased service costs entailed. Residential development would not generate such revenues in itself, and industrial redevelopment is unlikely. Therefore, urban renewal using land price write-downs, capital improvements, or tax abatements is currently not considered a wise investment for the city. It will not significantly improve the choices of low-income residents, nor will it generate revenues which could be spent providing such choices.

Block Grants

Another program that Cleveland has developed to counter the forces of deterioration is to make rehabilitation loans and technical assistance available to neighborhoods which have been subject to disinvestment and redlining (Cleveland Action to Support Housing, 1977: 1-7). In this program, block grant money is used to leverage private lending at a rate of five to one. In effect, the program uses private lending to stretch out community development funds, making more funds available to the city overall for rehabilitation. With block grant money, emphasis shifts to improving neighborhoods and arresting their deterioration.

The city is moving away from provision of massive subsidies in small, concentrated areas and towards increasing certain types of expenditures throughout large segments of the city. The city also hopes to invest in areas which are in the initial, not final, stages of deterioration. Along with this basic investment strategy are programs of health and safety code enforcement and technical rehabilitation assistance. This shift in emphasis suggests that investment in the neighborhoods is expected to generate greater local demand for downtown uses and perhaps an eventual subsidized renewal of the downtown. Investment in those neighborhoods with the fewest choices is expected to restore vitality to the city.

CONCLUSIONS

A great strength of the Cleveland approach to planning is that it succeeds in operationalizing the problems that are facing the city. Its precept is realistically and candidly to assess the conditions of the city. The report does not hesitate to address conflicts; in fact, it seems to seek them out. It recognizes that there are conflicts between economic growth and economic survival, conflicts among income groups in the community, and conflicts between the way that planners and politicians approach problems. These conflicts will not go away by ignoring or avoiding them. As planners, the members of the commission feel it essential to face the conflicts openly, to formulate a strategy based on clear-cut choices among alternatives, and to commit themselves to a given line of action.

On the other side of the coin, these strengths are counterbalanced by evident weaknesses in the commission's approach. If it succeeds in operationalizing problems well, then it also risks shortsightedness. Emphasis on addressing the immediate problems means that the long-term effects of the solutions can readily be overlooked. Even if temporarily solved, will the problems stay solved? Will the solutions chosen cause additional problems? Will low-income advocacy frighten away potential investors in the city? These questions are not dealt with in the report.

Another strength of the Cleveland approach is that it recognizes that a single city is part of a national system of cities; that its condition is the product of what is happening elsewhere in the region, the state, and the nation; and that what can be done realistically is often dependent on higher levels of government. Against such a background, the commission sees the need for communicating with many governmental levels and feels justified in expecting help from outside.

Significant issues have been raised by the heavy reliance on higher levels of government. There is no assurance that the flow of funds can be relied upon. As indicated, the heart of the commission's incomes strategy consists of obtaining substantial local income from federal sources. This strategy of dependence on the federal government has been criticized by Norton Long (1975: 13):

> The *Report* recognizes that the key problem of the city is disinvestment . . . (but) . . . does not address the reasons for the disinvestment nor whether it is possible for the city and its people to successfully alter these reasons. Failure to alter these reasons can only mean that Cleveland . . . becomes a charity case supported from without, powerless and dependent.

Is Cleveland looking to the federal government for the appropriate kinds of assistance so that it can avoid becoming a charity case? The Cleveland approach involves questions of the greatest significance for the future of American cities. The results of this experiment can be expected to have major impacts on urban planning in years to come.

Chapter 6
Planning in Phoenix: Land-Use Basics

BACKGROUND

Phoenix, one of the fastest growing cities in the United States, is known for its dry, healthy climate and thriving economy. The city grew as an agricultural center when irrigation projects on the nearby Salt River demonstrated the remarkable fertility of the desert. In 1940, manufacturing firms began locating in Phoenix. This trend accelerated rapidly after World War II, and today a diversified manufacturing base is the heart of Phoenix's economy, which is supplemented by agriculture and winter tourism.

The population as of the end of the 1970s was 704,000. This represents a 20 percent increase over 1970. The metropolitan total of 1,410,000 is an awesome 46 percent greater than in 1970. Many of Phoenix's residents, attracted by the lower cost of housing and abundance of jobs as well as the weather, have come from California and the Midwestern states. Racially Phoenix is more than 80 percent white, the balance is made up of blacks and Mexican Americans.

Phoenix is characterized by single-family homes in sprawling communities. The open space which once separated Phoenix from nearby Scottsdale, Mesa, Tempe, and Glendale has been swallowed up by the growth of new suburban communities.

As yet, there are few freeways, but traffic congestion on surface streets is a major problem. Another problem is the city's heavy reliance upon underground water supplies which are not being replenished as rapidly as they are pumped out. To ease the strain on subterranean aquifers, the state of Arizona is constructing the federally financed Central Arizona Project, an aqueduct which would bring more than 1 million acre feet of water to Phoenix annually as early as 1985. Despite the obstacles, the attitude toward the future is plainly optimistic.

Phoenix is governed by a manager and city council, with the council members and mayor being elected for two-year terms. The city manager provides the greatest continuity and is the strongest figure in this form of government. The organization of city government is such that the planning department is part of the Office of Development Services (along with engineering, building safety, and traffic engineering) while the offices of economic development, community development, and housing and urban redevelopment are part of a separate Office of Community Services. At least organizationally, planning is not seen as closely related to the latter activities as it is to the physical development of Phoenix. But the current planning effort may be changing this.

THE APPROACH TO PLANNING

The central theme of planning in Phoenix is growth and the related desire to preserve the city's amenities along with this growth. The planning department has projected a doubling of population between 1970 and 1990, and the economic trend for services and industrial relocation to the Southwest appears to be firmly established. There also seems to be little desire to stop or slow this growth. The prevailing sentiment was well characterized by a top city official who said:

> There is no way to stop growth. Growth is occurring because people don't like shoveling snow in Cincinnati. It will continue as long as this city is a more favorable place to live than other cities (Shuit, 1975: 3).

The problem for the city's planners is how to handle all of this seeming good fortune. Implicit in the planning effort is the confidence that this economic growth and expansion can be managed and reconciled with the desire to maintain the city's accessibility and pleasing character. This confidence pervades the city's planning literature.

Phoenix's approach to the future represents an effort to reconcile these two elements of growth and amenity and is explicitly future oriented. Currently, however, planning in Phoenix is experiencing an important shift in emphasis—from one dominated by physical land use and development to one which places greater importance upon the residents' need to identify with a particular community within the now vast city. This shift in emphasis is expressed in the "Phoenix Concept Plan 2000." The time frame of the 2000 plan can be called long range. However, the plan expresses only "the conceptual intent for future land use in Phoenix . . ." (Phoenix, 1979a: 1). Subsequent planning at both the citywide and community levels will certainly modify and refine this conceptual framework.

Phoenix's approach to planning the future has three basic parts: (1) the concept plan itself, (2) an interim plan, and (3) the forthcoming urban village plans.

The 2000 plan includes goals and policies which address the subjects of land use, transportation, public facilities, housing, environmental quality, social stability and sense of community, employment, and the role of government among others. Some of the major goals and objectives are as follows:

1. Provide a sufficient choice of adequate housing in all parts of the city to meet the needs of all individuals.

2. Develop a land use pattern that reduces the need to travel by shortening required travel distances.

3. Develop physical and social focal points in urban villages and neighborhoods.

4. Foster community spirit, friendliness, physical and psychological well-being, and high community morale throughout the Phoenix metropolitan area.

5. Provide opportunities for diversification of basic employment.

6. Minimize the level of government intervention necessary to achieve urban form goals (Phoenix, 1979a: 4-9).

The 2000 plan redefines the emphasis that the previous comprehensive plan for 1990 had placed on land-use patterns and is an attempt to more closely relate the future physical shape of the city to the residents' need for belonging to an identifiable subarea of Phoenix. Phoenix has grown so rapidly that its current planning boundaries measure 430 square miles, which is only 7 percent smaller than the city limits of Los Angeles.

> The unifying element of the 2000 plan is the concept of urban villages containing a mix of housing types, a variety of jobs and shopping, recreation and education facilities. These villages would help satisfy the psychological need to belong to an identifiable community with a sense of control over its own environment. An urban village will have clearly identifiable core and boundary. Its core will contain the most intense land uses and will be the aesthetic and functional focal point of the village (Phoenix, 1979a: 1).

The intensity of land use would diminish in each urban village as one approached its boundary. The character of the villages is expected to vary widely—from highly urban to quite rural.

The 2000 plan seems to imply that, as the psychological need for belonging to an identifiable community is satisfied through the new urban form, the future development of the city will also improve the quality of life in other respects and will contribute to a more equitable and efficient urban environment.

An innovative step in the development of the 2000 plan is the proposal that the city prepare a general plan to address citywide concerns and that it delegate responsibility for subareas to urban village planning committees. The 2000 plan contains parameters for the population, ratio of basic to service employment, total number of dwelling units, and average residential density for each of 11 villages by five year increments from 1980 to 2000. The plan concludes with a charge to urban village planning committees to "refine the city plan in accordance with the goals of their village and (city goals and policy) guidelines . . ." (Phoenix, 1979a: 19).

The 1985 plan is a supplement to the 2000 plan and is intended to "guide . . . the Planning Commission and City Council on zoning decisions" (Phoenix, 1979b: 1) until a citywide plan and the several urban village plans have been prepared. It briefly describes the concept of the urban village and outlines policies for land use and development which should bring interim decisions into alignment with long-range goals. The interim plan relies on the citywide goals and policies stated in the 2000 plan while offering specific policies for each of the 11 villages in Phoenix.

The forthcoming urban village plans, as indicated in the 2000 plan, are to be land-use planning documents which show ". . . future land uses and intensities in sufficient detail to serve as a basis for making zoning decisions" (Phoenix, 1979a: 19). These plans will feature both 25 year concept plans and more concrete plans in 5 year stages to demonstrate the location of development by intensity of land use and the corresponding patterns of circulation. Each village plan will also contain "quantifiable objectives and an implementation program for the first five year period" (Phoenix, 1979a: 19).

An important dimension of the 2000 plan has been the development by the planning department of a number of sketch plans which were designed to meet the goals statements in varying degrees. Four plans were eventually singled out as alternatives. The first is a simple extension of present trends. The second calls for 22 villages whose residential density would decrease moderately over the next 20 years. The third calls for eight villages with somewhat increasing density, and the fourth calls for eight villages but with an even higher average residential density to be achieved over the next 20 years.

These sketch plans were later extensively evaluated by four separate citizen committees to determine the comparative achievement of plan goals related to cost/revenue, man-made environment, and social fabric, transportation, and natural environment. Although the trade-offs are thoughtfully treated and both the advantages and disadvantages of each sketch plan carefully weighed, the goals were not prioritized and "the measurement techniques used by each subcommittee differed substantially" (Phoenix, 1979a: Appendix D, 26). A summary of the evaluation results is also provided in the appendix to the 2000 plan, but its findings do not favor any one plan conclusively. The choice of a single sketch plan for Phoenix appears to be left entirely to the city council.

The conceptual nature of the 2000 plan (and the fact that it is a draft) may account for some noteworthy deficiencies. One of its features—that of the city delegating village planning to bodies of local citizens—has already been mentioned. This is in line with an increasing trend toward citizen participation in most American cities over the past two decades. However, the plan does not explain how the citizens are to be linked to their village planning committees, how representation is to be structured, or how much decisionmaking power has been delegated.

The connection between the plan and the city's executive agencies is not discussed if, indeed, such a connection exists. No mention is made of any relationship which would presumably need to exist between the urban village planning committees and the offices of economic development, community development, or housing and urban redevelopment (all of which are organizationally separate from planning) (Phoenix, 1979c: 4). The coordination of public investments and services and their use as a planning tool is hardly mentioned in relation to the achievement of the suggested urban village format for Phoenix.

Another major omission in the 2000 plan is any treatment of the needs of special minority or disadvantaged groups in the city. While the language indicates that the villages will exhibit differing residential characters, the rapid economic growth which Phoenix has experienced has also brought with it problems for economically disadvantaged groups or those who do not partake in the general prosperity which surrounds them. While this concern is generally reflected in the goals and policies statements of the 2000 plan, simple confidence in the future or even in good urban design will not solve these problems. An examination of the special needs these groups would have for housing, employment, transportation, and other city services is necessary.

Perhaps more interesting than the goals statements of the 2000 plan are the statements of the major development decisions facing the city (Phoenix Planning Department, 1972). Included in the statements are decisions about the intensity of downtown development, the relative self-reliance of dispersed urban nodes within the city, the fate of agriculture in the area, the degree to which automobile traffic will dominate transportation modes, the type and strength of growth management to be used, and the relative intensity and character of residential development in the city. While the discussion of these decisions is neither full-bodied nor highly operationalized, it is at least a recognition of the actual decisions which face the city. As such, these serve to place in context both the goals statements and the proposed sketch plans.

While the plan 2000 presents an imaginative and thoughtful program for guiding city planning in Phoenix over the next 20 years, it also suffers from a lack of discussion about the implementation problems and strategies of a Phoenix of the future. The plan does not mention how various implementation tools could be built into the planning and development process to accomplish the goals set forth. There is no treatment of the connection between the proposed urban village form and the decisions being made to create the actual urban form, especially those services and structuring decisions which are within the power of the city. If this planning effort is actually to create a new urban form—the prototype end-of-the-20th-century city—then implementation must be addressed. One cannot help but remember the similar high hopes which were placed, early in its development, on Los Angeles as a new type of modern city. Without debasing Los Angeles, one can see that that city strayed from the visions of those early planners. Hopefully Phoenix can profit from that experience by learning to relate more closely the actual decisions made to the desired outcomes of those decisions.

When comparing Phoenix's goals and strategy statements with current problems, transportation surfaces immediately. The mayor of Phoenix concedes that "We have just about milked the capacity of our streets at this point" (Kovitz, 1978: 29). While the street network is overburdened, the public transportation system is grossly underutilized:

> The city does have a public bus system which it subsidizes to the tune of $4 million a year. However, it serves less than 1 percent of the population (Kovitz, 1978: 29).

Although one of the goals of the 2000 plan is to provide an equitable transportation system that will serve those without automobiles, in none of the sketch plans evaluated as alternatives for Phoenix "did total regional transit ridership exceed 5 percent of total trips" (Phoenix, 1979a: 38). The unspoken conclusion is that traffic congestion will be an even greater part of Phoenix's future than it is today as the automobile continues to be the dominant mode of transportation. And that those without automobiles will continue to experience problems of mobility.

An Additional Deficiency

One overriding problem should be noted in Phoenix's approach to the future. This is the failure to consider the long-range larger-scale social and economic picture. The planners do not consider the possible changes in the region and in the national system of cities. These conditions are presently the source of Phoenix's good fortune. What kinds of changes, therefore, might alter the fortune of Phoenix in the future? Might changes in lifestyles draw people away from Phoenix? Will changes in the national economy put Phoenix at a disadvantage? Will the growing importance of international trade make business bypass Phoenix or strengthen its commerce? Granting that such changes are not within the control of Phoenix, should they at least be the object of some consideration? A new urban plan can rather quickly become obsolete unless it is prepared to deal with changing conditions over time.

Chapter 7
Planning in the Atlanta Region: A Serious Attempt at Alternatives

BACKGROUND

The Atlanta metropolitan region, consisting of the city of Atlanta and a seven-county area (Clayton, Cobb, DeKalb, Douglas, Fulton, Gwinnett, and Rockdale), has been steadily growing since the turn of the century. Atlanta itself is a regional commercial and distribution center for the South due to its network of railroads, freeways, and airports. Wholesale and retail trade, manufacturing, government, and services are among the area's major employers. Transportation is seen as the key to the economic development and growth of Atlanta and the surrounding metropolitan area, a fact underscored by the recent completion of a rail rapid transit system that will facilitate access to the downtown center.

Between 1960 and 1970, the city of Atlanta grew only about 2 percent in population. Then from 1970 until 1978, the city experienced a decline in population that appears to have stabilized at approximately 440,000 (a drop of 12 percent). Meanwhile the Atlanta region has been growing at an impressive rate. By 1970, the regional population had climbed nearly 38 percent, from 1,053,000 in 1960 to 1,390,164 in 1970. Between 1970 and 1978, the region grew another 33 percent to 1,849,000. In 1970, Atlanta proper was 51 percent black, while the metropolitan area was over 75 percent white.

Regional planning in Atlanta began in 1949 with the creation of the Metropolitan Planning Commission, which developed a master plan for the two-county area of DeKalb and Fulton. In 1960, the planning area boundaries were expanded to include Clayton, Cobb, and Gwinnett counties. Concern focused upon the economic expansion of the region as well as special plans for rapid transit, water and sewerage systems, recreation, and airports. The Atlanta Regional Commission was created in 1971 to replace several areawide and regional planning functions. Two years later, the regional boundaries were expanded to their present size. The current regional development plan was developed in 1976.

APPROACHES TO PLANNING

Regional planning in Atlanta has focused on the construction of alternative long-range plans based on policy considerations related to factors that shape urban development. Major attention has been devoted to different forms of transportation and to land development controls.

An inquiry concerning approaches to the future in planning for the seven-county Atlanta metropolitan region elicited a useful detailed response from their director of community development planning of the Atlanta Regional Commission, Thomas H. Roberts:[1]

How are we using the future?

1. Of course, for one thing, we make long-range forecasts of total regional population and employment by socio-economic characteristics, and by five-year intervals, which we redo and revise periodically. The Commission has taken the position that it wants to accept the "normal growth" that will result from expanded job opportunities, etc., and attempt to manage that growth into a better future environment, as distinct from—say—a policy of slow growth or zero growth. Atlanta's growth rate is of such a magnitude—not too slow and not too fast—that this is a reasonable and manageable assumption.

2. We do not start out by allocating this future growth to geographic subareas. That is, we do not build regional allocations from the bottom up by locking ourselves into real estate trends. Instead, we construct alternative long-range plans based on various combinations of public policy such as different extents and types of transportation and land development controls. We then use a model to determine what geographic distribution of people, jobs, land use, densities, etc., would result from each of these alternative combinations of policies.

3. The Commission evaluates these alternative plans and their associated policies according to specified social, economic, and environmental criteria, and out of this evaluation and comparison process it selects a "preferred future" which it feels to be both optimum and achievable.

[1]Personal Communication, February 21, 1975.

Planning in the Atlanta Region 75

4. The plan so selected is then detailed and refined into component systems and for incremental time intervals.
5. The detailed plan is then translated into long-range system programs and a short-range regional improvements program, which (like a typical capital improvements program) looks five years into the future and is revised annually by the Commission.
6. The Commission repeats the above process cyclically.
7. We do not expect our long-range picture of the future to be precise. It is neither a "prediction" nor is it an immutable Utopia. Instead, we do long-range planning in order to:
    a. get a better fix on the short-range future;
    b. establish policies and criteria for public programs which are necessarily of long durability and permanence, such as the installation of a rapid transit system or the construction of a freeway;
    c. get a better feel for goal and policy interactions and trade-offs in making short-range incremental decisions.
8. As we repeat this planning cycle every four to six years, I do not expect it to be the same each time. At least, in my experience it never has been. The Atlanta Region has gone through at least five regional plan cycles: the early 1950s, the middle 1950s, the early '60s, the late '60s, and now the middle '70s. Each time the ground rules, values, processes, actors, and available methodologies have always been different. You can state more eloquently than I can the add-on nature of these additional layers of values: efficiency, equity, environment, energy, and God knows what next.
9. As I indicated above, I personally do not take the Utopian view of long-range planning. We are not trying to put together *the* best physical or regional design for the future or for all time. Instead, my goal is to foster a planning program which will increase people's opportunities to grow, change, and exercise relatively free choices as to life style, etc., in future ways which I cannot fully predict, and in such a way that their individual differences can be compatibly pursued with minimum friction. You will note the difference between the alternative policies approach described above (in which distributions and effects are compared) and the more traditional end-state physical form alternatives (e.g., wedges and corridors versus satellites versus salami-shaped nodules or whatever, etc.) . . .
10. We are assuming that implementation tools (whether regulatory, direct public action, or finance mechanisms) will continue to evolve as they have in the past, and that they will be different in the future. Therefore we think it is reasonable to base future implementation strategies on an increasingly stronger and more diverse mix of available tools. (Who in the world thought a few years ago that sewers would have sex appeal, or that land use and zoning would win and lose elections for politicians?)

11. Not only is the future a moving target, but we aren't going to get there in one fell swoop. We will get there in bite-sized chuncks (i.e., many little decisions, not one big decision), so we must translate our broad long-range goals and plans into component short-range programs and projects that public managers and decision makers can deal with. Inability to realize this is where most regional planning programs have fallen down, I believe?

Here is a conscious effort to move away from planning based on an idealized end-state physical development toward planning centered on alternatives keyed to policy areas that presumably shape urban development. The rationale is explained in the regional development plan:

> It was decided early in the planning process that the use of alternatives was critical to producing an effective plan.[2] A choice process for decision-makers and the citizenry could not be posed in all-or-nothing terms. Alternative scenarios of how the region could choose to meet the continuing challenges of growth and change were required to provide a real choice—a choice that would be based on the knowledge of what would result if various actions were taken.
>
> This thinking led to the next decision: the kinds of alternatives to be defined and evaluated. Alternatives employing a physical design approach, such as "linear city," "radial corridors," or "spread city" have most commonly been used in regional planning but suffer from several key deficiencies, the most notable being the difficulty in relating short- and medium-range policies to an ultimate pattern of development. Put another way, it is relatively simple to sketch a year 2000 development pattern, but quite another matter to define how to bring it about. Consequently, it was decided to use another approach, one in which alternatives were built around key policy choices that shape urban development in the Atlanta region: transportation investments and land use policies. The three initial alternatives featured three different transportation systems along with the existing land use policies prevalent in the region. A subsequent set of three alternatives featured three refined transportation systems coupled with a set of more extensive, strengthened development control policies (Atlanta Regional Commission, 1976: 17).

The transportation systems selected for testing in the initial alternatives represented extreme directions in transportation policy. Alternative 1 was designed to evaluate the implications of providing a transportation system

[2] Paul Kelman, chief of environmental planning at the Atlanta Regional Commission, commented: "The main continuing problem with the planning process is that serious alternatives analysis wasn't begun early enough. Several overall regional population forecasts were considered, but not extensively enough to satisfy many people. Because of the continuing controversy over the regional "control total" for population, subsequent efforts (such as the transportation and development control policy scenarios) were viewed by many people as being somewhat suspect and tainted by their association with 'wrong' population forecasts. I have some doubt that this problem could have been avoided even with extensive ventilation of alternatives, because some critics use population forecasts as the issue to get at their real targets, such as highways and sewage treatment plants" (Personal communication: January 8, 1979).

Planning in the Atlanta Region

with a realistic maximum number of new highways in addition to the committed rapid rail and bus system. Alternative 2 emphasized even more transit service for the region and no new freeways. Alternative 3 featured no new transportation facilities beyond the already committed rapid rail and bus transit lines, with only a limited number of arterial improvements to facilitate transit service. The land-use policies included in these alternatives in the first instance assumed continuation of present low and moderate densities reflecting existing zoning and development. The evaluation of each of the alternatives consisted of developing information about the expected distribution of regional growth up to the year 2000 and the accompanying effect on various indicators of lifestyle based on the transportation and land-use policies embodied in each alternative. The evaluation indicators are shown in the second column of Figure 7–1.

Information about each of the indicators was prepared for these three alternatives for 1970, 1980, and 2000. The purpose was to attempt to estimate the extent to which each of the alternatives would help achieve certain designated objectives (see column 1 of Figure 7–1). Testing was carried

Figure 7–1. Regionwide Evaluation Matrix

Housing		A	B	C
Increase Housing Diversity	% Multi-Family & Single Family Households			
Increase Housing Diversity	Housing Demand			
Increase Housing Diversity	% Low Income Families			
Preserve Existing Housing	Households Taken for Transportation Facilities	■	▓	
Minimize Neighborhood Disruption	Land Taken for Transportation Facilities	■	▓	
Land Use				
Encourage Compact Residential Areas	Net Residential Density			
Encourage Balanced Development	% Land in Different Uses			
Maintain Urban Land Reserve	% Vacant Developable Land	■	■	
Protect Critical Areas	Land Withheld From Development	■	■	
Accessibility				
Increase Opportunity	No. Jobs Within 30 Minutes by Highway			
Increase Opportunity	No. Jobs Within 30 Minutes by Transit		▓	▓
Increase Opportunity	No. Regional Parks Within 45 Minutes by Highway			
Increase Opportunity	No. Regional Parks Within 45 Minutes by Transit		▓	▓
Increase Opportunity	No. Cultural Facilities Within 30 Minutes by Highway			
Increase Opportunity	No. Cultural Facilities Within 30 Minutes by Transit			
Serve Special Transportation Needs	No. Aged Services Facilities Within 30 Minutes by Highway	▓		
Serve Special Transportation Needs	No. Aged Services Facilities Within 30 Minutes by Transit	▓	■	▓
Serve Special Transportation Needs	No. Hospitals Within 15 Minutes by Highway	▓		
Serve Special Transportation Needs	No. Hospitals Within 15 Minutes by Transit		▓	▓

Objective	Indicator	Evaluation
Facility Requirements		
Provide Adequate Facilities	Water Demand	Lowest
Provide Adequate Facilities	Wastewater Generation	Lowest
Provide Adequate Facilities	Area Developed but Unserved by Water Facilities	Highest
Provide Adequate Facilities	Area Developed but Unserved by Sewerage Facilities	Highest
Provide Adequate Facilities	New Schools Required	Middle
Provide Adequate Facilities	Park Land/1000 Persons	Lowest
Conserve Regional Heritage	Park Land/1000 Persons	Highest
Environmental Impact		
Enhance Air Quality	Air Pollution Generated by Highway Travel	Lowest
Conserve Nonrenewable Resources	Energy Consumption	Middle
Minimize Noise Level	Airport Noise Effects	Highest
Minimize Noise Level	Highway Noise Effects	Middle
Transportation		
Maximize Balanced Travel	Transit Patronage	Highest
Decrease Travel Time	Travel Time to CBD by Highway	Lowest
Decrease Travel Time	Travel Time to Buckhead by Highway	Lowest
Decrease Travel Time	Travel Time to Airport by Highway	Lowest
Decrease Travel Time	Travel Time to CBD by Transit	Lowest
Decrease Travel Time	Travel Time to Buckhead by Transit	Lowest
Decrease Travel Time	Travel Time to Airport by Transit	Lowest
Minimize Congestion	Volume/Capacity Ratio for Highway	Middle
Maximize Efficiency	Transit System Characteristics (Utilization)	Middle
Improve Accessibility	Households Within 1/2 Mile of Transit	Lowest
Improve Accessibility	Land Within 1/2 Mile of Transit	Middle
Improve Accessibility	Average Peak Period Highway Speed	Middle
Fiscal Impact		
Reduce Capital Costs	Capital Costs for Highway and Transit	Highest
Reduce Operating Costs	Operating Costs for Highway and Transit	Highest
Reduce Net Costs	Net Cost/Revenue Impact for Local Governments	Highest
Small Area Impact		
Multiple Objectives	Small Area Impact	Middle
Historic, Cultural and Recreational Impact Site		
Protect Critical Areas	Historic, Cultural and Recreational Site Impact	Highest

Evaluation Code
- ■ Highest level of objective achievement
- ▨ Middle level of objective achievement
- □ Lowest level of objective achievement

Source: Atlanta Regional Commission, Regional Development Plan, 1976, p. 21.

out for each county and the city of Atlanta as well as for each of 34 planning subareas into which the region had been divided for evaluation purposes. (Figure 7–1 portrays estimates for the region as a whole.)

After exposure of the initial alternatives to local jurisdiction planning staffs, various policy groups, and the public in general, a set of refined alternatives was developed. These represented certain modifications in the transportation features of the three initial alternatives coupled with a set of stronger, more extensive development control policies. These modified development control policies, to be tested as the next stage of the planning process, cover policies related to certain natural features (flood plains, high water table, rock, steep slopes, and high shrink-swell rates) as well as to "densities/open space/ development centers" (covering airport flight zones, transit station areas, parks and recreation, redevelopment areas, new communities, and preservation areas). Both the technical and legal implications of these development control policies have been or are to be evaluated. The technical analysis is being done through the use of a computerized "activity allocation model" and a series of evaluation techniques which address the social, economic, and environmental impacts of the policies. The main objective has been to provide information necessary for deciding on such key issues as whether to restrict development in flood plains and other questionable areas; whether to encourage development in planned redevelopment areas, transit station areas, and new communities; whether to increase the amount of public open space; and whether to attempt to preserve viable neighborhoods and historic areas.

Parallel to this aspect of planning has been an examination of how the modified development control policies might be implemented if adopted. Reports were prepared on the constitutional and legislative basis for modified development controls in Georgia covering (1) public regulations or ordinances setting conditions for private action, (2) taxation, and (3) public investment. Included in the analysis were proposed implementation tools in addition to those already established.

Efforts to involve the public have been characterized by the issuance of popular reports, a TV show coupled with a survey of views concerning major regional issues, and meetings throughout the region. This survey established that popular support for development controls was quite high. At least two thirds of the respondents in each of the counties supported the preservation of scenic and recreational open spaces and the restriction on development by insisting "that adequate community facilities such as sewers and schools are available before permitting development of new residential and commercial areas" (Atlanta Regional Commission, 1974). But the planning staff reports do acknowledge that citizen involvement is still marginal due to the nature of a regional, intergovernmental planning process. This is improving as the planning progresses and tackles more controversial issues, thus attracting the serious interest of a greater number of citizens.

CONCLUSION

It is interesting to note that a new planning agency, coming into being in the 1970s and unencumbered by inherited planning approaches, seeks to provide a useful base for decisionmaking on urban development and urban services.[3] The planners wish to make these decisions by (1) emphasizing *alternative* patterns of development and services rather than a single projected end state, (2) emphasizing policies rather than specific physical patterns, (3) viewing the possibility of greatly expanding development controls, and (4) concerning themselves in a serious manner with involving citizens groups in every stage of the planning. At the same time, the effort underlined the fact that the conceptual and factual base for carrying out a detailed evaluation of developmental alternatives involving many natural and man-made features was limited. Many of the questions raised by considering developmental alternatives cannot yet be answered. But the Atlanta Regional Commission is making noteworthy progress in coming to grips with both the uncertainties and the potentialities of the future.[4]

---

[3]Kelman again writes: "We may not have been encumbered by planning approaches, but I feel that we were encumbered by inherited plans and projects, particularly highways. It was a long and arduous task to give some of them a decent burial" (Personal communication: January 8, 1979).

[4]That the commission has a long way to go in realizing the goals it has established is underlined by the difficulties it has encountered in evolving a consistent pattern of development for the new rail rapid transit system and the extension of the highway system. At points they are in clear competition (Eplan, 1980: 129-43).

Chapter 8
Lessons to be Drawn from a Review of Current Planning

Generally accepted standards do not exist for judging the quality of city planning. A key criterion is the extent to which urban planning within a community provides effective guidelines for the developmental operations of the various city departments as well as for private and community group activities significantly involved in urban development. Effectiveness in this sense has both a technical and a political dimension. *The technical standard* is whether the content and processes of the urban planning that is carried out provide guidelines capable of being used for operational decisions. *The political dimension* refers to the will to use such guidelines. Technical effectiveness implies the degree to which planning makes it easy and attractive for politicians and departmental heads to follow the guidelines. This might be thought of as the political inducement standard. The matter of political will, however, goes beyond inducement to encompass such factors as how the economic leadership sees its own interests advanced or hurt by the planning and the extent to which the political leadership is influenced by this interpretation.

Earlier studies of planning implementation (for example, Pressman and Wildavsky, 1973; Rabinovitz, 1970) as well as the examination of planning in the preceding chapters underline the importance to planning effectiveness of two factors: (1) the extent to which the planning provides guidelines for matters that are of major public (political) concern and (2) the exent to which the plans are readily translatable into decisions being made by the political leadership and action agencies. In short, is the planning politically significant and operationally useful? Viewed in light of such standards, the individual planning operations that we have examined have both strong and weak features. Interestingly, only a few common elements could be found among all the cities examined. Most city planning operations reflect special approaches for coping with current problems and for dealing with the future. Each has unique sources of strength which undoubtedly reflect the planning traditions of the community, the nature of current issues, the political support for those issues, and the quality of the planning and political leadership among other factors. If *all* the points of strength identified in the various city planning activities were to be combined into a single planning operation, it would result in a fairly sophisticated and effective planning operation. The few significant weaknesses would lie in large measure in the treatment of the *time* dimension: in the failure to close the gap between the long-run and more general future on the one hand and the specific and more immediate on the other. This is a lack of functional operationality.

FEATURES OF URBAN PLANS UNDER STUDY

Some of the more significant features of the urban planning programs previously examined are subject matter, goals, planning tools and execution, and the time dimension and approaches to the future.

Subject Matter

All of the plans examined treat city form and a small number of major elements (often mandated by state and/or other laws), such as land use, housing, environment and open space, and transportation. Jobs and economic development are of central concern in only a few instances (such as, Boston and Cleveland); the specific strengthening of downtown economic activities is a more frequently expressed concern. Changing the status of the poor and redistributing income and services are subjects of overriding interest to Cleveland alone. Most plans make only limited references to the poorer and more troubled neighborhoods. Treatment of policies and programs for such neighborhoods is even more limited. More common is treatment of the issue of low- and moderate-income housing. The tendency for urban planning to encompass certain social and economic concerns, initiated gingerly in the 30s, is very slowly gaining momentum. A great deal of ambiguity can be found about the legitimate extent of city planning's involvement in these matters and the appropriate relationship of physical to economic and social concerns.

Surprisingly, relatively little mention is made in the various planning documents of the dynamics of urban change or of those issues that are likely to be more concerned with the future than the past or the present.

Goals

A certain commonality can be found in goals, a further indication of the matters which tend to be of major concern. These, include in most cases:

1. Efficient and orderly pattern of land use.
2. Enhancement of city's role in the regional economy and especially the role of the downtown area (Transportation plans are particularly focused on this goal).
3. Preservation of neighborhoods.
4. Conservation of amenity resources, particularly open space.
5. Efficient community services (but less frequently, adequate revenues to cover the costs).
6. Increase in low- and moderate-income housing.

Any distinction is rare between short- and long-run goals. Equally rare are discussions of priorities or conflicts among goals. With the exception of Boston's planning, rarely are goals quantified, with the implications of achievement or shortfalls spelled out.

The long-range urban-form goals of Phoenix and Los Angeles are notably similar. Each calls for identifiable high intensity nodes at various points on their sprawling urban landscapes which will serve as foci for urban life and offer a broad range of services.

The Los Angeles concept plan is the most far-reaching of the long-range planning documents studied—extending some 30 or 40 years into the future. It is an attempt to address the need for improving transportation efficiency and preserving the single-family lifestyle while at the same time providing for new growth and development. What is significant here is that a city is willing to consider the potentialities of the very long-range future. If further developed, such an approach could lead to more future-related decisions on current issues and debates, such as governmental decisions on capital maintenance and new construction (see Chapter 17). The Los Angeles concept may prove equally important in the near-term future as American cities launch efforts to conserve energy through changing land-use and transportation patterns.

Phoenix's 2000 plan, although rich in its potential for efficiency, is more directly a response to its citizens' need for a sense of community identification. The psychological effects of urban formlessness has led to framing a physical goal in terms of its psychological benefits. Thus, quality of life is uniquely related to the goal for urban form in Phoenix.

The urban village planning model offers the opportunity for high levels of citizen participation at the community level in formulating long-range plans (25 years) for the urban form directions of the several villages. The Phoenix plan also presents a guide for sequencing the development of these villages in line with a policy toward balancing population with job opportunities and for balancing basic employment with services-oriented employment. This is one of the few examples of sequencing encountered in any of the plans.

The unique contribution of San Francisco is its emphasis on the goal of preserving the character of a whole city. Here is a strong sense of the value of the inheritance from the past and of the importance of preserving features that are pleasing. While other plans treat conservation and preservation rather generally and as tools or techniques of planning, these concepts are a major theme in San Francisco planning. The role of these preserved features is that of a guide to the future-built form of San Francisco.

Boston's special planning emphasis is on economic development: job creation, reduction of the city's unemployed, raising income levels, and expanding the municipal tax base. Decisions about priorities have been made, and the relationship of the highest goal to other goals is of conscious concern. The treatment of the relationship between economic and physical development is particularly innovative—resulting in a keen awareness of the effects of both public and private investment in the city.

Planning Tools and Execution

That urban planning has not yet discovered the best framework or foundation for specifying the various steps and measures to be taken to achieve selected goals emerges strongly from the review of city plans. Planners are not certain whether to rely on the traditional physical master plan (or general plan) idea, to move entirely towards a policy planning approach with social and economic factors at the center, or to evolve a specific and understood combination of these. Regional planning in Atlanta and planning in Boston are exceptions to this rule. In each case, the relationship between physical factors and social and economic factors and between the general plan and operational features play a more explicit role in the formulation and execution of the plans. Boston perhaps comes closest to fully operationalizing this relationship. The unresolved nature of this key issue in the other cities' plans makes those plans seem vague and only partially operational at best.

While alternative approaches to carrying out goals, policies, and programs are widely discussed in the various plans, only in Atlanta can regional planning be seen as the concept of alternative approaches integral to plan formulation. In this case, the major alternatives are based upon transportation and land development controls.

The use of alternatives serves to illustrate the problem both city and regional planners face by only partially resolving the differences between a physical master planning approach and a policy planning approach. How essential to the achievement of general goals is physical specificity (where and how to build, the designation of particular public facilities or specific open spaces) as opposed to relying upon standards and broad policy statements? Planning in Atlanta does not fully resolve this key issue, but its approach has great promise.

Another common problem is the limited treatment of diversity. Most of the plans seem to be dealing with a uniform average, whether in neighborhoods or people or commercial establishments. General references are made to poverty neighborhoods and poverty groups, but rarely are policies and programs geared specifically to the different conditions to be found in a city. Nowhere can one find full-bodied recognition of lifestyle differences. The planners act as though they were dealing with a homogeneous clientele. Only the poverty groups receive any special recognition (and even in this case, the poverty is an averaging of income rather than a consideration of specific people and neighborhoods with a variety of conditions and traditions).

The most carefully elaborated and integrated use of multiple planning tools is found in the case of Boston. This planning operation has gained sophistication by borrowing substantially from the experience of national and regional developmental planning in less-developed countries. Several interrelated plans and programs have evolved within an economic-physical developmental context including the following:

1. A general plan over a ten year period.
2. A specific downtown plan aimed at strengthening economic activity.
3. A ten year program of capital improvements.
4. A ten year transportation plan.
5. A long-term program of housing fix-up and neighborhood revitalization.

6. Ten year targets for housing construction and investment targets for commercial construction and for revival of retail trade.
7. Survey information on planned investment in medical facilities and institutions of higher learning, on public utilities investment, and on the investment plans of the federal government and state agencies.
8. Employment and investment targets by economic sector and by type.
9. A neighborhood revitalization program aimed at stimulating private investment to provide increased employment opportunities and programs to increase personal incomes and the municipal tax base.

Investment, both public and private, is seen as the main vehicle for the implementation of goals, policies, and general development plans. The sources and impacts of such investments are matters of major concern.

An operational focus on making the best possible use of both public and private investment is only found in Phoenix. Even more than in Boston, the Phoenix planners recognize the significant role of current investment in creating the forms and conditions of the future—an approach long employed in the planning of individual business units but rarely found in public planning and operations. In Phoenix, more than elsewhere, the value of using relative returns on investment is explicitly recognized as a basis for making public decisions.

Apparently the newer tools of evaluation and impact analysis are only partially used within the various cities reviewed. They are largely geared to individual projects with little if any examination of relationships to broader programs and long-run objectives. Cost/benefit analyses and environmental impact reports are the most commonly employed tools, generally following mandates of various federal, state, and local laws and regulations. Phoenix has employed goal-achievement matrices and a type of fiscal impact study called cost/revenue analysis in the evaluation of its alternative sketch plans. Social impact studies were even more rarely employed at the time of the review.

Even more important is the fact that few regularized feedback mechanisms could be detected. Few techniques for monitoring changes underway had been developed to provide a base for being able to revise goals, plans, and programs on a continuing basis, a claim made in almost all of the cities examined. Boston is the exception since its planners revised the focus of its neighborhood revitalization effort when unemployment among the city's residents continued to mount during the mid-1970s.

As has been noted in many previous studies of urban planning in the

United States, provision for the execution of plans is a weak link in the planning process, probably the weakest link. Ideally, one would like to see plans for execution built into the planning (as some of the cities are already doing on a limited scale) with selected goals, policies, and programs emerging as a result of careful implementation analyses.

The Time Dimension and Approaches to the Future

The weakening of the physical master plan concept, combined with the political pressures for planning attention to matters of current political interest, has lessened urban planning's concern for the long-run future and its capacity to deal with it. This is apparent from the examination of urban planning in various cities across the country.

To be sure, urban plans do have time dimensions, including long-run time periods. The plans examined generally treat time in two or three segments: short range (4 to 6 years), middle range (10 years) and long range (20 years or more). However, these time segments are not treated consistently or operationally since there does not seem to be any special principle involved in the choice of the period, the relationship of plans to the expected longevity of capital improvements, or the decision cycles. Only in budget planning is there an understandable relationship of plan features to specific decision points; and budget planning is still fairly rare among the cities of the United States.

A serious lack of contingency planning exists. The plans seem to include no provisions for failure, for major surprises, or for new and unexpected opportunities. At the very least, cities should be examining the possibility of an energy-short future and the allocation choices that would have to be made in such an event. Instead the future is seen as more of the present with only slightly changed conditions (those brought about by the planning). There is little attention to the dynamics of urban change.

On a more specific and technical level, a problem arises with regard to the forecasts of population, land uses, and other subjects of major planning concern. In many cases, there seems to be an unexplained mixture of expectations and preferences. Throughout the plans, no real distinctions are made between projections of existing trends and preferred future situations. Nor does one come across treatment of what can and cannot be changed in a specific planning category (say, the economic activities in the downtown area) within a given period of time. Similarly, the amount of effort and resources it would probably take to achieve desired futures in the face of existing trends is not even treated.

Instead, the plans deal largely with generally preferred directions, broad policy proposals, and programs without time or quantitative features. There may be good reasons for this, but such an approach severely limits the functional operationality of the plans produced.

LOOKING AHEAD

Taken together, combining the more advanced features of individual city planning approaches, urban planning as a decisionmaking tool can be seen to be moving ahead in several important directions. Economic, social, and natural environment elements are being more firmly incorporated in city planning than in the past. Significant experiments are being carried out in trying to combine the long-run considerations and those of more immediate concern. Policy planning is finding a surer ground for itself, where it can incorporate physical elements in an operational manner without relying on the traditional physical master plan.

All these features can be built on. The remainder of the book addresses concepts and methods that can encourage progress in these directions; specifically, that can encourage city planning to be **in league with the future.**

PART 2
PRINCIPLES OF TIME-CONSCIOUS PLANNING

Chapter 9
Recent Progress in Theory and Practice

Urban planning has been and can be defined in many ways. It has evolved as an idea under greatly different contexts over many centuries and has been given a wide variety of tasks over the years. At the core is the concept of a set of activities that helps to guide the functioning and development of an urban community into the future towards certain goals or by means of preconceived strategies. Like many other societal concepts with a practical dimension, urban planning has life as an idea and symbol, as well as variable forms in actual practice.

At the idea level, it has come to stress the desirability of being operationally concerned with relationships among people, physical objects, and ecological forces; of bringing information (including forecasts and other future-oriented materials) to bear on public and private action; of trying to see things whole; of setting goals and trying to figure out the best way of achieving them; of coordinating and providing frameworks for activities carried out by local government; of reconciling continuity and change; and of aiming at and working towards a better future.

At the operational level, urban planning in the United States has been essentially *additive,* moving from an early emphasis on aesthetics to encompassing concern for the efficient functioning of the city, then focusing largely on the evolving of sound land-use patterns and controlling the uses of land, then encompassing social considerations and stressing the human element, and most recently encompassing many socioeconomic, political, and environmental elements in the functioning and development of local communities and metropolitan regions.

Since urban planning practice branched out from its concentration on land-use planning and control, a divergence has occurred in the content and form of planning among the various municipalities and regions across the country, as noted in Part 1. The dominant master-plan/land-use paradigm (or conceptual framework) of urban planning has given way to experimentation and a search for new frameworks for practice. Not unexpectedly, a certain amount of confusion has accompanied the moving away from the previous dominant paradigm and the experimental search for effective new approaches to the problems of planning in our complex, troubled cities.

While there is confusion, there is also much to draw on in looking ahead to the evolution of a new framework for planning practice appropriate to the next stage in U.S. urban development. Such a framework must undoubtedly have substantial openness and flexibility since it must accommodate the wide variety of urban conditions across the country. Based on a review of both urban planning history and current practice, the critical feature of a new framework is assumed to be the *search* for ways of (1) reconciling the concerns for the current *immediate* problems and the *long-range* considerations and possibilities; (2) learning to live comfortably with being involved in both the needed *technical* activities (particularly centering on information, research, and forecasting) and in the *political* life of the community; and (3) effectively relating *national and state* urban policies and programs to *local* needs and aspirations. The first of these receives the greatest attention in the following because of the author's feeling that there is great danger in what is happening currently in that urban planning may find itself not really effective in either the immediate matters or the long-run concerns. If planning loses its unique relationship to long-run considerations, it probably will not be an effective mechanism for *current* management in local government.

The outlines are clear for the development of a new framework for planning practice in the latter part of the 20th century. (The author is assuming that paradigm change will be a continuing matter.) A number of the more general principles are discussed in Part 2, and others of a more operational nature are discussed in the parts that follow. What is implied is that a new framework for planning practice is not to be found in some *parallel substitute* for the physical master plan focusing on land-use considerations, but rather that it is to be found in a set of principles and in understandings about processes and structures centrally related to political decisionmaking on urban functioning and development.

The principles discussed in this part of the volume are a distillation of certain theoretical and conceptual developments of recent decades that have direct relevance for urban planning, particularly for the considerations identified as the critically important ones for the next stage in the evolution of the field. The theoretical constructs are largely from outside of planning, but that should not be surprising since outside developments often provide the new frameworks and tools that are particularly fruitful for one's own field. Some of the concepts have already been seriously discussed in the planning-theory literature; some have not. What is more important in the present context is that they have yet to be fully incorporated into planning practice. Together, these principles provide a platform on which to build a new planning paradigm.

Chapter 10
Contributing to Societal Learning

One of the most important recent advances in social science theory, in terms of applicability to urban planning, is the *theory of societal learning*. This theory holds that society plans and takes action based on what its human components or agents have been learning about how to function successfully under varying conditions. Such learning can occur in two ways—observation and practice. In the former, learning is by observing what has taken place outside the given society or community. Behavior of others judged to be successful is copied; (for example, the United States borrowing certain features from the British legal system or people emulating those cultures which have learned to "live with nature"). The second form of learning can be essentially internal, out of the society's or the community's own experiences. This practical learning approach has been termed *creative learning* (Dunn, 1971: 27-30).

The theory of societal learning holds that history does not repeat itself even if some features of a current situation have some resemblance to the past. There is instead a constantly evolving process based on learned reactions by the members and leaders of the society or community. The problem is not mainly one of learning how to do the old tasks better—although there is certainly some provision for this—but rather one of learning how to meet new situations effectively. Discovering how to improve learning skills becomes one of the most important processes.

The theory of societal learning has obvious roots in the theory of culture which has long been concerned with the ways in which the young learn the accepted rules of the game. Some anthropologists, in fact, see *culture* as the product of what is inherited from generation to generation, or the accumulation of learned experiences. Because anthropology has been largely concerned with traditional (and relatively static) cultures, the learning features of the theory of culture were not developed very extensively. It remained for those who started from a base of the economically more advanced and highly dynamic societies to push the theory of learning into new realms. Most intriguing is the relationship of societal learning to social change. As Edgar Dunn (1971: 30) suggests, "An important part of social change—indeed the most important part—is the product of an open process of creative learning." In a constantly evolving situation, learning how to deal with change is probably the key to everything else.

The theory of societal learning has not only borrowed from the long-standing theory of cultural evolution but also from the study of biological evolution, the field of human development, and so on. The concept of *paradigm change,* as developed by Thomas Kuhn (1964), has been particularly influential. While Kuhn introduced paradigm change to explain the flow of scientific research, the concept was seen immediately to have great relevance for social research and social practice. Kuhn pointed out that scientists work under the influence of common paradigms which are essentially frameworks and standards within which they do their research. Such paradigms, as frameworks of thought or unifying theory, emerge out of earlier scientific practice because they have been successful in helping to solve problems. The promise of the paradigm is realized by progressive testing and refinement to best approximate its correspondence with nature. The acceptance of a paradigm by the scientists who follow its tenets sets up restraints on what they try to do and how they see nature. But, intriguingly enough, this very process tends to generate novelty. Kuhn (1964: 52-53) explains:

> New and unsuspected phenomena . . . are repeatedly uncovered by scientific research and radical new theories have again and again been invented by scientists. . . . If this characteristic of science is to be reconciled with what has already been said, then research under a paradigm must be a particularly effective way of introducing paradigm change. That is what fundamental novelties of fact and theory do. Produced inadvertently by a game played under one set of rules, their assimilation requires the elaboration of another set. . . . Assimilating a new sort of fact demands a more than additive adjustment of theory, and until the new adjustment is completed—until the scientist has learned to see nature in a different way—the new fact is not a scientific fact at all.

Each paradigm shift brings a newly emerging world view, which then becomes the accepted framework for further research.

The parallels to societal practice were evident to those who read Kuhn's work. Slightly preceding the Kuhn volume, Donald A. Schon wrote along similar lines of theoretical development. He traced the way in which new societal concepts or metaphors arise out of the old ones and displace them as the old concepts are applied to new situations. Schon (1963: 64) maintained, "The old theory becomes new as it changes to meet the demands placed upon it as a projective model for restructuring the new situation." The ability of society to achieve such paradigm or metaphor change is, clearly, a key feature of societal learning.

Planning theorists were quick to see the significance of the ideas embodied in the theory of societal learning. Planning, they suggested, must become a key instrumentality in society's effort to learn (Dunn, 1971; Friedmann, 1973; Michael, 1973; Schon, 1971). In fact, Donald Michael (1974: 47) has related this to the organization of planning itself:

> A variety of societal factors, exemplified by a growing appreciation of the need for orientation to a novel and uncertain future rather than to a familiar and reliable past, and the steady accumulation of evidence showing how little we understand and control our environment, will lead to increasing attention to the theory of design of organizations that can learn their way into the future. The necessary components of the planning process constitute a paradigm for cognitive and effective learning. I expect extensive theoretical efforts aimed at the design of organizations that can learn how to plan.

While societal organizations have been less adaptive or flexible than might be desired (Schon, 1971), urban planning organizations have actually been among the more adaptive ones. Over recent decades, planners have rapidly encompassed new social and political concerns (for example, urban renewal, economic development, freeway planning, social planning, and environmental planning), new methods (particularly quantitative methods), and a new interest in involving community residents in planning. (It is this history of flexibility in urban planning organizations that gives one hope that a volume such as this one can have practical as well as theoretical relevance.) At the same time, it is evident that the incorporation of societal learning into planning practice has not yet been sufficiently accomplished.

Looking at government in general, there has been a tendency to see the public institutions as sharply delineated problem-solving machines. Governmental social organizations are supposed to solve the problems of the poor, renewal agencies to redevelop blighted areas, police departments to prevent and solve crime, and planning agencies to create plans that make the city a desirable place in which to live. But it is one thing to ask a water agency to lay pipes to new homes as they are built, and it is another to ask a police department to prevent all crime. It is no trivial matter to distinguish between the things that people know how to do reasonably well and those that they do not. At the present time, people find it difficult to conceive of any public agency as engaged in a learning situation. Learning to deliver a service is different from actually delivering it in an accepted and approved manner. Thus, if adding more police officers again and again under different circumstances does not reduce crime, one should take that as a lesson being learned and look for quite different approaches to delivering that particular service, maybe even redefining the service itself quite substantially.

Urban planning has much to learn in carrying out the tasks assigned to it. First and foremost, not nearly enough is known about how the urban system works within a local jurisdiction or a metropolitan region to be able to help it function efficiently without a very heavy tax burden or how various forms of new urban growth add to or detract from overall efficiency. Ways to achieve racial and income integration—a reasonably unified society—without using unacceptable coercion have not been found. Ways to safeguard the environment without putting some jobs in jeopardy, frequently the unskilled and semiskilled jobs so badly needed by inner city workers, are unknown, although it should be possible to provide for reasonable economic growth while protecting our environment. The list can be enlarged because the urban scene is remarkably complex and residents of American cities have ambitious goals.

Much of this learning falls into the category of the need for additional research, but, even more, it suggests the necessity of building research into the planning process itself. It can thus become an open organizational recognition of the concept that "we plan as we learn" and a legitimization of experimenting on a small scale before launching larger-scale efforts.

But there is also the problem of a troubling lag in the *application in practice* of what seems to have been learned. For example, city officials are aware of the importance of national urban policies and programs and the often counterproductive results produced in cities. The reaction to this recognition seems to be not to press hard for more careful monitoring and study of national urban policies and their impacts but is limited to improving the art of getting the largest possible amount of federal money, no matter under what constraints. There has been very little reaction with regard to entirely new organizational and process relationships between the federal government and local governments that is clearly implied in the central fact of federal dominance. Similarly, the importance of involving all operating agencies of municipal government in urban planning has long been known, but it is hard to detect the practical follow-through of this learned lesson. Of course, efforts—and in some cases substantial efforts—have been made in individual cities to involve operating agencies in the planning process, but as with federal-local relationships, the near impossibility of effective local planning without the organizational changes has not been declared in ringing, constant, and attention-getting ways.

Other examples can be given, but without going into detail it is evident that there is much scope for strengthening urban planning's learning (and follow-through) capacity. Some of this is discussed in later sections of this volume, but two of the most urgent needs might be referred to here. One is for substantial improvement in techniques of *monitoring* so that lessons learned are thoughtfully and carefully recorded, thus providing a firm basis for follow-through on what is learned. The other is for intensive effort *to learn from the future*—and not from the past and present alone. Much of what follows is concerned with this need. In fact, a highly significant part of future orientation in planning derives its value from permitting us to learn from the future—its constraints and its alternative possibilities.

Not only is planning itself in the need-to-learn category because of the tasks which have already been assigned to it, but, following Michael's reasoning, urban planning is one of the governmental institutions best situated to help a community develop a learning posture. This is because planning, more than any other institution, can use the activity of *reaching out to the future* as a key ingredient in societal learning.

Chapter 11
The Use of Images
of the Future

A number of scholars, writing over the past two decades, have developed the concept of *images of the future* as playing a key role in human affairs—both for the individual and for communities and societies as a whole (Bell and Mau, 1971; Evered, 1973; Polak, 1961). One's image of the future determines to an important extent how one thinks and acts, and the same is true for collectivities, whether with optimism or pessimism, in short- or long-range terms, and whether one assumes that events are within or beyond human control. The concept is highly suggestive when considering approaches to the future in urban planning.

This concept has been given its most extensive treatment by Fred Polak, a Dutch sociologist whose two-volume work, published in 1961, carries a title that characterizes the central theme: *The Image of the Future: Enlightening the Past, Orienting the Present, Forecasting the Future.* Polak (1961: vol. 1, 49-50) analyzes past cultures to establish his thesis that the rise and fall of civilizations is preceded or accompanied by the rise and fall of dominant images of the future:

> As long as a society's image of the future is positive and flourishing, the flower of culture is in full bloom. Once the image of the future begins to decay and lose its vitality, however, the culture cannot long survive.

He points to the decline of many cultures, including the Greek and Roman, as following this principle.

Polak highlights the danger to present-day Western culture because of its lack of an idealistic image of the future. Creators of positive future-oriented images are needed. "Man is in a better position to fashion the kind of society he desires than ever before, but without new images of an ideal future to guide his striving, his civilization is doomed." The vigor and potential of the society of tomorrow can be detected in the society of today. Today's image of the future needs elaboration, refinement, and revision if it is to help realize the better life in the future.

Polak is not clear on how an image of the future can, and does, come into being. At times, he emphasizes that image-creation has been the role of a select few individuals (such as, prophets, poets, philosophers, artists, and political and humanitarian thinkers). On other occasions, he refers to groups such as the French philosophers and the American founding fathers. In the cases of the ancient Greeks or the ancient Jews or "the Americans," he refers to an entire civilization as creating an image. Of the American, Polak (1961: vol. 1, 50) says: "Is it not striking that an off-shoot of European culture during the period when its faith in progress was still virile made this faith its own in the 'American Creed' and rose to further heights independently of its parent culture?" He specifically distinguishes between images of the future which must be utopian or idealistic in content and politics, including even the politics of social reform, which is short term and pragmatic. However, Polak (1961: vol. 1, 426) also argues:

> . . . Through the centuries the politics of social reform, or "social engineering," moving in short hesitant steps through time, has been profoundly enriched by preceding and current utopian images of the future and has in many respects gradually transformed the utopian ideal into social fact. Concrete politics has thus always been influenced by the effective working out of the preceding utopian images, to the extent that these images have directed coming events through their foreshadowings.

In *The Sociology of the Future* (1971), Wendell Bell and James Mau devote equal emphasis to the value of the concept of images of the future in human affairs generally and the concept's specific role in social decisionmaking. Their main concern in the book is with the latter as the cornerstone of a theory of social change. Bell and Mau (1971: 18) make use of what they call a *cybernetic-decisional model* which treats the process of change as:

> . . . a feedback cycle resulting in a spiral of progressive interaction between information and action. Motivated individuals, acting as individuals or members of groups, their images of the future, and their resultant behaviors are the key elements that keep the system moving and bring a future into being in the present. The behavior is viewed as largely the result of decisions (or in some cases decisions not to decide) which are essentially choices among alternative futures. . . . Images of the future are of critical importance in influencing which of the alternative futures becomes the present reality.

Bell and Mau (1971: 23) define an image of the future as:

> ... an expectation about the state of things to come at some future time. We may think most usefully of such expectations as a range of differentially probable possibilities, rather than as a single point on a continuum.

Before action takes place in a community, some decisions occur which are the result of choices among alternative futures. Such decisions involve the specification of particular goals and the selection of means in the light of beliefs about the past, present, and future and about values as they have become congealed in images of the future. This process varies in its deliberateness, consciousness, and rationality, but Bell and Mau see an increasing trend toward an attempt at human mastery over the unfolding of events and, therefore, more deliberate planning of political, economic, social, and cultural change.

The Sociology of the Future is essentially an attempt to record the images of the future held by individuals, groups, and nations. Because the authors wish to deepen the understanding of the concept and of its role, they attempt to lay a better basis for its use in practical affairs.

Although the models of the sociologists and others employing images of the future as an intellectual construct are directed at scholarly research, they are highly suggestive for planning. Planning has, in one sense or another, always been involved with images of the future. There is value, however, in greater awareness in urban planning of the role that individual and group images of the future play, and should play, in arriving at the goals and general strategy intended to guide local decisionmaking and action. The Bell–Mau construct suggests, for example, that if such goals are to have more than the superficial support of the community, more is needed in evolving the goals of planning than an occasional goals committee.

Referring back to the first planning principle of societal learning, it seems evident that in employing the *cybernetic-decisional model* urban planning must develop feedback loops that permit learning, over time, more and more about the role being played by individual and group images of the future in local decisions and actions. Beyond that, there is the philosophical issue of whether planning is properly a translator of images already held or more appropriately a creator of images that will have a future impact on such decisions and actions. Ideally, it could—and, in the author's view, should—involve each of these. Even philosophical issues can be enlightened by societal learning. Individuals involved in urban planning should understand those images, including the images of the future, that are significant for and meaningful to the members of their community. At times, events and experimental efforts can provide valuable insights into such images. It was intriguing to watch Seattle in the mid-1970s bounce back from the pervading pessimism that had resulted from the rather sudden and sharp decline in the dominant aerospace industry. The recovery of a spirit of optimism was due in no small part to the cultural activities that accompanied a concerted effort to diversify the city's economy. And the people of Seattle reacted very affirmatively and joyfully to a new arts thrust. They liked the picture of themselves as appreciating the manmade arts as well as the natural beauty of their surroundings of which they had always been proud. As an outsider, it was exciting to see the events of the mid-70s bring out a deeply rooted, optimistic, and beauty-oriented self-image.

The plans discussed in the first part of this volume supposedly reflect specific images of the communities for which the plans were being prepared (see Chapters 2-7). One cannot help wondering how accurate these images are, and whether the planners are even aware of the extent to which they are dealing with community images. Asking whether the images that are employed can, and do, stir the people of the community is relevant. It is not necessarily Burnham-like grand plans that "stir men's blood" but plans of whatever scale that fit community images and strivings.

Discovering and projecting community images and strivings are, however, no small matters. The goals committee efforts in several cities in the last few decades have been an initial step in a sound direction. But such efforts have severe limitations. A broad enough spectrum of the community's variable population is often not involved since only certain kinds of people are willing to sit through many committee sessions to discuss community goals. Personal goals and actions are often not related to community-oriented ones. The goals discussed are normally not related to potential resources and alternative future situations. Nor do they lend themselves to testing out major departures from present living patterns or lifestyles.

Clearly, the discovery and projection of community images and strivings must involve a great deal of learning for communities and for planners, building on what has already been learned from the various goals efforts. Major possibilities exist for working with school children, particularly in stimulating the often dormant imagination of potentially imaginative young people as to the kind of environments and societies in which they would like to live, work, and play. Important possibilities can be found in the creation of museums of the future, giving opportunities to individuals and industries to graphically and in other ways project their ideas about the future. The specific forms are not, at this time, the subject of major concern. What is more important is to bring the concept of images of the future to the center of the planning stage.

The planners (the mayor, the city council members, and the professional and lay planners) do not have a passive role in the development of images of the future. They, particularly the professional planners, have a built-in responsibility for continuously holding out images of the future focused on what might be called *life-support* and *moral* concerns. It is at the very core of the urban planning concept itself to seek for survival and betterment. The planner should always make the case for the human beings as the primary resources of the community and always reach out for a future which involves improvements in human capacity and the human condition. The planner should always hold out the natural resources, including the land resources, as in *trust* in the community, seeking perpetual protection of the precious amenity resources and a land ethic which views that critical resource as not a commodity to be simply traded (even though that may be our current mechanism for providing for community needs) but as indeed a community trust. And the planner should, appropriately, serve as an activist seeking greater and greater equity into the future.

No matter how much the members of the community will want to be central to the projection of images of the future, they will respect the rightful role of planners to hold out the importance of life support and moral issues as a key to the future.

Chapter 12
The Need to Develop Knowledge for Action

Drawing on new developments in communications engineering, with its extensive use of self-steering and self-monitoring automatic processes, Norbert Weiner (1961) and others developed the concept of *cybernetics*. The use of cybernetic models has since been extended into many other areas of human affairs. This concept has provided a framework for dealing with the accumulation, storage, and communication of knowledge and its use in human activities, particularly in societal decisionmaking and societal guidance or self-steering. Weiner had pointed out that organizations are held together by communication. Communication enables a group to think together, to see together, to act together. A self-modifying communications net is essentially a learning net which permits what is learned to be used in guiding an activity or set of activities.

In developing a model of government as a system of communication and control based on cybernetic concepts, Karl Deutsch (1963: 245) highlighted social change as deriving from images of the future. He sees a governmental system like any other autonomous system acting out the future "implicit in the distributions of its memories" as well as in the nature of its communications channels. As it acquires new memories through its own behavior and as it learns to improve its communication patterns, it, in effect, is remaking itself and its future.

> If the system has consciousness, if it monitors its own behavior, and derives and remembers images of itself that it applies to its own actions, then it may well also derive and use images projecting its behavior into the future. It will thus use goal images and entertain explicitly formulated aspirations.

Deutsch sees the promotion of the public interest or the common good, over and above all special or lesser interests, as being closely related to survival. In turn, he sees survival as an outcome of growth, adaptability, and learning capacity. In explaining that a key dimension is the growth of autonomy or self-determination, Deutsch (1963: 250-51) contends that:

> This implies, on the one hand, a growth in the resources and functions that bear on social cohesion, that is, the growth, range, speed, and effectiveness of internal communications, both among individuals and among institutions or parts of the society or political system. On the other hand, it implies growth in the steering performance of the system, in the effectiveness of its use of data recalled from memory, and of information received from outside. It will require, therefore, a growth in the facilities of memory and recall, and thus of institutions of learning, record-keeping, and the like; a growth in the variety and effectiveness of channels for the intake of new ranges of information from the outside world; an improvement in goal-seeking operations.

At the same time, a governmental system must be able to change its own patterns of communications and organization so as to overcome the possibility of not keeping up with growth or other changes in scale. Deutsch (1963: 161) says:

> It must resist the trend toward increasing self-preoccupation . . . and it must reorganize or transform itself often enough to overcome the growing threats of internal communications overload and the jamming up of message traffic. One of the most effective responses to these threats—highlighted by such writings on politics and administration as "Parkinson's Law"—consists in *strategic simplification*.

Amitai Etzioni (1968) further developed the concept of societal guidance and particularly the application of knowledge to societal action. Etzioni's primary concern is with a societal guidance system which would enable a community to act effectively in attempting to solve its problems and achieve the aspirations of its members. Employing a cybernetic model, he evolves a theory of societal guidance which is based on three major elements: knowledge-units, decisionmaking, and power. Knowledge-units, or cybernetic capacities, reflect society's ability to collect, analyze, and disseminate knowledge about itself to societal decisionmakers and members. The second element, decisionmaking, concerns not only how society uses knowledge in the formulation of policies but also how society implements the policies and guides change. Societal power is viewed as a key force which affects the relationship between knowledge-units and decisionmaking. Power both affects and is affected by the distribution of assets among the members. According to Etzioni, these three elements must be integrated into a single guidance system in order to bring about change in desired directions.

Etzioni sees great disadvantages in both the pure rational-comprehensive approach and the incrementalist approach to decisionmaking. He proposes a *mixed-scanning* strategy as a useful middle ground. Mixed-scanning seeks to integrate worthwhile elements of both approaches while avoiding their pitfalls. Mixed-scanning involves two sets of mechanisms: (1) high-order, fundamental policymaking processes which set basic directions and which are adaptable to either changes in values and norms concerning the desired future or to changing priorities and (2) incremental processes which prepare for fundamental decisions and work them out after they have been reached. Thus, mixed-scanning is making long-range, fundamental decisions concerning the future which serve as the evaluative criteria for short-term, more detailed decisions.

Under this integrated approach, the knowledge requirements are neither as unrealistically high as those of rational-comprehensive planning nor as slight as those of incrementalism. Etzioni (1973: 224) explains:

> A mixed-scanning strategy would include elements of both approaches by employing two cameras: a broad-angle camera that would cover all parts of the sky but not in great detail, and a second one which would zero in on those areas revealed by the first camera to require more in-depth examination. While mixed-scanning might miss areas in which only a detailed camera could reveal trouble, it is less likely than incrementalism to miss obvious trouble spots in unfamiliar areas.

Etzioni regards current planning and decisionmaking processes in American society as overly incremental. Extremely little long-range and comprehensive planning is based on solid knowledge. Instead, the tendency is toward muddling through, making limited adjustments on the basis of limited knowledge. Totalitarian societies often go to the other extreme of formulating highly ambitious long-range plans which assume a great capacity to control and direct change and which are then carried out at the expense of personal freedom. The middle ground is seen as essential to preserve freedom for the members of the community and also to be realistic about our own capabilities in acquiring the knowledge needed in anything more than mixed-scanning.

Etzioni has, in effect, provided a theoretical base for planning practices that have evolved over the years in both the United States and Britain. Several cities in the United States have been using the concept of a long-range framework plan or a general plan as providing the broad-angle view. These are intended to make possible the preparation of detailed plans and programs which zero in on specific areas of concern, thus furnishing the base for the short-term, incremental decisions. In Britain, the nationally mandated structure plans and local plans fit Etzioni's concept quite closely.

The effectiveness of something like a mixed-scanning approach depends on the scope and quality of knowledge available to decisionmakers and to the community as a whole as well as the quality of the communication of such knowledge. Only if urban planning has the push-pull capability for both (1) in-depth analyses of trends emerging from the past and (2) the imaging of desirable futures that reflect converging and negotiated values among various groups, can it hope to create Etzioni's "high-order, fundamental policymaking processes which set basic directions" for the more immediate, incremental decisions.

Intensive work is needed on the framework—or Etzioni's "broad-angle lens" idea. First and foremost, urban planners (including the municipal political leaders as well as the technical planners) must accept the difficult task of periodically working out broad, future-oriented strategies and policies which can provide useful guidance to the more immediate political and technical decisions. The concept itself has to be given more politically meaningful content than it has at present so that its usefulness will become more apparent. Some ideas in this direction are presented in Chapters 26 and 27 of this volume.

Chapter 13
Determining the Appropriate Sources of Knowledge and Political Power

Practical events and concerns, as much as theoretical developments, point to the need for urban planning to determine the appropriate sources of knowledge on which to base decisions and the appropriate governmental and private linkages for action and implementation.

The 1960s and 1970s have been marked by an increasing concern for bringing government closer to the people. This concern has encompassed the search for new ways to effectively include citizens in governmental decisions and operations. It has also focused on the appropriate division of authority and resources among the various levels of government.

In urban planning, these interests have given rise to the increasing importance of neighborhood plans, often prepared with substantial inputs from neighborhood residents, in the city's general plan. In some cities, a broad effort has been made to reduce the amount of top-down planning—typical of past practice in which the planning product was largely the result of ideas generated by the professional planners—and to increase bottom-up planning which better reflects community views of what should happen in individual neighborhoods. *Advocacy planning* has been developed in which technical know-how is provided by professional planners to the poorer neighborhoods and groups in the city to increase their leverage on the political process. Advocacy planning is sometimes interpreted to require professional planners to play a major role in promoting the position of the more disadvantaged members of the community in order to achieve an equalizer effect. Such advocacy would be dictated by the fact of the usual political weakness of such disadvantaged groups. This position has characterized the work of the Cleveland Planning Commission, as noted in Chapter 5.

The location of authority in urban matters among the various levels of government has been a subject of intense discussion. Limited shifts in authority have been brought about by the establishment of general and special revenue sharing. These shifts have accompanied the creation of "a new federalism" which seeks greater decentralization of government, with more authority in decisionmaking for the local mayor and city council. Federal categorical grants are important in determining what local jurisdictions can undertake in the developmental realms. Therefore, federal-local relations are still focused largely on grantsmanship.

Urban planning is at the vortex of many of these developments and issues concerning the appropriate roles of various actors in urban affairs. It must try to find some solid ground on which to stand in carrying out its complex tasks. A key question is how best to involve citizen views, concerns, and aspirations in the planning process, while incorporating what professional knowledge can bring to bear on the process.

In discussing this issue, John Friedmann (1973) has argued that a new style of planning, *transactive planning*, is appropriate to the modern learning society. This style involves a process of mutual learning between the expert and the client (citizen) groups. Its success depends on developing effective means for interrelating the personal knowledge upon which the lay person or nonexpert in community groups must inevitably rely with the processed knowledge of the expert. The latter is "built up from symbols that stand for particular dimensions of reality and is expressed in the form of models that can be formally communicated, critically examined, and revised on the basis of new observations." Personal knowledge is ultimately inadequate as the sole approach to urban planning, but processed knowledge is also severely limited in its contributions and often provides distorted models of reality. Processed knowledge must be connected to personal knowledge "so that both, those who know primarily from experience and those who know about the world chiefly through the prismatic images of models, may increase their capacity for learning" (Friedmann, 1973: 101, 106). Mutual learning is essential. Who assumes the roles of expert and client in this process of mutual learning in the carrying out of planning tasks? How they can be expected to react in these roles? What is the probable scope of their interests?

Most community groups involved in urban planning activities will devote their attention and energies to measures that would be of direct, essentially personal, gain. Those from relatively poor neighborhoods, facing many personal and neighborhood problems and deprivations, must inevitably view planning decisions in terms of their own immediate welfare and in terms of the current services provided in the close-in neighborhood. Equally, those from the wealthier areas can be expected to concern themselves chiefly with current policies and actions that influence their well-being as they understand it. Thus, they are more likely to be concerned with the diversion of traffic from their neighborhoods than with the issue of creating an efficient transportation system for the entire region. They are much more likely to press for the strengthening of zoning restrictions in their own community than for a regional fair-housing policy. Such immediate and narrow concerns are familiar enough in a democratic polity. But what of the future and what of the welfare of the entire region (and of the nation—not to mention the world at large)? Who is the client for the consideration of issues that have a broader impact and can only be achieved in the more distant future?

At minimum, broad representation is important. Particular efforts must be made to involve a wide range of interest groups, lifestyle groups, and age groups in a dialogue on the future. This is evident from a consideration of the different age groups. Naturally, young people have a different kind of interest in and view of the future than older people. Furthermore, they are less tolerant than older people of community meetings. If they are to be involved effectively in planning operations, they would have to be reached through discussion in classrooms (rather than community halls), through gaming techniques, television, and other means. Similarly, firms that have substantial investments in the city will have a different interest in the long run and in the larger regional area than will individuals whose total investment is in a single-family home and whose only regional interest may be related to commuting to and from work. Citizen participation and the question of who is the client are far from simple matters. It is difficult to determine from a study of planning practice in various cities as to how much thought has been given to the issue of who represents what and how to get a balanced representation from the community in terms of the subjects with which planning must deal. (The author feels that representation in planning is a topic that deserves much more study than it has received.)

Even the broadest kind of representation of separate current interests is not enough if citizen participation in urban planning is to be both meaningful and effective. There must be a strong learning component in the exchanges between professional planners and the various interest groups. Neighborhoods and other groups must increasingly come to understand how their interests fit into the larger scheme of things, for example, with regard to the broad picture of housing provision and not just the immediate neighborhood housing situation, the impact over time on the special interests of the changing local economy, the requirements of regional transportation and of basinwide air quality, and so on. Special groups can never be expected to forego their own interests entirely, but they *can* learn to see their welfare in a broader context and over a somewhat longer period of time. In fact, this kind of learning is a very important part of the very reason-for-being of a planning operation.

The urban planner does not automatically qualify as the expert (on the other side of the client/expert equation). This is particularly so when the long-range future is considered. To be an expert when the long-term future is at issue requires an understanding of the requirements and possibilities for systemic changes in socioeconomic-political forces and human behavior needed to achieve the agreed upon community goals. Current planning practice involves such expertise in only limited ways. When the master plan—which traditionally provided a broad physical design for the community—was accepted as a legitimate and effective framework for dealing with the urban future, the expertise of the design-oriented planner could be readily accepted. However, the issue is more complex today. As will be argued in later chapters, the skills for dealing with the long-run future must necessarily extend to a wide variety of subjects. These include such matters as asset accounting, urban systems analysis, forecasting methods of various kinds, and analyses of institutional change. Other kinds of skills are involved in dealing with the more immediate issues and particularly the skills involved in policy analysis. A spectrum of expertise needs to be drawn upon, and at least some of this must come from outside traditional planning agencies.

Much of the knowledge needed in urban planning as well as much of the power needed to make and to implement planning decisions must come from the action agencies of the local government. The planning operation must itself be set up so that all the operating agencies are *in fact* part of it. The central planning agency should not need to plead for cooperation which, even if forthcoming, currently still leaves planning a weak and limited governmental activity. The expertise (and authority) of the entire local government must be involved in urban planning if it is to be something other than a peripheral activity.

The question of expertness extends to the vertical plane, particularly in regard to that important part of knowledge which covers the larger context within which local planning must function. Expertise on subjects of regional, state, and national import, many of which directly affect local planning and some of which are affected by such planning, cannot normally be expected to be available within the local planning agencies or even local government in general. Even in the case of large central cities, the local planners and the citizens from individual neighborhoods cannot be expected to be very knowledgeable about regional, statewide, and national developments—nor do they adequately reflect the interests of these larger areas. The gap in expert knowledge that this leaves can be appreciated when consideration is directed at the subjects which can be understood in any depth only if treated mainly at regional, statewide, and/or national levels. This encompasses such critically important subjects for urban planning as major shifts in employment and unemployment, industrial location, population and family structure, and interarea family migration. Thus, as with expertise that is involved in dealing with significant time components, unless more knowledge is provided to extend over the whole urban hierarchy, mutual learning in urban planning can only be among different kinds of amateurs.

Beyond the issue of knowledge is the broader question of political effectiveness and political legitimacy. The current weakness of urban planning is in no small part related to its narrow relationship to the higher levels of government. Even the most impressive kind of grantsmanship on the part of a local jurisdiction, and cleverness in obtaining more than a proportionate share of federal and state largess, cannot overcome the tenuous relationship between the unplanned, "ad hocish" urban activities of the national government and the states and what is needed to achieve the goals of local planning. Local planning is normally carried out as if the plans were being made for jurisdictions with the internal powers of the old Greek city-states rather than jurisdictions that make up a limited part of a regional urban system and an even smaller part of a national system of cities. Urban planning must put great stress on making it clear to everyone that cities are dependent on national developments, policies, and resources (as Cleveland has begun to do in its planning). Cities need to join forces to bring pressure on the federal government and the states to plan their urban policies and programs so that they reflect the needs of local jurisdiction in carrying out local plans.

SUMMARY

A new framework is needed to fit the requirements of urban planning in the period ahead. This can be evolved in the first instance by bringing together the principles that should guide planning practice. These call for urban planning to be essentially an instrumentality of societal learning, seeking to learn from future history as well as from past and current experience in community functioning and development. It should also be the prime instrumentality for discovering, creating, and projecting images of the future that can help fuel community action and arrive at the goals and general strategy intended to guide local decisionmaking and implementation over time. These need to come together in planning practice through the creation of processes for the making of long-range, fundamental decisions concerning the future (brought together in policy or strategy plans) which can serve as the framework and evaluative criteria for short-term, more detailed decisions and actions. And, finally, local planning must continuously determine the appropriate sources of knowledge and of political power and legitimacy across the local horizontal spectrum (including the citizens and municipal agencies) as well as the vertical spectrum of the different levels of government. Urban planning must involve many actors in the urban drama.

PART 3
THE PAST COMPONENT OF THE FUTURE

Chapter 14
The Future as Containing Elements of the Past, Present, and Future

A community is, at any moment in time, made up of the old and the new. This is significant in thinking about and acting for the future. Try to imagine a given community ten years from now; you would see much of what is already in place at the present moment, plus the new features which would be added between now and then. Probably 80 percent of the present housing would still be where it is now. Much of today's infrastructure and urban patterns would remain in place. A large proportion of the people now in the community would still be there, and many of those who left would have been replaced by people with fairly similar demographic characteristics. Most of the familiar institutions would still be functioning. Think back ten years and note the similarities and differences between then and now. This suggests the important of **inheritance** when thinking about and acting for the future. This is the **past** component in the future.

Similarly a **present** component can be found in the future. All decisions and actions are taken in the present no matter how far into the future one is deciding and acting for. Somewhat less obvious, but closely related, is the fact that present ideas, present images of the future, present processes for deciding and acting, present methods and tools of forecasting all influence strongly what is being done for the future. The present is a filter for all thinking and actions about the future, a filter that must inevitably have a here-and-now impact on decisions and actions aimed at the future. But there is also the reverse. Images of the future and ideas about the nature of the future have a major impact on current policy concerned with the most immediate matters. Individuals act today, even if it is literally for today, because of the view of future history as much as of past history. Individuals act in terms of what one intends to experience as much as in terms of what has already been experienced.

Finally, there is a **future** component to the future—the *new* things, people, ideas, and institutions. New possibilities and opportunities will arise. New problems will have to be faced. And some small and large surprises are undoubtedly in store for each individual and community.

Important insights can be gained into what might be done to plan for the future (so that the future is more to one's liking) by probing these three different elements of the future and being aware that *all of them will ultimately come together into a single future.* The usual view of the future, stressing the elements of change (that is, the newness elements), tends by its very nature to bring to the forefront the uncertainty feature. It generates a tendency to overlook certain subjects about which decisions need to be made and action taken—for example, specific decisions on how long various physical and nonphysical features of the community *should* last into the future. In a broader context, the centrality of the task for urban planning of reconciling continuity and change must be appreciated for all three components of the future are of major concern in such planning.

Continuity and change converge because the old and new often meet and because the here-and-now and the yet-to-be are involved in the same decisions and actions. Thus, new structures or land uses frequently have to be added to old ones, and provisions have to be made for the renewal of out-of-date urban elements and for projected, as well as existing, needs and desires of people. The present and the future are involved in holding back on building in given areas to save open space for future use or in holding back present production in order to provide for a cleaner environment in the future.

Defined in a narrow way, continuity and change would seem to be inevitably in opposition to each other. Yet what looks like an impossible task of reconciling seemingly opposing forces becomes a logical possibility when it is realized that things can only be held on to by making certain necessary changes. Even consensus on the desirability of retaining some cherished feature of our society (for example, substantial homeownership) would require a carefully thought-out set of changes. Such changes might well require public action in the social, economic, and political realms, such as tax regulations, efforts to influence industrial and residential location, or new subsidies. Only such planned changes will allow for the preservation of the desired feature in the face of the many changes that are taking place. Probably the hardest thing to achieve would be the complete maintenance of *status quo*.

One does indeed have to "run very fast to stay in the same place." Retention can be very difficult. This is easily seen in the examples of past (basically unplanned) efforts to keep intact small farming operations and small farm community life. Generally, if continuity or retention is to have a fair probability of success, substantial planning is required which involves making many changes to achieve the given end.

The cherished values and features of our lives are lost in the jumble of unplanned changes. We have not attended seriously enough to the problems involved in holding on to the things we would like to continue to enjoy. At a relatively simple level, people are just beginning to appreciate the effort and cost it takes to preserve buildings and districts of historical and architectural significance that should be kept for the future. The conservation of natural amenities, which are rare and precious because they cannot be reproduced, requires new laws and many substantial changes in behavior patterns. Retaining a sense of family or neighborhood or community requires great efforts and often a variety of new institutions and procedures.

Continuity does not imply sameness. Attention is focused on the fact that some 20 percent of American households move each year. America is, seemingly, a nation of transients, a rootless people, always on the move. Yet, a closer look at these moves reveals that while many people change their addresses, they do not change their lifestyles, physical environments, or the *kinds* of people with whom they associate. That is certainly true of young executives who are moved by their companies every few years from one town to another. This is also true of the transient farm worker who ends up each time in a very similar environment. That is not to say that there are not disruptions in moves, but there is a degree of continuity involved. Continuity can be found in the level and style of living, in a familiar kind of surrounding, in a familiar kind of job, and in the trappings of life.

Politics and planning face major problems in attempting to reconcile the wishes and demands of those who are essentially satisfied with their lot and seek continuity in most features of urban life with the aspirations of those who want to move up. Significantly, even the contented ones will not be satisfied by continuity alone, and many will insist on achieving something better, for example, in the quality of air. Members of this group often attend community meetings and demand improvements in urban life. Those who wish to advance will certainly press for changes in those areas that they see as determining relative advantages (including power). However, in other realms they, too, will insist on elements of continuity. Those who try to improve the neighborhoods of the poor from above tend to learn some interesting lessons about the desire for continuity.

Urban planning can contribute to this extremely difficult governmental task of reconciling desires for continuity and change in several important ways. It can highlight the benefits and costs of retaining over time the capital-in-place and features of the natural environment within the community, as well as those of retaining the patterns of living of different lifestyle groups. It can also contribute by evaluating the impacts on different groups and the community as a whole of alternative policy proposals looking to changes in the future. Finally, urban planning can provide a helpful framework for decisions influencing continuity and change by holding out images of alternative futures which largely reflect the views of community members as to areas in which improvement is desired.

Against this background, the chapters that follow probe what have been described as three components of the future (past, present, and future) and analyze specifically the implications of each of these components for planning practice.

Chapter 15
Inheritance as an Aspect of Planning

The future that is likely to be the concern of local decisionmaking will have many inherited elements in both physical capital and other urban features.

The endurance of capital and other urban features involves benefits and costs. Significant benefits can be found in the additional resources (assets) that longevity makes available for carrying out the city's functions. The inherited urban assets continuously constitute a large share of the nation's total wealth (as well as of the wealth of individuals). Benefits can be found in the comfort given people by the availability of familiar features. Novelists have frequently recorded the joys of returning to familiar scenes of one's childhood. Costs of longevity appear in the form of constraints on the introduction of new technologies such as when a new means of transporting people and goods is delayed by the existence of the old or when an old school building delays the introduction of new approaches to education.

The endurance of urban capital and of urban patterns means that major urban transformations of the kind discussed at the beginning of this volume can only be carried out over a long period of time, barring unrealistically large resources dedicated to such changes in only a few years. Downtowns are not reconstructed to meet the requirements of a postindustrial society in less than several decades, nor can cities' layouts and work-residence locational relationships be made more energy efficient in short order.

VALUE OF A PLANNING ORIENTED APPROACH

We cannot decide in advance that the longer things last the better. It takes some fairly extensive analysis to be able to decide on the relative costs and benefits of the longer or shorter lifetimes of major urban features. The question for the community is whether certain of the decisions about capital longevity should be guided by urban planning. A very strong reason for such guidance is that each urban community has already decided to make many of the physical and nonphysical features of the community subject to collective (public) decisions and actions which can probably benefit from guidance by a time-conscious planning operation.

Many decisions must be made about features of urban life which loom as all-important over the next decade or two that strongly relate to urban infrastructure and urban physical patterns. These include decisions about:

1. The changing character of the downtown and other dense activity centers, including an appropriate balance of functions and balance between work places and residences.
2. The alternative techniques for changing from high energy consuming locational patterns to patterns that are much less so.
3. The best ways for conserving neighborhoods where this is an important objective of the residents.
4. The best way to conserve housing for lower-income residents and to find locations for new housing for such groups.
5. The most cost-efficient ways of maintaining the city's public infrastructure and providing for needed replacement (for both physical and functional reasons).
6. The public and private infrastructure that is needed over the next decades to be able to hold on to existing productive enterprises and to attract new enterprises that would strengthen the local economy.
7. How best to conserve existing park and recreational areas and to make changes strongly desired by users (such as more capacity for active sports).
8. How to make changes in existing structures for educational and health purposes to meet the newer demands and new technological opportunities.
9. How best to incorporate arts facilities (as well as activities) in major new development and redevelopment projects so as to provide adequate cultural outlets for the community and to attract visitors and industries to the city.

These are only illustrative; many other facets of anticipated urban planning tasks will involve infrastructure and other physical features.

A planned approach would also benefit asset management by providing increased coordination among the governmental decisions and actions on construction, maintenance, rehabilitation, and demolition that the planning operation would bring to bear. Greater coordination reduces expenses and promotes efficiency. A more important benefit is the increased control that the community would have over what is actually inherited over time, particularly in public infrastructure and other public capital. This can mean substantial savings in resources and greater capacity to achieve valued goals. It is not enough for a community to want to replace buildings or urban patterns that have become obsolete. It must have the resources, including local government funds, to make such replacement possible. This may well call for the accumulation of reserves and the expansion of revenue-raising capacity over time so that the necessary resources are available when needed.

Time-conscious planning also requires the accumulation of know-how in determining the relative usefulness of assets over time. The usefulness of urban assets is the product of a complex mix of factors including the rates of introduction and diffusion of new technologies, changing relative prices, and the current view of what is considered functional and appropriate. Given its inherent complexities, this kind of know-how can only be amassed over time by the continuous monitoring of the outcomes of relative longevity and of the different approaches employed to deal with assets and urban patterns. Only when an institution—logically urban planning—has the responsibility for monitoring the impacts of longevity in the different components of urban life and of relating what is learned to public decisionmaking can the community hope to plan and act in timely fashion.

What is inherited at any point in the future is neither subject to total control by the collectivity nor beyond control. The durability of buildings depends partly on the quality of maintenance, a matter subject to conscious decisions. The same is true of urban patterns, including locational relationships among different land uses and the urban infrastructure. The useful life of all of these features can be extended or cut back by governmental decisions and actions.

The idea of influencing what is to be inherited by a community at various periods in the future extends beyond the issue of physical assets and urban patterns. The quantity and quality of the people of a given community at points in the future are also inheritance questions and raise issues of the most profound type. Quantity issues that are now being discussed, mostly under the rubric of *growth management*, include the question of the rights of individuals to live where they wish and of others to control the character of their community. Quality questions raise even more difficult moral, legal, and socioeconomic issues, including the issue of the appropriate role of urban planning in addressing the human resources *assets* of the community—since clearly the people of the community are its greatest assets.

The longevity of institutions and their activities is also an inheritance question since such longevity is a product of conscious decisions. Even ideas, values, and human behavior patterns persevere or change as a result of deliberate decisions (for example, through the kind of education that is promoted in urban public schools, or through public propaganda to save energy, water, or other resources that are in short supply).

While all of these questions are of great importance, they are beyond the scope of this study. This book concentrates on the question of physical assets as a way of highlighting the importance of inheritance to urban planning. This question is appropriate at this stage in the evolution of the planning field and can be discussed on a more solid basis than can many others. Over time, however, all of these questions must be addressed by modern urban planning.

Before discussing the *operational* features of planning related to the inheritance of physical assets, some of the planning issues involved must be considered. Urban renewal and preservation/conservation will be used to illustrate many of the planning issues related to the **past** component of the future.

SOME INHERITANCE ISSUES

Housing and Urban Renewal

In a highly stimulating article, Marion Clawson (1968) asks how great the urban renewal problem of the future will be. This is a critical issue in urban planning. Housing and commercial structures filter down to lower-income users except in rare instances. This filtering-down process must someday come to an end when it no longer pays to restore the units. Good maintenance of individual property and of public infrastructure may forestall depreciation and decay for relatively long periods, but even the best of maintenance cannot obviate the need for eventual rebuilding. Postponing the day of renewal may, however, be extremely important for racial and income groups dependent on older housing. This is a matter for community concern.

Since age of the stock is an important factor in the value and functionality of housing, Clawson (1968: 173) points out that it is possible to estimate how much housing of various ages will exist at any future date (and where it will be) through "a housing demographic approach." He provides an estimate of housing-unit age on a national basis from 1890 to 1960, showing in an appendix how it was derived and indicating that the same sort of analysis can be made for individual cities or metropolitan areas.

Table 15–1 provides an estimate of past patterns of demolition and

Table 15–1. Estimated Total Housing Units at Each Census, 1890 to 1960, by Decade Originally Built

Period built	Housing units (millions)							
	1890	1900	1910	1920	1930	1940	1950	1960
Before 1890	(13.5)[b]	(9.6)	(7.4)	(6.2)	(3.4)*	(3.9)*	(4.7)*	(2.9)
1890–1899		(6.9)	(6.7)	(6.5)	(6.2)	(5.8)	(5.4)	(4.9)
1900–1909			(6.9)	(6.7)	(6.5)	(6.2)	(5.8)	(5.4)
1910–1919				(6.6)	(6.4)	(6.2)	(5.9)	(5.6)
1920–1929					(9.5)	9.2	(8.9)	(8.6)
1930–1939						6.0	(5.8)	(5.6)
1940–1949							9.6	(9.3)
1950–1959								16.0
Total	(13.5)	(16.5)	(21.0)	(26.0)	(32.0)	37.3	46.1	58.3

Source: Marion Clawson, "Urban Renewal in 2000," *Journal of the American Institute of Planners* 34:3 (May 1968): 174.

* These figures are probably in error.—H.S.P.

Table 15–2. Housing Units Removed and Remaining by Decades (in millions)

Period built	Number (millions) in 1960	Estimated number (millions) remaining in				Estimated number (millions) to be removed in decade of			
		1970	1980	1990	2000	1960's	1970's	1980's	1990's
Before 1890	2.9	1.6	.5	.1	0	1.3	1.1	.4	.1
1890–1899	4.9	4.0	2.3	.6	.1	.9	1.7	1.7	.5
1900–1909	5.4	4.9	4.0	2.3	.6	.5	.9	1.7	1.7
1910–1919	5.6	5.2	4.7	3.8	2.2	.4	.5	.9	1.6
1920–1929	8.6	8.1	7.5	6.8	5.5	.5	.6	.7	1.3
1930–1939	5.6	5.4	5.1	4.7	4.3	.2	.3	.4	.4
1940–1949	9.3	9.0	8.6	8.2	7.6	.3	.4	.4	.6
1950–1959	16.0	15.5	15.0	14.4	13.6	.5	.5	.6	.8
Total	58.3	53.7	47.7	40.9	33.9	4.6	6.0	6.8	7.0

Source: Marion Clawson, "Urban Renewal in 2000," *Journal of the American Institute of Planners* 34:3 (May 1968): 175.

replacement of residential structures. Because it is not inevitable that this pattern will be followed in the future, Clawson stresses that his estimates are based on past practice and show at each census period up to the year 2000 the number of housing units remaining from the 1960 stock and the number expected to be removed in each decade (see Table 15–2).

A continuation of past patterns of demolition portrays the number of removals as rising steeply over the decades to 7 million in the 1990s nationally. Analysis of his own data leads Clawson (1968: 174) to urge government to stimulate private urban renewal to meet the requirement concerning total number of units. He also points out that policies which would stimulate the renovation of older residences could add significantly to the supply of older housing. "This would be especially important to low income tenants who are highly dependent upon very old housing."

Using this or a similar approach introduced by Wolfe in 1967, it is possible to estimate the age of any city's housing by areas, provide information on maintenance and other factors that influence longevity, and determine when renewal would be necessary. The general costs and benefits of different policy alternatives which seek to change the trends in desirable directions can then be calculated.

As early as 1949, when a national urban redevelopment program was first legislated, officials recognized that not only individual housing units but entire sections of cities become obsolete over time. As a result, publicly assisted renewal will be required if cities are to maintain their plant in efficient working order.

A detailed review of the U.S. experience over a generation with publicly assisted urban renewal suggests that the national program suffered from several rather serious weaknesses (Perloff, et. al., 1975: chapters 4 and 5). The lack of clear objectives was particularly damaging. While the very title of urban renewal suggested the importance of modernizing and revitalizing the older cities, the program soon became associated with the objective of eliminating slums and blight. Rarely were individual projects related to a strategy for the future development of the city as a whole. Renewal programs were vague on the issues of poor families and redistribution of income and opportunity. In many cases, urban renewal projects simply forced poor families to relocate to other rundown areas of the city. The net impact of urban renewal in many cities was to reduce the quantity of lower-cost housing.

Drawing on the substantial urban renewal experience and the much more limited experience with "new-towns-in-town," a recent study (Perloff et. al.,

1975) suggested that modernization[1] might most appropriately be aimed at objectives of efficiency, equity, and quality of life (the general objectives underlying the urban-system element in urban planning, as discussed in Chapter 25). In the present context, these objectives can be defined as follows:

Efficiency considerations involve the objective of adjusting the urban fabric to those functions logical for the current and future city at a scale and density appropriate to both present and anticipated needs. Particularly important are modernization of infrastructure (including the transportation system) and of locational relations among work, residence, and other activities (essentially closeness), as well as ensuring the competence of governmental institutions to guide and manage these functions.

Equity considerations imply adjustments to achieve a fairer balance of gains and losses among social groups than has occurred to date in the redevelopment of the city's plant and in the provision of governmental services and facilities. Something is seriously wrong with a renewal program where the poor pay the largest share of the social costs, with their homes torn down, neighborhoods destroyed, and where they are forced to pay higher rents in relocation.

Quality-of-life considerations in modernization are those factors which touch on the city as a satisfying and healthy place in which to live and work. Beyond efficiency and equity, qualitative aspects exist that determine whether people will want to live and work in the city or will live there because they have no other choice. Developments of the past decade have highlighted the fact that the desirability of a city as a place in which to live and work determines to a large extent the economic vigor and fiscal health of the city (Perloff et. al., 1975: 384-85).

The ability to carry out a continuous modernization program which is effective (that is, getting optimum returns from the resources that can be applied to such a program) depends in no small way on the information available about the condition of, and changes in, the urban fabric and the evolving functions of the urban system. Much more is required than information on existing slums and blight. A system of information is needed that cannot only report the condition of the city's physical plant at any time, but which allows analyses of the relationship of physical condition to significant developments in the life of the people. Such information would permit relatively firm projections to be made of probable future conditions and requisites for improvement and modernization in specific geographic and functional areas.

[1]This term is used to avoid the connotations that have grown up around the term *urban renewal*.

Preservation and Conservation

The preservation of buildings and districts rests on an idea similar to the inheritance concept: a conscious decision (usually collective in nature) to maintain certain assets for future generations. Originally directed toward individual buildings of unusual architectural or historic interest, the concept has in recent decades been broadened to include entire historic districts. The implications often extend beyond simple preservation. Preservation could encompass the restoration of a building to its original condition or the recreation of an historic area with substantial rebuilding. Through preservation, the current generation wills something considered unusually precious to future generations.

In quite a few instances across the country, the creation of historic districts has turned out to be an excellent real estate investment for both private investors and the government (through substantially increased tax returns). Many urbanites are attracted by the special flavor of an historic environment and the extensive controls over development which accompany their establishment. Often preservation has strong class overtones; poorer families are displaced through the process by wealthier ones. It is a process that the British have come to call *gentrification*, the moving in of the gentry. The culprit is the shortage of housing that the lower-income groups can afford to rent or to own. When individual preservation projects go their own natural way, the amount of housing for lower-income families is reduced in a given section of the city; or in the case of large projects, it is reduced in the city as a whole.

Parallel to the development of the preservation movement has been the extension of the concept of urban conservation. This is an attempt to save somewhat declining neighborhoods of the city from further deterioration. Common aspects of a conservation program are efforts to get owners to repair their homes, to encourage the city to improve public services and facilities in the neighborhood, and (often) to hold down density. As in the case with preservation, conservation programs serve to maintain physical (and other) assets for the future; they thus influence the inheritance picture. Conservation programs also tend to impact the various income classes differently. They are often begun in the absence of a built-in evaluation of impacts of such programs on the city as a whole (Goetze, Colton, and O'Donnell, 1977; Public Affairs Counseling, 1975, Stegman, 1972).

Only a few of the larger communities (most notably San Francisco and Philadelphia) have tried to bring such efforts into some coherent framework by including preservation and conservation in the general city plans. Such frameworks are essential to guide action if high priority general goals are to be achieved.

In encompassing preservation/conservation in urban planning, consideration should be given to the following:

1. Processes and methods must be developed which can serve to designate individual buildings, areas, and districts for preservation (even if initiated by private groups) through local political-decision procedures. The objective is to fully evaluate the net impact of all the individual projects taken together, against the flow of such projects over a decade or more. The normalization of such processes is necessary to assure ordinary governmental budgetary financing. Preservation and conservation should become a built-in part of the developmental activities of the community—the part of the process that covers construction, maintenance, rehabilitation, adjustment, demolition, and renewal activities.

2. The preservation concept should be expanded to include the study of structures, artifacts, and areas of historical significance because of the commonness of usage in given periods in the past or because of importance in the lives of various ethnic groups in the community. Keeping something of the lives of people from each epoch of the past has value for the future.

3. Plans must be based on multipurpose operational goals, such as the establishment of historic districts, in order to strengthen efforts at rehabilitation, to stabilize areas, to help provide focal points of interest in the city (and thereby help revitalize it) and/or to increase the economic base of the city (for example, by providing a tourist attraction).

4. Analyses must be performed of the actual and potential *negative* impacts of preservation and conservation, taken as a whole, and in terms of individually proposed projects, such as blocking the implementation of needed new developments and the displacement of lower-income groups. Such cost/benefit analysis becomes possible only if preservation and conservation are an integral part of the city planning process.

5. Finally, in terms of the thrust of Part 3, decisions on preservation/ conservation need to draw on the information that can be provided by asset accounting. These two types of activities must be related to all the other activities that help to determine which physical assets are to be inherited by future generations.

The broad planning issues involved in two complex sets of urban development activities—renewal and preservation/conservation—have been discussed here in some detail to demonstrate the kinds of considerations that can be expected to surround the use of information on asset inheritance; specifically the use of asset accounts and of capital programming and budgeting (treated in Chapters 16 and 17). While asset accounting, capital programming, and capital budgeting can be used for many purposes in governmental management, the central concern of this book is with their use in *planning decisions on inheritance*. The present chapter illustrates the planning context within which these kinds of information should be used. In reading Chapters 16 and 17, this context should be kept in mind.

Chapter 16
The Inheritance Component: Asset Accounting

Planning for the maintenance of assets into the future may not seem like the most exciting activity. Perhaps, planning for the future should be focused on the great *new* things that will or might happen. However, if the desired changes are to be implemented within the limits of resources likely to be available in the latter part of the 20th century, such changes must be introduced by carefully timing the maintenance and removal of existing assets.

Unfortunately planning is not presently equipped to deal effectively with the inheritance component of the future. Only limited informational capability is found in most American cities for long-range planning decisions about physical plant. A number of problems exist. Asset accounting and other types of asset information are geared specifically to current, short-range management of fixed assets. City planning departments are rarely involved in determining what asset information is to be collected, and such departments can and do use the available information in only limited ways. Information on land use that is of central concern to planning departments can provide only limited guidance on inheritance decisions. Actually, most land-use projections and land-use proposals made by planning departments are not time specific; they do not indicate how long existing patterns are expected to remain or should remain or when changes should take place. In fact, information about longevity and other features of the physical plant are important for land-use decisions themselves.

Fixed-asset accounting (covering land, buildings, equipment, and so on) is a well-established fixture of many municipal governments related to the management of public assets by operating agencies (most importantly the public works department) and to fiscal management. Fixed-asset accounting is a highly developed field. The National Committee on Governmental Accounting, associated with the Municipal Finance Officers Association, has been prescribing a model form (which is periodically revised) for asset accounting as part of a model system of governmental accounting, auditing, and financial reporting. Certificates of conformance have been granted to governmental units by the Municipal Finance Officers Association since 1945 indicating they have met the established requirements, including the fixed-asset accounting requirement. The main concern has been to ensure adequate governmental accountability and fiscal efficiency, including effective safeguarding of assets owned by the government (for example, adequate insurance coverage) and effective management to meet needs for replacement of existing property and equipment, as well as a sound presentation of financial position and results of operations.

While clearly important to basic governmental management, the scope of current public accounting is limited. It is particularly limited in terms of urban planning. The information provided does not extend to the larger picture of the capacity of the urban plant to meet new community needs and demands, changing economic forms, or the requirements of community betterment over time. Communities seem suddenly to realize that their streets and parking system are obsolete and that traffic congestion is driving business away. Urban rehabilitation and renewal in many cities is undertaken on a haphazard, project-by-project basis, weakly related to the long-run functional needs or fiscal capacity of the city. The physical plant can be worn down while funds are channeled to new projects without the true situation coming to decision points in a compelling way. Recently the problem of urban physical decay has come to public notice mainly because of reports pointing to the crisis conditions in New York City ("Repairs Lag, N.Y. Called in Peril of 'Wearing Out'"; "New York Fast Becoming Old York"). Reports of bridge closings and a widespread water loss and sewer disrepair in northern urban areas have also helped to focus public attention. Discussion of crisis in urban infrastructure may have provided the atmosphere for serious attention to the inheritance component in the coming decade.

Public accounting which provides a planning-oriented picture of the condition of the community's assets is needed to make reasonable projections of the economic and fiscal future of the city. Such public accounting should be able to provide a basis for community policy on various kinds of incentives for modernization of private plants as well as public plants and for the use of tax policy and other public levers for initiating and expediting necessary community transformations. The housing, economic development, and neighborhood development elements in city plans, if they are to be soundly grounded, need this kind of accounting as part of the information base.

The encompassing of information on private property deserves special attention. Asset accounting in private enterprise is highly developed, but, not surprisingly, it is aimed at the specific and limited decisionmaking requirements of individual firms. The community interests in such assets are normally not registered, except for the purpose of estimating near-term public revenues. But the longevity of private housing is a major *community* concern since it is a key element in the adequacy of housing for the various income groups. Even such factors as the relative obsolescence of private productive plant and equipment can be of the greatest moment for a community. In many of the older cities of the Northeast, such obsolescence—which has influenced productivity and the contraction of operations—has had a great deal to do with the economic and fiscal difficulties of these cities in recent decades.

In general, then, what is covered by asset accounting should be determined by the need for basic information about physical plant and urban patterns in the making of community plans and in the making and carrying out of policy decisions about the city's development.

AGING AND OBSOLESCENCE IN BUILDINGS

What a community inherits in the physical realm at any point in the future is significantly related to the rate of obsolescence, the quality of the maintenance, and the rate of replacement. These are specifically determined by private and public decisions over time. Private decisions are made within the context of the economic market; public decisions are substantially influenced by the market. These decisions are normally related to immediate business and near-term governmental considerations and not to the question of asset inheritance by the community as a whole over the long run.

Obsolescence, which is a key to decisions on assets, is usefully conceived as having both physical and functional aspects (the latter covering a wide variety of technical, social, economic, and financial considerations).

Physical Obsolescence

Physical obsolescence, a measure of structural deterioration of physical assets, is related to the level of regular maintenance during the asset's life. Cowan (1962/63) presents an interesting chart, reproduced in Figure 16–1, which relates structural degeneration to maintenance and demolition costs. Because deterioration is a gradual process, the curve is smooth and downward sloping with degeneration measured by some indicator of satisfactory functioning. By assumption, the initial level of performance is very high, even above what is estimated to be the optimum level. The degeneration process begins when performance drops below the optimum level, at which point four options are available: (1) complete rebuilding, after which there is a return to the very high performance; (2) regular maintenance, which supposedly keeps the level of performance above a certain minimum level for a very long period of time; (3) demolition, exercised when the level of performance is at a minimum; and (4) the do-nothing options (curve 3). The decisions are made on the basis of the relative costs and benefits of each option at each point in time.

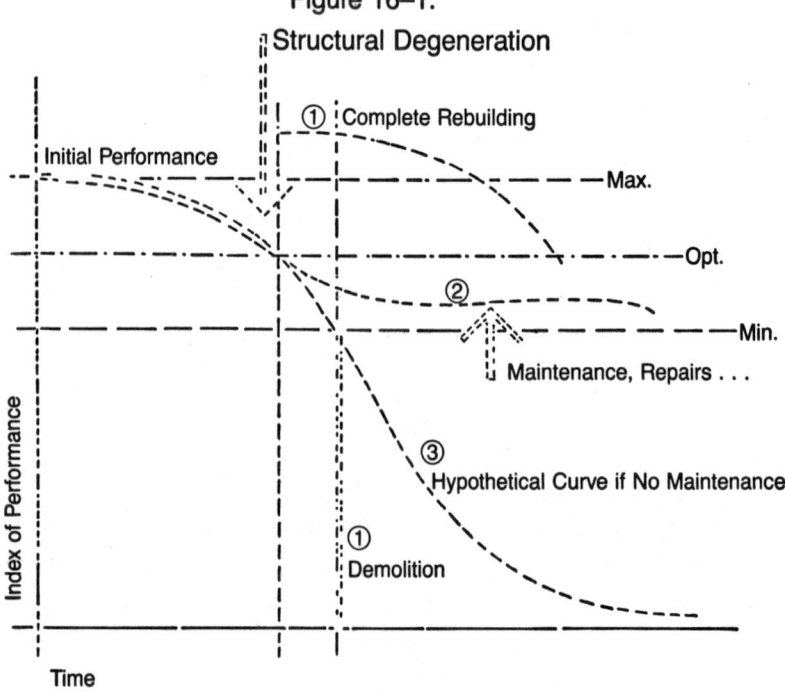

Figure 16–1.
Structural Degeneration

Structural Degeneration   Hypothetical Curves

Source: Peter Cowan, "Studies in the Growth, Change, and Aging of Buildings," *Transactions of the Bartlett Society 1962/63,* vol. 1: p. 68.

Private enterprises generally account for physical deterioration of both buildings and equipment by writing off the asset through depreciation over a predetermined life cycle. The period is usually determined by considerations related to taxation. Traditionally, public property (except in the case of public business enterprises) is not depreciated because there is no tax deduction as in the private sector (Goldberg, 1960). However, there are some good reasons for considering the establishment of depreciation charges for public assets. Depreciation is a source of information on physical deterioration. It can conceivably be used as the basis for establishing a fund earmarked for replacement; then dependence upon transient political considerations would be unnecessary at the time of replacement. Depreciation would force the public agencies involved in asset maintenance to plan replacement in advance and to define the expected lengths of an asset's life cycle. These are planning reasons, not operational reasons. They become valid only when a community decides that it pays to plan asset maintenance and asset inheritance over relatively long periods of time.

In the absence of this type of measurement, government agencies tend to follow rules of thumb which may be substantially removed from rational cost/benefit decisions. An example from Los Angeles is the tendency for the Bureau of Public Buildings to maintain the public property at the highest possible level for a given budget size, without regard to the possible need for replacement because of problems other than physical deterioration. Considerations of relative costs of different approaches—that is, of doing nothing, of demolition, or of rebuilding—are considered irrelevant when the regular maintenance is automatically at a very high predetermined level.

Functional Obsolescence

A building may become obsolete for many reasons before it physically deteriorates. These can be encompassed in the very broad concept of functional obsolescence. Cowan (1962/63) graphically contrasts this type of obsolescence with physical obsolescence in a chart which is reproduced in Figure 16–2. This time the curve is not smooth but decreases in a series of discrete points in time, mainly because such causes as technological change occur at discrete times and may speed up the rate of obsolescence. Figure 16–2 also illustrates the fact that, in most cases, functional obsolescence occurs before physical obsolescence; this second curve is below the optimum level of functional performance before there is any physical need for demolition or rebuilding. An option that was not present in Figure 16–1 is the physical adaption of the building so that the level of functional performance is raised above some optimum level. Cowan recognized that a major difficulty lies in devising proper indicators of functional performance. He also points out that "in the past functional change occurred slowly, and buildings could be pulled down as they became obsolete. Nowadays almost every building becomes obsolete long before it is ready to fall down" (Cowan 1962/63: 72).

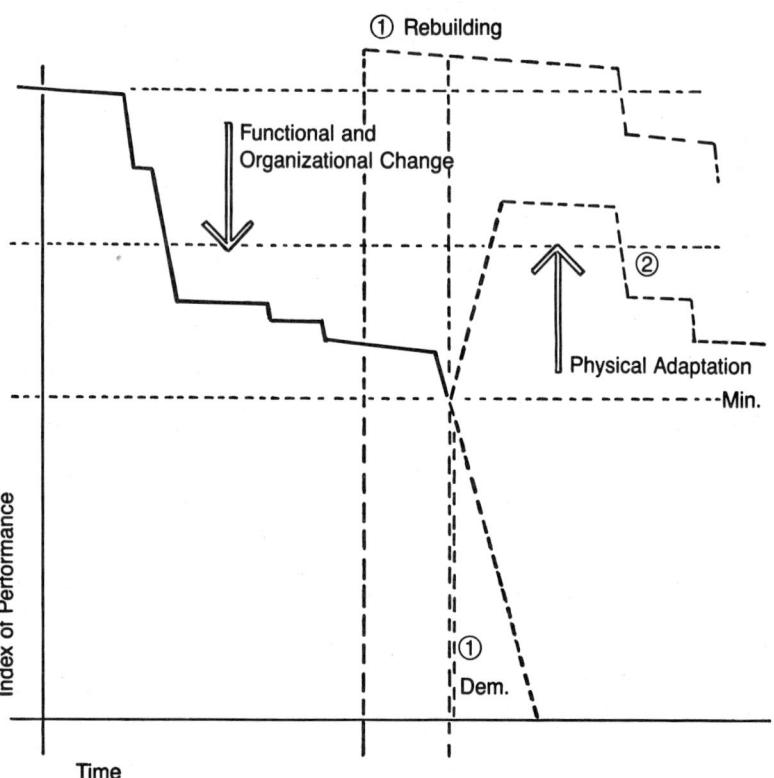

Functional Obsolescence
Source: Peter Cowan, "Studies in the Growth, Change, and Aging of Buildings," *Transactions of the Bartlett Society 1962/63*, vol. 1: p. 69.

Unlike the situation with physical obsolescence, where regularized procedures exist for coping with the needs for maintenance, no specified check points are available to indicate that a given facility is becoming functionally obsolete because of changes in technology, tastes, needs, and so on.

The planning department is generally not called upon to bring new ideas and influences that could postpone obsolescence. The issue of building obsolescence is barely mentioned in the city's general plan. Nor is the planning department normally utilized in decisions about new facilities, the design of new buildings, or even the design of new sections replacing worn out districts of the city.

PLANNING APPROACHES TO THE QUESTION OF INHERITANCE

No easy solution has been found to the problem of dealing with public assets as a way of guiding future developments toward publicly desired goals. The issues are many and complex, and this book has only touched on the surface of them. Three general areas hold promise of major improvements over present practices and deserve further study by researchers and some experimentation in local government. These are (1) planning-oriented asset accounting, (2) the introduction of long-range planning considerations into the capital programming and budgeting process, and (3) changes in local government structure and operations. The first two will be explored in this chapter.

At the present time, information provided by city planning agencies and decisions based on such information have only a limited impact on the factors that actually guide the development of the city over the succeeding generation and the extent to which the goals of urban planning are approximated. An important factor in determining the fate of the city of the next generation is what is done about the physical assets of the city—how long the assets are kept, how they are maintained, changed, and replaced. If all assets magically disappeared every ten years, city planning would largely have to become the art and science of new town building. Instead, the future, at least the physical future, is significantly influenced by the decisions made about *existing* urban capital. These decisions merit thoughtful consideration.

Asset Accounting and Reporting

Accounting for urban assets, both public and private, would ideally give city officials and the general public a status report of the city's physical condition, indicating strengths and weaknesses in the urban plant (as well as land uses). It would also provide a basis for decisions about the long-run future. With this knowledge, the city government (as well as state and national governments) could decide whether major physical transformations—for example, substantial changes in the size and functions of downtown areas—were needed to meet the evolving requirements of urban health. Furthermore, such data would aid officials in more properly appreciating the kinds of urban futures to which urbanites were aspiring.

Government accounting has traditionally concerned itself with flows (financial transaction moving through a system) rather than stocks—that is, the assets of the system at any point in time. The accounting system of the federal government functions in this manner because the nation's major economic and fiscal decisions focus on issues such as money and credit, fiscal policy and prices and international trade—all requiring information on financial transactions. Local government accounting systems also emphasize flows, but, in this case, it is to provide accountability to citizens and other governments for the use of money and property for which the local government is custodian or manager. This has been logically related to the earlier limited role of local government as a provider of services.

However, an increasing proportion of local governmental decisionmaking is now focusing on investment in infrastructure and on the issues of urban development and redevelopment. The aging of the plant has been a factor in this greater focus on capital stock, as has been the increasing importance of transportation. With the major transformations that are taking place within cities and with the serious economic and fiscal problems that many have come to face, decisions which focus on *development* are becoming more important. Considerations of development and redevelopment loom large when a city attempts to strengthen its downtown or to halt the rapid decline of certain neighborhoods. This increasing concentration by local governments on physical stock and the fact that the wealth of the city exists in large part in the form of existing fixed assets suggest that planning-oriented asset accounting has become an important undertaking for cities. Physical plant inventories are already a fixture of governmental accounting in many large cities. These can be strengthened by periodic condition and performance assessments which provide direct ratings of conditions or recording of system failure or breakdown rates, assessing conditions normally in relation to evolving use patterns of the system as a whole—whether transportation, warehousing, education, or whatever. The next stage in the development of local accounting should aim to meet several important requirements that would make such accounting more useful in making decisions that influence the long-range future.

Under today's conditions and those anticipated for the near-term future, a base of information is needed that can guide expensive public investments in infrastructure and other capital assets for *developmental* purposes. Accounts must serve more than a custodial function and should be able to provide the base for broad planning analyses that can help determine where obsolescent infrastructure and other assets are particularly damaging to the city's economic and social evolution. Such obsolescence is damaging if it imposes high costs on carrying out business operations within the community. Obsolescence is also damaging if it encourages higher-income individuals who work in the city to move away. Transportation facilities are important in this regard, but so are all the other major public facilities, including health, protection, education, the arts, and recreation. Information that can permit assets to be placed into a number of categories estimating broad ranges of obsolescence in planning terms would greatly help in ascertaining requirements for, and impediments to, economic and fiscal improvements within cities. Given the complexities of the task, only by monitoring the progression of developmentally viewed obsolescence of assets over a period of time may such calculations be made with any sense of reliability.

Naturally other kinds of information—essentially of a social, economic, and political character—would be equally vital in accumulating estimates of the type suggested here. However, many of the economic and fiscal difficulties of central cities have been attributed to physical aging and obsolescence, so that the physical causes of this phenomenon need to be monitored closely and considered in planning decisions. Oddly enough, this phenomenon has not received serious planning or operational notice.

In treating Clawson's suggestion that cities can project urban renewal needs, much insight for decisionmaking can be provided by rather basic information on aging alone. However, more accurate data are needed (mainly in accounting for functional as well as physical obsolescence) to support major public investment decisions. Researchers from the Joint Unit for Planning Research of University College in London, England, have developed a model for the analysis of obsolescence in housing (based on a theory of obsolescence) which is suggestive of the kinds of models which can be built for this purpose (Nutt et al., 1976). The further development of indicators of structural and functional performance is critically important. Local government interest in planning-oriented asset accounting would surely stimulate research along these lines so that, over time, both the techniques of monitoring and the usefulness of models of aging and obsolescence could be expected to be developed.

A more ambitious development of asset accounting for planning purposes would go substantially beyond the recording of the current physical *condition* of assets. The information sought might well include estimates of the degree of underutilization and above normal pressures in use; considerations of alternative uses of the assets (including adaptive reuse); economic values of existing and alternative uses; and the interrelationships among assets as well as the relationship of assets to their support systems and to the surrounding environment. Particularly important for planning is the grouping of the various assets in terms of (1) location, such as districts or neighborhoods; (2) functions, such as education, health, manufacturing, private services, and the like; (3) special groups, such as so-called life-support systems; and (4) other groupings for various broad decision needs. These are only illustrative. The actual questions asked of the asset accounts would depend on the situation of the individual municipality, including the nature of its politics.

An economically troubled city might well consider using the concept of liabilities as a counterpoint to assets. Such a concept of liabilities would cover not only the usually recorded public debts but also provide a recording of those elements of the physical plant which block the achievement of the planning goals. Specific negative features of the downtown, of the transportation system, of overly impacted natural resources, and so on might be recorded as liabilities to provide a greater understanding of the resources available for the achievement of goals.

The economic health of a city is influenced not only by the condition of its public infrastructure and other public assets but also by the condition of its private productive plant (in manufacturing, wholesaling, and so on). Publicly oriented accounting for the private plant poses major problems, but since the condition of such plant is so important to the welfare of the city, it becomes a matter of governmental concern. The most realistic way of proceeding by periodically studying the condition of the city's private productive plant (possibly carried out every five years, with year-by-year updating if that is deemed appropriate). Such studies would provide signals of highly damaging obsolescence (that is, where the plant is so outmoded that productivity is down, employment is down, and total demise threatens). The studies should, ideally, also highlight features that can be influenced by government action, such as location, availability of space, transportation, parking, and various public services and facilities. Such studies could also be expected to provide a base for municipal, as well as state and national, policy decisions which might encourage modernization through special tax- and public-expenditure measures. Such special studies could be carried out only if private firms were convinced of the ultimate value of the studies and if confidentiality could be guaranteed.

The availability of this kind of information might conceivably provide the basis for negotiation between municipal government and private industry for an agreed upon level of commitment to capital maintenance and improvement where needed to strengthen the local economy. Government commitment to long-term capital improvement would be essential to this kind of negotiation. Under conditions of energy shortage, the negotiations might well involve mutual commitment to a changeover to more energy-efficient capital installation and use. By considering these kinds of measures, planning is beginning to move into a realm where the achievement of community goals are not left to vague paper plans built on vague land-use ideas, but rather involve a direct approach to the use of community resources for the achievement of community goals.

Unless a municipal agency—logically the planning department—has the responsibility for reporting on the condition of public and private assets and its impact on the development of the city, asset accounting can only be useful for specific operating decisions. Planning-oriented reporting is, then, a major instrumentality in decisionmaking on matters that have long-range impacts. Such reporting can be quite useful if the municipal planning agency has established channels for the regularized flow of information from municipal departments maintaining the asset accounts, in exchange for keeping these departments posted on the impacts that the aging asset structure is having on developments in the city. These two-way exchanges are important if the whole asset accounting system is eventually to serve both the purposes of long-range planning decisions and the operating decisions that the executive departments must make.

Planning-oriented reporting would need to be done with some care to convey timely information about capital assets to decisionmakers and the general public without drowning them in details. Ideally, such reporting should provide firmer base for major decisions on the five to six year capital program and budget and for the operating decisions on assets so that maintenance, rehabilitation, demolition, and renewal have some sensible relationship to the developmental needs of the city over the ensuing decades.

Chapter 17
Governmental Decisions on Capital Maintenance and New Construction

Public decisions on capital maintenance, improvement, and new construction are made in most cities within the context of a capital program and budget. The preparation of five to six year capital programs and budgets has generally had a close tie to city planning, and in some cases, both the capital program and budget are prepared by the planning agency. Even in these instances, however, often only a tenuous tie exists between the capital program and budget on the one hand and the main work of the planning agency (for example, concerns with land use, zoning, housing, transportation, environment, and so on) on the other. A major reason is that planning agencies have not become significantly involved with the problems of maintaining, improving, and building public assets. Only if the assumption that urban planning in the latter part of the 20th century must focus on the need to bring about major transformations in urban life and functions is accepted, and that this, in turn, involves detailed attention to the changing urban infrastructure and other capital assets, can a new relationship of planning agencies to capital programming and budgeting be expected.

DIFFICULTIES IN THE PRESENT SYSTEM

In the cities studied earlier, little interaction was found between the urban planning agency and the operating agencies with regard to the capital portion of the budget, the place in which the decisions are made that affect the physical form of the city directly, with all its long-range implications.

Key questions are what are the priorities for spending money and how are they determined? Some insight into what is currently involved is provided by a look at some recent decisions about capital in the city of Los Angeles.

The first answers about priorities for capital expenditures in Los Angeles, as in most cities, come from the five year capital program. For the period 1976–77 to 1980–81, it was estimated that the city must spend over $1.9 billion for improvements and additions to existing infrastructure. Over $350 million was to come from outside funding sources. So the actual cost to the city was figured at roughly $1.5 billion. About $600 million of specific projects was detailed in the five year program, with over $900 million estimated as required in general categories in later years. Of the $600 million, approximately $100 million was budgeted for the next fiscal year, so that of the almost $2 billion put into the capital budget on a supposed priority basis, only 5 percent was scheduled for the next year. One cannot help but suspect that the remainder was essentially a shopping list of capital expenditures that agency personnel thought would be useful.

In the actual proposed budget for 1976–77, the total allotted to capital improvements was $72.6 million. This means that over $25 million in assumed needed improvements had to be cut out of the budget to balance it. The $25 million in capital budget cuts came from projects that did not have outside sources of funding or specially earmarked funds that could only be used for designated projects. Sewers, parks and recreation, off-street parking, streets, bikeways, and several other items with independent funding were not cut, at least not in the first round. Office buildings, landfill sites, animal shelters, repairshops, maintenance yards, libraries, and other items without independent sources of funding *were* cut.

Libraries, for example, have no special fund for capital projects. At least two high-priority needs have been identified by library officials: to bring libraries built before 1933 up to earthquake standards and to extend library services to the underserved regions of the vast San Fernando Valley. For many years, these needs have been recognized by the inclusion of library projects in the proposed capital programs, but in none of these years have expenditures for these purposes been included in the next year's general budget. The first year of the 1976–77/1980–81 capital program contained an item of $3 million for libraries, but in the general budget for that year only $800,000 was included for two libraries that could be placed under the community development fund. Their location was determined by the availability of money for the selected areas, not because they were in the best locations. Finally, no money was included for the long-recognized needed improvement of the outmoded central library that is important for many persons in the inner city.

The reason for the unusually large budget cut in the following year's budget (25 percent of the amount proposed for 1976–77) was the desire of the mayor to divert most of the general fund and revenue-sharing monies from capital projects to pay for the operating costs of the city. This was a move undertaken to avoid raising taxes. Over $16 million of these funds was removed from special municipal facilities projects and made available to finance general city operations. This had the effect of drastically reducing the amount of flexible money that the mayor felt could be spent.

The outcomes were that the city had little flexibility in what capital projects it could undertake, and that short-term gains rather than long-term benefits were to be emphasized. The major determinants were (1) whether a proposed expenditure had earmarked funds associated with it and (2) whether the project was eligible for federal money. Since the federal government provided up to 83 percent of the costs of some projects, it had a major impact on which programs were actually implemented. This suggests that federal monies often dictate much local capital spending.

Los Angeles is far from unique in this regard. Other cities react the same way to financial pressures. In *Urban Outcomes,* Levy, Meltsner, and Wildavsky (1974: 108) report that Oakland also diverted capital funds to meet operating expense requirements, and that decisions on capital projects were largely based on whether the costs were shared with outside entities.

What this adds up to is that the budget for the first year of a five year capital plan is used as the starting and ending point for decisions about what actually gets implemented. The items allocated for later years in the program are not taken seriously. In the case of Los Angeles, less than half of the programs which have been included in the later four years (supposedly as a result of specific plans for the future) are normally funded. Each year, a rather thorough evaluation is carried out, and priorities are largely determined by the current fiscal and political situation.

Since the first year of the capital plan and budget is used in actual decisionmaking, the next question is how rational is the first year plan and how much consideration does it give to the future? Again, the situation in Los Angeles is fairly typical. The decision process is tied in with capital-improvement-program meetings organized along city councilmanic districts. There the individual council member informs the Technical Committee for Capital Programming (made up of members of the various agencies with building responsibilities, in addition to the city administrative officer and representatives of the planning department) of his or her priorities. This would seem to have a dominant influence on which departments are to undertake projects in various areas of the city and the order in which projects are to be undertaken. The rationale for the choices is not readily apparent. One council member indicates an interest in street lighting and pays no attention to street improvements or parking. Another does not care much about street lighting but wants to make sure that the streets do not flood. The total amount allocated to each district (at least in the case of streets) is equivalent, but the money is spent, within certain limitations, according to the wishes of the council members representing the various districts.[1]

The council members work with materials prepared by the various operating departments concerned with capital improvements. The approach of such agencies to the treatment of public assets is of major significance. A closer look at the Los Angeles Department of Public Works, which is particularly important in the capital improvement decisions of that city, provides some insights into the current situation. Its Bureau of Engineering is responsible for capital investments in streets and highways including major reconstruction and street widening, involving an annual budget in excess of $20 million. This work is critical to the modernization of the city's infrastructure in line with future requirements. Rather than receive policy guidelines from the city's general plan, as might be expected, the highways and streets shown in the plan are the result of *inputs* by the bureau and other agencies, and the plan is adjusted periodically as major changes are initiated by these agencies. This type of action serves to highlight the facts that official planning in this city is not necessarily leading the way and that connections of urban planning to operational capital programming are hard to find.

Most of the 7,200 miles of streets in the city of Los Angeles were built in the 1940s and 1950s and are consequently nearing the end of their life expectancy (25 years for asphalt pavement). The choice between performing

[1] A long-time city manager, in reviewing this section, made the following noteworthy point: "I assert that Los Angeles brings the city councilmen into capital improvement programming at too early a stage and thereby truncates the administrative contribution and increases pork barreling. Very few communities bring in ward legislators prior to the time when the administration completes its formulation of a recommended capital improvement program. From my city manager and other administrative experience, I would assert that good government depends on generalist administrators being able to fully develop recommendations on their own within their sense of political reality, upon creative debate between them and elected officials as the elected officials consider their recommendations, and upon elected officials making all the final decisions." Interestingly, he does not refer to the role of the planning department in this process.

street reconstruction or including the streets as part of normal maintenance (carried out by the Bureau of Street Maintenance) seems to depend on factors such as fund availability and political pressures. During the latter part of the 1970s, the city government was devoting most of the gas tax funds to street maintenance and using federal funds for major capital improvements. The main reason for this was the fact that during the period under consideration the gas tax remained almost constant (measured in cents/gallon) in a time of aging streets and increasing costs of maintenance and reconstruction. This funding approach clearly served to more or less freeze the critically important transportation infrastructure of the city. The organization and procedures made even the constrained type of street reconstruction difficult. An area of interbureau conflict was referenced in the city budget proposal for 1976–77/1980–81:

> During the preparation of the Program . . . it was learned that a section . . . which was scheduled for reconstruction in 1978–79 had been resurfaced by the Bureau of Street Maintenance. Generally, a project is scheduled for reconstruction when resurfacing and other efforts by street maintenance crews is deemed not cost effective. It is urged that the Director of the Bureau of Street Maintenance obtain specific Council approval before including any project in his Resurfacing Program which has been identified as a reconstruction project in the Five Year Capital Program (Los Angeles, 1976–77/1980–81:5).

Aside from the obvious problem of coordination that is evident in this memo, the lack of long-range planning and programming information, which could aid in making decisions on public-asset management in terms of the changing needs of the city as well as its changing fiscal and operational capacity, is evident.

The Bureau of Street Maintenance in Los Angeles resurfaces and/or reconstructs only 60 miles of street per year. At that rate, it would take over 100 years to service all of the streets. Clearly, a good bit of patchwork is going on. If one were to use the standard reported as applying in Oakland (resurfacing streets every ten years), Los Angeles should be working on 700 miles of streets a year, over ten times the present rate. This raises some questions about the rationality of the decisions made about asset maintenance in this particular instance at least. A similar issue develops on the lack of restriction on the use of buses in the city. Because of the grid system in the San Fernando Valley, the Southern California Rapid Transit District is running buses on secondary streets, which were not built for loads that heavy. This must have a significant effect on asset preservation, but the effects are not known, and the Bureau of Street Maintenance does not seem to be able to deal with the long-run considerations involved.

THE MULTIYEAR CAPITAL PROGRAM AND BUDGET

The specific events in this illustration serve to underline the fact that the existence of a multiyear capital program and budget does not guarantee that long-range considerations about the city's assets will determine the actual decisions made and actions taken. The dominance of the immediate political and fiscal considerations in such decisions and actions tends to discourage a genuine effort at long-range programming of asset maintenance, improvement, and new construction by the operating agencies and their reliance on long-range policies developed by the planning department. The lack of meaningful multiyear fiscal planning and of substantial provisions for contingencies is particularly damaging to a planned approach to city development and redevelopment. If there is no reliance on the availability of fiscal resources for a number of years beyond the next one, the approach to capital programming and budgeting is almost certain to be *pro forma,* a simple exercise not to be taken too seriously.

While looking ahead over a period of 10 to 25 years, a city's general plan is supposed to provide the basis for the 5 or 6 year capital improvement program (Snyder, 1977: Chapter 4; Hirsch and Sonnenblum, 1970: Chapter 11; Burkhead, 1956: Chapter 8). That program, in turn, is to provide the base for the capital budget, encompassing proposed capital outlays and the revenues to finance such outlays. In rare instances (for example, certain aspects of transportation in some cities), that is what happens. More frequently, the capital program is pieced together through the independent proposals of the various operating departments. Few of those preparing such proposals for their departments even know what is in the city's general plan, let alone follow it closely. In one case mentioned in Chapter 2, the capital improvements proposed by a department were inserted into the general plan to bring the two into agreement. That is hardly a useful congruence, however. Genuine congruence would occur if there is actually a long-range, capital-improvement strategy translated into specific standards for capital asset management, as well as locational and other guidelines for public capital investments. Such strategy, standards, and guidelines have to be specific enough to offer a basis for joint development of the five or six year capital improvement program by the planning and operating agencies. Financial considerations, including the availability of special funds and of grants from higher levels of government, will inevitably have a major impact on the capital improvements included in the capital program and budget. Yet, the availability of the planning strategy, standards, and guidelines would provide a groundwork for choosing among alternatives—no matter how constrained—for weighing the long-run future against more immediate requirements. It also represents an opportunity for more conscious control of asset inheritance at *various* points in the future.

If the intermediate-range capital-improvement program and budget were not already in existence, they would have to be invented. An operational hinge is needed between the really short-range decisions of a one year budget and the long-range considerations involved in building and managing public assets. However, this hinge cannot serve its purpose effectively if the long-range planning materials are only tangentially related to the content of the intermediate-range program and budget. Finance officers, budget officers, and heads of operating agencies, all of whom normally have significant roles in the design and implementation of the five or six year capital program and budget, do not exactly go out of their way to invite planning agencies to play a larger role in the programming-budgeting process. In fact, in many instances, they tend to resist. Thus it is the responsibility of the planning agency itself—hopefully supported by the mayor and the city council—to evolve approaches and to prepare materials which can give a planning orientation to the process.

WHAT LESSONS SHOULD BE DRAWN FROM PAST EXPERIENCE

At the present time, danger exists that wrong conclusions will be drawn from the observed limitations of the older physical approach to urban planning. The lesson that some seemed to have learned is that the physical component is not centrally important in urban planning and that planning should substantially play down this component in the future. But another conclusion is more appropriately to be drawn from our experience with the limitations of the earlier approach. A physical master plan is based largely on idealized land-use concepts and a limited number of proposed physical features does not provide a useful framework for municipal government decisionmaking (or county or regional decisionmaking). The other part of the lesson is that the earlier master plan approach totally underestimated the importance of specific decisions on urban infrastructure and provided little lead to important decisions on maintenance, rehabilitation, and removal of existing plant and construction of new plant.

Urban planning has a unique and important contribution to make in community decisions as to how to manage the inheritance of assets over time so as to help approximate the community's goals and more general image of the future. Important moves in this direction have been made in some cities across the country—as in Boston, Cincinnati, Dallas, and New York—but these are only a beginning. Urban planning needs some new approaches and new tools to cope with this critically important matter.

These must encompass (1) appropriately designed general policy plans that provide a strategy for the development and management of infrastructure over the long-run, for top-down guidance, (2) asset accounts that provide a continuous picture of the condition and impact of existing capital, for a ground-up view, and (3) multiyear capital programs and budget that serve to bring the other two to a decision focus.

In developing strategy suggestions for the construction and management of infrastructure, planners will have to develop models of asset construction and change that permit an ever-improving view of the impact of such changes on the economic health of the city and the welfare of its residents. Planners will have to produce compelling information on the role of infrastructure in achieving community goals (as well as of land-use and zoning proposals) to play an appropriate role in the guidance of decisions on public and private assets. Urban planners will have to evolve long-run fiscal plans to parallel general plans for the development of the community over time, essentially to demonstrate the fiscal implications of different approaches to development and redevelopment and to the use of the jurisdiction's fiscal authority and capacity. Planners will also have to show what needs to be done to change from present systems of asset accounting to planning-oriented systems (discussed in Chapter 16) as well as what needs to be done to make multiyear capital programs and budgets serve decisions that have long-term impacts on the community.

These are extremely difficult and complex objectives which will take many years to achieve. The effort will be made only if planners appreciate their importance for urban planning in the decades to come. Once they appreciate their importance, then it becomes a matter of skill in institution building. Political and administrative leaders must, in turn, be convinced of the value of such efforts and included in the activity of thinking through how best the objectives can be accomplished. The public must also become supportive of such efforts. With the ever-greater resistance to tax increases and expansion of governmental operations, the concentration of urban planning on methods for obtaining optimum results from existing city assets and from new public investments should please the public.

In general, everyone concerned with the future of the city must come to see that a planful approach to the inheritance component (the **past** component of the future) is the key to our ability to guide future urban development into desirable directions.

PART 4
THE PRESENT COMPONENT OF THE FUTURE

Chapter 18
The Emerging Planning Paradigm

An appreciation of the importance of the inheritance factor in dealing with the future brings the value of such concepts as asset accounting, capital budgeting, and, most of all, fiscal planning, to the forefront of city planning.

Along the same lines, an understanding of the role of the **present** aspects of the future highlights the importance of a strong information (intelligence) capability to city planning. Planners must grasp how the present situation has come into being and is evolving into the future and how present decisions are likely to impact people and places in the future. The importance of this capability has already been anticipated in the discussion of the key role in planning the principles of societal learning and of self-directing cybernetics in government.

TIME AS A THREE-FOLD PRESENT

"Time, said St. Augustine, is a three-fold present: the present as we experience it, the past as present memory, and the future as a present expectation" (Bell, 1967: 639).

Planners must be particularly conscious of time and how individuals and communities relate to it. Decisions about the future—to achieve a given goal or to avoid a given evil—are filtered through the current views about the present and the future. Images of the future and views about the nature of the future influence decisions being made and actions currently taken about the most immediate matters. The present and the future (as well as the past) are thus inevitably intertwined.

One of the major problems is the dominance of current difficulties (for example, traffic congestion, energy shortage, or urban crime) in current decisionmaking about the future. As a result of the overbearing presence of such immediate problems, a tendency exists to see the "better" future—when setting goals and working out strategy and policies to achieve them—as essentially a *later* present in which the difficulties have been removed. The limitations of this approach, which is central to so much current planning and decisionmaking, is apparent. It concentrates on overcoming the *effects* of decisions made or not made in the past (as in the case of traffic congestion, past decisions about locations of homes and places of work, the transportation networks constructed, gasoline price policy, and the like). Unfortunately, overcoming past decisions and actions is extremely difficult in most cases.

Another difficulty is that the "bads" that we want to eliminate are often tied in to the social structure itself—the "system." It is not easy to remove the unwanted feature in isolation, that is, without making some necessary changes in the system as a whole. An example is the large cluster of problems found in central city ghettos (poor housing, unemployment, crime, and so on). Such problems are tied in to the established patterns in the distribution of resources, education, freedom of locational choice of the more advantaged (the ability of white middle-class families to move away from the central city to single-class suburbs to avoid the costs of dealing with poverty and disadvantage), and other elements of the urban system as it has evolved to the present. The "bads" and the "goods" are all part of the same urban system. The future cannot be the present with only the undesirable features removed.

A related problem stems from the "past as present memory." Planning tends to attack the difficulties and crises of the present without adequate consideration of the past. Memory can be rather poor. If policy aimed at overcoming present difficulties is to be effective, it is important to know how such difficulties evolved, what kinds of efforts in the past (with regard to the same or similar problems) succeeded or did not succeed, which of the community institutions were effective in dealing with which problems, and the like. It is equally important to try to conceive how the future community's urban structure (system) may evolve—what might be called "future history." A sense of what is involved in the stability and change of a highly interrelated system over time is needed. This is an *operational* imperative. It is necessary for sound decisionmaking, that is, for decisions that have a high probability of success in the present and the future. When a city in the 1970s (*post* Pruitt Igoe) constructed large institutionalized public housing, it was essentially overlooking decades of experience with the imperfections of this kind of housing. And when public housing is built today, the kinds of assumptions made about the future in regard to such housing is important. If the future is not treated in a conscious manner—asking hard questions about evolving social structures, aspirations of the poor, and housing patterns—the assumptions may well be unrealistic. The results over time could then be unduly costly or damaging to the community in other ways.

THE SHIFT TO A NEW PARADIGM IN URBAN PLANNING

In a practical sense, the present can be viewed as a useful transition from the past to the future. A very important task for planning is to make the transition as efficiently, humanely, and goal oriented as possible. In this, the importance of the *intelligence* function must be appreciated. It is essential to grasp the changes from the past and understand the major forces underway while at the same time reaching out to the possibilities of the future. Obtaining as much knowledge as feasible about the past, present, and future is essential to sound urban planning. Urban planning in the United States (and in other industrialized countries) has been moving toward trying to provide a stronger and broader base of information for decisionmaking than formerly while trying to conceive the future in broader terms as well. The move away from the earlier paradigm towards a new framework for planning activities, not unexpectedly, has been partial and disjointed. In what follows, an attempt is made to conceive the new framework in model (or idealized) terms. This will hopefully stimulate discussion as to what a desirable urban planning framework should consist of as a guide to planning activities in the future.

The earlier paradigm of urban planning was based on a specific *focus* for its activities—a physical master plan presenting an idealized future picture of land uses and of transportation interconnections. This focus was sustained even as planning encompassed newer concerns in the economic and social realms, as is apparent from the descriptions of planning in various cities across the country, as was described in Chapters 2 to 7.

What should urban planning focus on in the next stage of its development? This is not only an intellectual question but an operational one as well. The extent to which urban planning should limit itself operationally to physical development has been a hotly debated issue among both city planners and municipal officials. Limitations on what city planning may legitimately cover are included in some city charters; in other communities, the limitations are essentially traditional—what has been acceptable over time. While the scope for urban planning will undoubtedly continue to evolve on the basis of political and economic interests and events within each community, the *logic* of planning's development in its next phase must be considered.

The new paradigm of urban planning must start with the conception of the *subject* of urban planning as a city composed of a number of closely interrelated elements—an urban system. The system evolves over time so that its past, present, and future are all relevant to the decisions that have to be made—decisions that have pertinence for both the present and for the future. One of planning's major reasons for being is to try to *interconnect* the more significant elements of the community in decisionmaking so that the goals chosen by the community can be achieved, or at least approximated.

COMPREHENDING THE COMMUNITY AND URBAN SYSTEM

One of the many complexities that urban planning must face is the fact that the political/territorial municipality (the community for which the planning and the political decisions are made and actions carried out) does not fully encompass certain of the elements with which planning must be concerned, elements such as the regional economy, the air and water basins, and the transportation network. To some extent, the difficulty is mitigated by the existence of county and metropolitan regional planning which treats some of these metropolitanwide features. But the connections among the various local levels are generally so informal and haphazard that the municipal planning departments do not have the information to develop a broad enough picture of what has been taking place, and is likely to take place in the future.

To achieve a sense of the community changing over time, a systemic municipality-within-a-region base of information needs to evolve.

The importance of this can be appreciated by looking at a limited practical example. Suppose very strong political pressures have built up for a municipality to do something about the inability in many cases of the lower-income groups within the city to acquire decent housing. An initial requirement would be for firm information on the state of housing (all the supply factors, including the land-use situation in poor neighborhoods and housing currently available to lower-income groups, potential new areas, rent levels, history of filtering, and so on). Demand factors would have to be examined simultaneously, including income levels of households (looking at the changing nature of households); projections of the job situation would be needed. Consideration would have to be given to feasible targets for, say, the next decade (with estimates of how quickly housing could be provided under various assumptions). The resource (fiscal) assumptions would be particularly important, and here revenue projections would be needed (relying on the capital budget and fiscal plan if available). The strategy and policies to meet the housing targets that had been set would then have to be worked out. Only one of the various alternatives to be considered would be the direct provision of lower-rent housing by the municipality (with aid from higher levels of government). Other approaches would have to be tested through detailed policy analyses. This, in turn, would require several forecasts—made either openly or implicitly. One of the most important considerations would be whether strongly stepped-up efforts in the job and income realm (rather than the direct provision of housing) would be both feasible and politically attractive. The role of the federal and state governments in these matters would be crucial. The municipality would have to consider effective ways in which it can make its needs known to the federal and state governments and in which it could influence federal and state policy in directions supportive of its needs.

A key point here is that even a limited example demonstrates how extensive the information requirements of municipal decisionmaking must be—and how closely that information is tied to the concept of an evolving urban system—if effective policy and action is sought.

It would be very comforting indeed if there was a firmly based general theory of how the urban system functions and changes and stronger notions about the scope and limits of societal control over change. Such would provide the framework for gathering information, carrying out analyses, and preparing policies and plans. However, while there is no general theory, partial theories have been derived from both the natural and social sciences. As stressed in Part 2, the key role of being in a learning posture has been discovered (or rediscovered). The opportunity, is available, through monitoring and study, to learn as one goes along and to record and to act on what one is learning. Useful concepts have been developed on the role of images of the future, on the role of self-directing and directed cybernetic systems, on transactive planning, and on decision frameworks, as outlined in Part 2.

There is much to draw on in conceptualizing an idealized information base for time-conscious urban planning, keeping in mind the different needs for information of operating agencies as compared to a central planning office (Dunn, 1974; Friedmann, 1968; Garn et al., 1975; Goodman and Freund, 1968: Part II; Hirsch and Sonnenblum, 1970; Holleb, 1969). A broad, generalized information base (that can be conceived of as an informal cybernetic system) is called for—one which permits the drawing out of a limited number of data sets geared to key governmental decisions and local government operations. In practice, this would involve substantially broadening and deepening the present systems of information in municipalities so that they can soon approach the idealized system suggested.

Chapter 19 will explore the key elements of such a system. The objective is the elaboration of an intelligence function sturdy enough to assist urban planning in making the transition from the present to the future as efficiently, humanely, and as goal oriented as possible.

Chapter 19
Information Needed for
Time-Oriented Planning

Urban planning needs information that can reveal the urban system changing over time, from the past to the present and into the future.

MAJOR ELEMENTS OF AN INFORMATION SYSTEM

First, certain broad categories of information must be considered that would be particularly useful in municipal decisionmaking when noting how the urban-system information fits into the larger scheme of things. (The focus here is on information needed by a planning agency—working together with the operating agencies—in a municipality of medium to large size. The major categories, as highlighted in Figure 19–1 are (1) contextual information (that is, information on the nation as a whole and on the state as the context for the individual municipality); (2) information on the basic urban system in change—the municipality-within-the-region; (3) analyses of needs for system improvements and ways of achieving them; (4) analyses of special problems and difficulties and ways of mitigating them, and (5) analyses of future opportunities and possibilities. The kinds of analyses needed would determine the types of raw data that would be sought within the information setup (always remembering that the collection and use of information are costly).

URBAN SYSTEM INFORMATION

Information on the urban system (item 2) is at the core of the scheme and gives form and substance to the other items. Information on what has been

Figure 19–1.
Major Components of a Time-Conscious Urban Information System for Municipal Planning

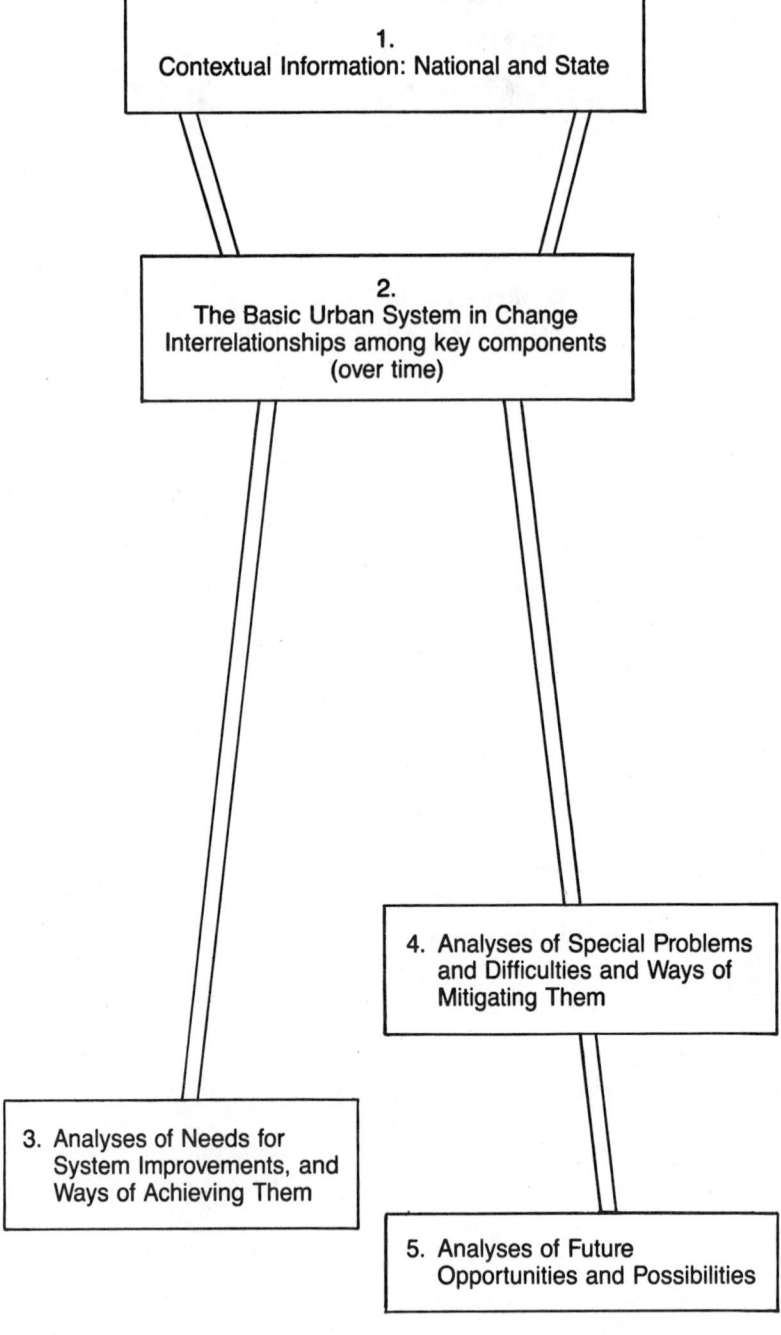

called "the basic urban system in change" should reveal the important relationships among the major components of the functioning city in the context of the metropolitan region. Municipalities need two sets of urban-system data: one for the region and another for the municipality itself as a political/territorial entity. This poses several problems, not the least of which is the problem of the differing geographic boundaries that tend to be employed by data-generating agencies.

Certain elements of the city loom large in most issues with which a municipality must cope. This becomes apparent when one examines a broad range of comprehensive urban studies by both scholars and planning departments. (Cowan, 1973; Gakenheimer, 1965; Goodman and Freud, 1968; Klaassen and Paelinck, 1974). These elements are not only the key to understanding how the city functions, but they are central to the definition of city problems (where it does not function well), to an evaluation of resources available to deal with the problems and to achieve goals for the future, and to the creation of policy and program proposals. They are dominant threads of the urban fabric and of the content of urban planning. This multiuse feature is what can be said to characterize urban system information in contrast to other types of information.

These elements are set out in Figure 19–2. The form and position of these clusters suggest the interrelationships among the key elements. (Arrows are not employed because too many would be needed to show all the possible interrelationships.) A distinction is made between asset items (people and things), financial flow items, major institutions, and functioning systems (economic, social, environmental, and governmental). The emphasis throughout is on *changing* status or condition. Unlike items are brought together for convenience mainly to *characterize* the urban system which must be comprehended in urban planning. The purpose here is to be suggestive of some of the needed features of the new paradigm or framework for planning, rather than attempt to be definitive. The key features of such a framework can be highlighted by reference to the items in Figure 19–2.

Individual and family (or household) welfare should be the focal point—or literal center—of urban system information. This is suggested by the circle (A) at the center of Figure 19–2. Without going into too much detail, net change in household income can be seen as a useful indicator of changes in welfare. (The household encompasses all persons who share their income, from a single individual to a joint family or a collective.) Since income alone cannot tell the whole story of welfare, other objective and subjective indicators are

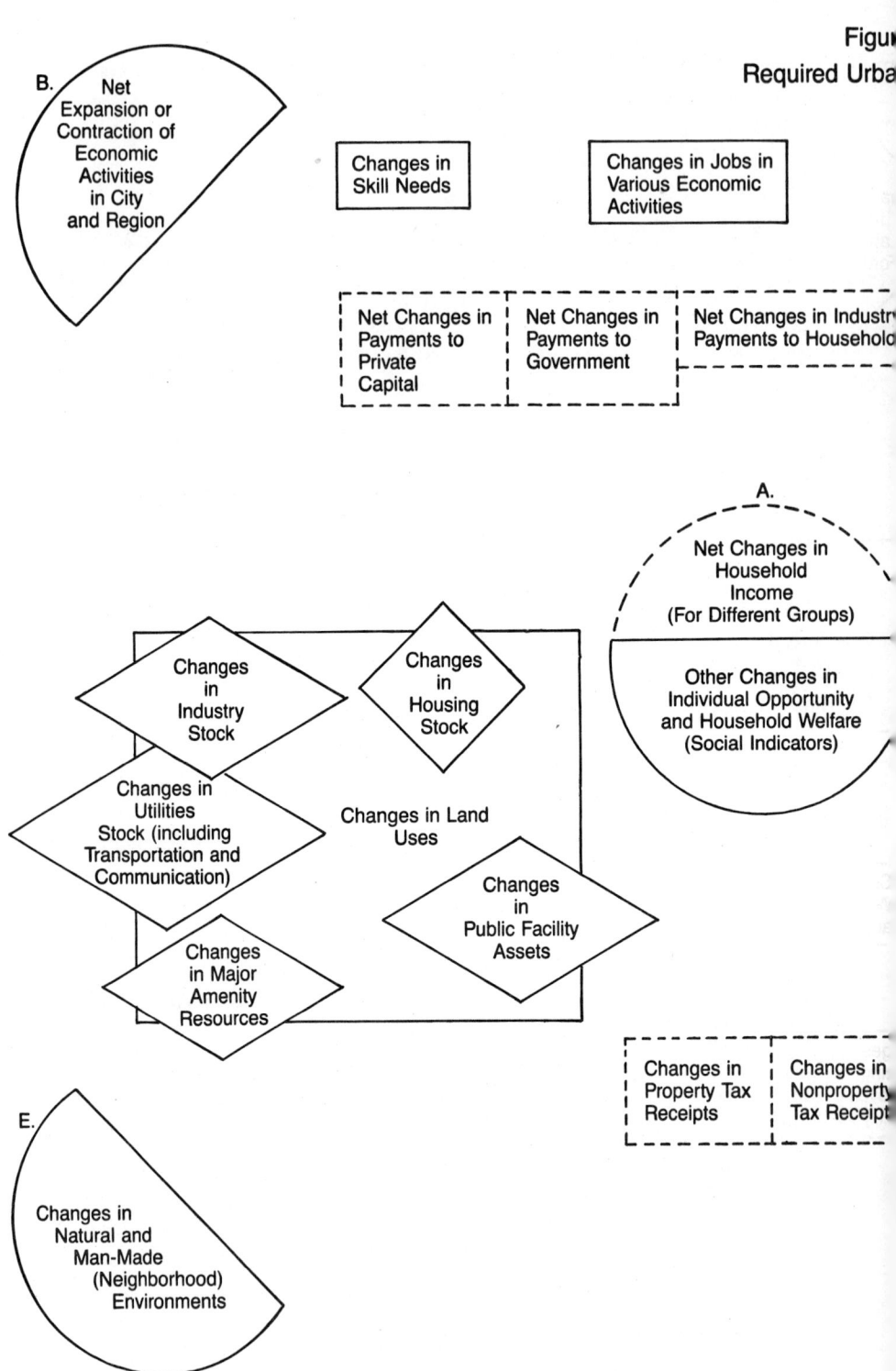

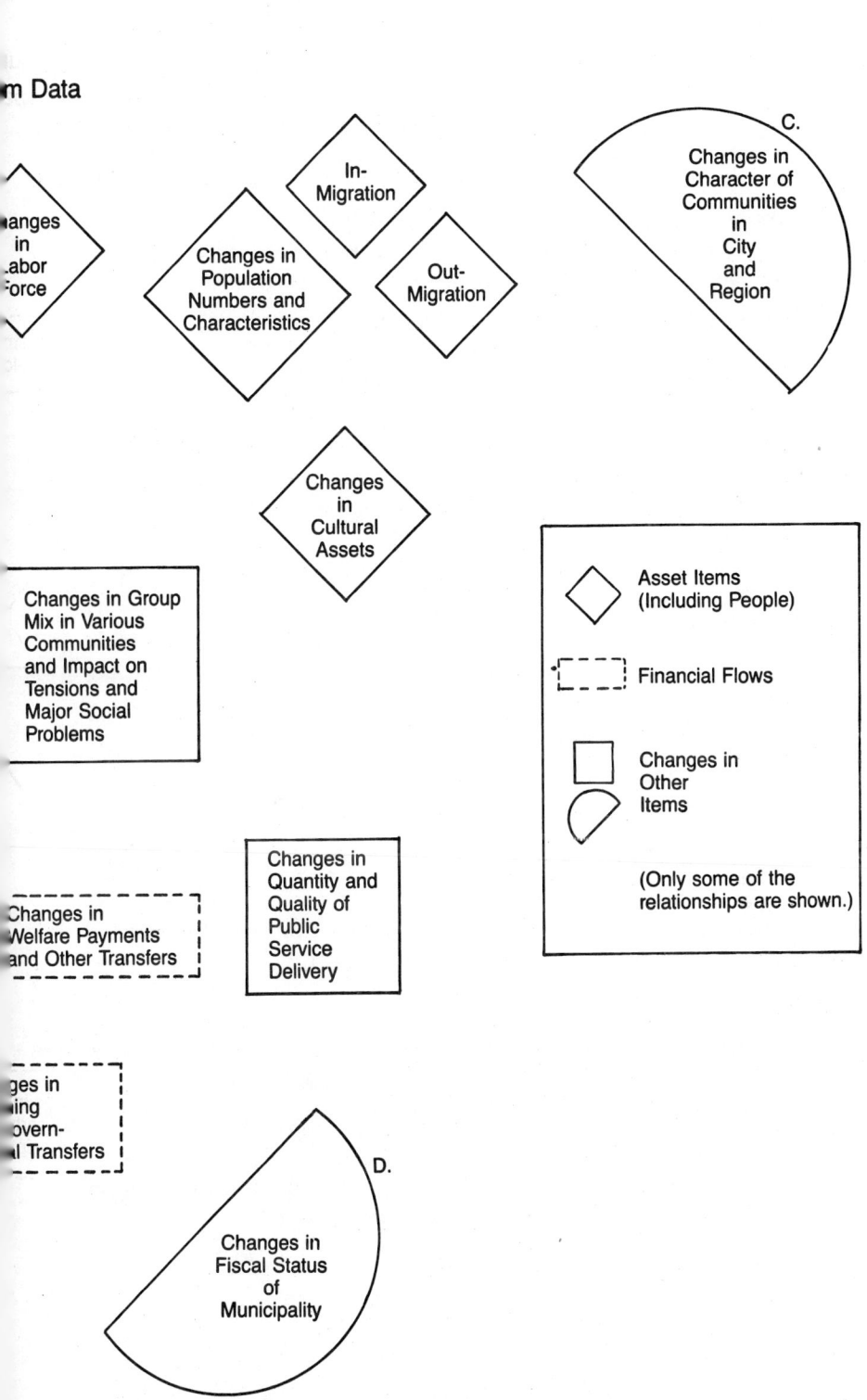

needed to reflect satisfactions and dissatisfactions, access to opportunities of various kinds, and so on. Other welfare measures (for example, unemployment and subemployment, the latter encompassing underemployment and the number of people earning below the poverty level) can provide a variety of important kinds of information when compiled for different groups within the city (for example, racial, ethnic, age) and for the different sectors of the city and region (Mier, Vietorisz and Giblin, 1975). Some useful kinds of indicators of welfare have been proposed when long-run considerations are involved. One of these is a lifetime-earning-power index which can reflect the anticipated income situation for various groups in the community over time by measuring changes in longevity, job opportunities, education, and other factors that affect earning power over a lifetime. This index and related indicators can be used to improve estimates (over perhaps a generation) of anticipated demands on public facilities and services, on the urban environment, and on other matters of major concern to urban planning.

Figure 19–2 highlights the various sectors that must be included in trying to understand—and to influence—the functioning of the municipality (within the region). They are (moving clockwise from the upper left) the economic (B), the social (C), the political/governmental (D), and the physical/environmental sectors (E). These broad categories encompass the key urban *functions* (the reason people are in cities), including the productive (jobs and income), the residential and neighboring, the recreational, the cultural, and the large array of public and private services and facilities. The primary concern is to be able to determine how well the urban system is functioning, the ingredients essential to its functioning, and to identify the changes required to bring the system into an improved future state. Urban planning's contribution lies in its participation (along with other agencies of government) in trying to achieve broad objectives of the basic urban system such as:

1. Helping to strengthen the economic base of the city, to enlarge residents' opportunities for jobs (Economic development has been an increasingly important objective of federal assistance to the cities).

2. Helping the less-advantaged to improve access to the whole range of opportunities that the city has to offer (This has also been an increasingly important objective of federal grants to cities and of federal regulations).

3. Preserving, and if possible increasing, the value of the city's asset base, including the natural and man-made features.
4. Providing space for all urban functions and uses in an orderly and satisfying manner (the traditional land-use objective broadened).
5. Providing facilities and services for the urban functions, sometimes called life support systems (for example, transportation, communications, power, water, sewerage, education, health, and so on).
6. Enlarging the housing services (direct housing provision or subsidy).
7. Helping to ensure that governmental instrumentalities and financing are available to enable these items (1–6) to be carried out in line with decisions about priorities and about the division of responsibilities between the public and private sectors.

Viewed in this broad context—reflective of what municipal governments are trying to achieve—land use (and its planning) can be seen to be an important *but limited* part of the larger whole. The economic, social, broad environmental, and political/governmental sectors are all integral parts of the total picture and must be of central concern to urban planning if the goals and objectives of the community are to be achieved or approximated. All of them must be encompassed not only to understand how the municipality-within-the-region (the urban system) is evolving over time, as indicated earlier, but also to be able to analyze how to improve the system and how to approach the problems and possibilities of the future.

A major problem in establishing an appropriate information system for planning is the lack of a single unit of measurement to *characterize* the elements of the urban system as they function and to measure outputs and outcomes. Instead, a variety of measures must be used—some physical in nature (for example, the quality of air and water, the physical condition of housing or of public facilities), some monetary (for example, in certain of the economic features and governmental finance), and others using yet different bases (for example, to describe satisfactions and dissatisfactions of residents or of the quality of relations among ethnic groups in the community) (Wilcox et al., 1972). However, inability to use a single unit of measurement throughout does not alter the fact that planners are dealing with an urban system the parts of which are linked and do or do not produce desired outcomes (for example, efficient functioning, equitable access to opportunities, and high quality of environment).

While all the components shown in Figure 19–2 are interrelated, the form of the chart suggests the logic of seeing the system changes as being triggered by significant changes in the volume and quality of economic activities that provide jobs and income (symbolized in the upper left-hand corner of the chart) (Conroy, 1974; Sonnenblum, 1968; Thompson, 1966). The changes in skills demanded through the jobs provided can be expected to have an important impact on the nature of the labor force needed, including requirements for migrants.

Related factors come into play which are too complicated to be shown on the chart; for example, the pull of the city for people living on income transfers—including retired persons and individuals on welfare. The in-migration of such persons, independent of jobs, also affects the expansion of economic activities.

The upward and downward features of social mobility are significant (see C in Figure 19–2.) The changing population structure has an expected impact on changes in group mix and social behavior in various communities of the city. The communities themselves are undergoing change both socially and geographically. This, in turn, affects the nature of the social problems the city faces and the services and facilities to be provided. All of these changes have a discernible impact on the capital assets of the municipality (housing, productive plants, utilities and facilities, and so on), including the existing stock and the requirements for new stock, as well as an impact on the natural resources and amenities (see the items near E in Figure 19–2). The changes in activities, stock, and amenities correspondingly change land-use requirements while the changes in stock have an impact on the needs which the government (as well as the private sector) must meet. Of course, changes *initiated* by government in the man-made and/or natural environment—through land-use controls and development measures—can trigger changes in the social and economic realms. In fact, a significant reason for urban planning is to trigger desired changes in these realms through such land-use controls and developmental measures.

All of these various changes can be expected to have significant impacts of governmental finances and management requirements (suggested by the items clustering around D in Figure 19–2), while governmental policies and activities can be expected to impact all the other realms—hopefully, in line with effects desired.

In various ways, all of these factors alter individual and household welfare.

Getting to understand these impacts on welfare, as already noted, is the key to the whole informational exercise.

CONTEXTUAL INFORMATION

Comprehending the functioning of the municipality-within-the-region is not possible without seeing the individual city as a part of the national and state setting. Thus contextual information (see 1 in Figure 19–1) is a necessity. Ideally, this would encompass information concerning major socioeconomic-political developments, such as changes in national and state demographics, migration patterns, and labor markets; changes in national and state urban policy, strategy, and funding for cities; and the introduction of new regulations on housing, the environment, and other items of planning concern. Every city planning agency currently collects a substantial amount of this information, but it is rarely complete or systematic enough to permit any in-depth analyses of a contextual nature.

Cities should be able to rely on up-to-date information from national and state sources but, unfortunately, neither national nor state reports on urban development are adequate in this regard. Some of the most pertinent information available—such as the National Planning Association's Metropolitan Area Projections on population, employment, and industry—is provided as a commercial service and acquired by only a limited number of communities. (Cities, through their central organizations, would be well advised to bring strong pressure on the federal and state governments for the generation and distribution of the needed "contextual" data.)

Today, analyses and projections on national and state developments that are prepared by scholars, research organizations (for example, the Urban Institute), and upper-level governmental departments find their way to city planning agencies only slowly, if at all, and are rarely an integral part of the ongoing work of such agencies. In considering policy and action programs, the mayor, the city council, the planning commission, the operating agencies, and the people of the city should all be able to see their city within the context of national and state as well as regional developments over time.

A reverse flow of information is also needed. In a later chapter, the case is made for periodic reporting *from* municipal planning agencies *to* federal and state governments describing internal developments over time so that specific requirements for major transformations (rather than grantsmanship) can become the test of federal and state assistance to cities.

SYSTEM IMPROVEMENTS

Other than by accident or good luck, urban planning can hope to achieve (or at least approximate) the goals that are set for it only by increasing its capacity to understand the workings of the urban system and to evaluate cost-effective methods of bringing about system improvements.[1]

Urban developments over the past generation have amply demonstrated the relative importance of the various components of the urban system (for example, changes in the job structure, in the population structure, in activity centralization and decentralization, in the governmental effectiveness of handling fiscal matters, and the like) and have helped put the traditional planning tasks which are related mainly to control of land uses in the proper perspective. With the aging of cities and the decentralization of activities, the need for major city transformations has also become more apparent. Against this background, urban planners must become much more skillful at policy and action-program analyses which encompass total system improvements. Certain features of Boston and Cleveland city planning and Atlanta regional planning, as described in Chapters 4, 5, and 7, suggest the next logical stage in the development of urban planning. However, even these efforts do not encompass adequate consideration of the economic, social, political/ governmental, and physical/environmental factors (as suggested in Figure 19-2)—clearly needed to achieve the relatively ambitious goals of system improvement established in these communities.

Sparked by grants from the U.S. Departments of Commerce and Housing and Urban Development (HUD), the recent interest in urban economic development has encouraged some planning departments (and/or other agencies of the municipality) to do studies of the forces behind the changing urban economic picture and of the programs needed to strengthen the city's job base. If the economic development thrust continues for some time (federal

---

[1]This is not to suggest that all of this capability must be in-house. There is every reason to involve university and research-center scholars just as there is every reason for cities to get help from the federal and state governments. But outside assistance can be helpful only if a continuous flow of pertinent data is made available within the municipality and if there is a regularized system for monitoring the impacts of urban policy and action programs.

programs are notoriously uncertain), a growing appreciation of the schematic nature of urban change can be expected. It is hoped that, over time, attention to systemwide improvements will be a normal part of cities' economic development efforts along with the design of citywide programs for asset maintenance, preservation, urban renewal, and neighborhood improvement.

A close look at the jobs picture in any of the large, older U.S. cities is suggestive of why it is appropriate to use the term "major urban transformation" and to speak in terms of changes that will have to be carried through over future decades. The economic bases of these cities have been going through profound changes which have made it difficult to provide employment for the cities' residents, particularly for the most vulnerable segments of the cities' populations. Major changes will be needed in the future to improve the job situation.

Looking ahead, cities will have to decide on many issues associated with these transformations including whether to concentrate on strengthening the downtown areas or the many subcenters that have grown up; whether to encourage population growth or to accept a stable or even declining population and plan accordingly; whether to take action to change the proportion of poverty-level families in every part of the metropolitan region or to accept whatever proportions eventuate; whether to place the greatest economic development effort on retaining the old manufacturing industries (and possibly attract new ones) or to concentrate on capturing service activities; whether to use urban renewal as a major tool of revitalization or to concentrate on nonphysical programs. These and many other issues that must be decided are essentially issues of urban system improvement.

A similar set of considerations—leading to the conclusion of the need for urban system improvements—emerge if one starts with other major concerns, such as high rates of urban crime and violence, tensions among ethnic groups, or the deterioration of the quality of air and water. All of these are outcomes of the functioning of the urban system. Urban planning should be particularly concerned with such considerations since, of all the staff institutions of municipal government, it is most responsible for a comprehensive view of such functioning over time. The traditions centering on the earlier paradigm of an almost exclusive focus on land-use planning have been a major block to accepting this view both within the planning profession and among municipal officials in many cases. The departures from this tradition, as pointed out earlier, have been slow and disjointed. Unless it is to continue to be a peripheral activity in municipal government, urban planning must quickly get itself into a position to provide well-based analyses of systemwide functioning and of the best approaches to urban system improvements.

SPECIAL PROBLEMS AND DIFFICULTIES

Improving the basic urban system in order to solve (or mitigate) the more troublesome current problems is not always possible or feasible within the time horizon that is realistic in political and human terms. Problems often have to be attacked directly because some people or groups are suffering too much to wait for an improvement in the basic system (for example, problems, such as the inadequacy of housing that poorer families can afford to rent). A good municipal data base should be able to show the relationship of the perceived problems to the workings of the urban system.

A data base may provide the raw materials for sound analyses of problems, but it does not guarantee that such analyses will be conducted. A capable municipal planning agency should be able to provide reasonable figures on the costs and benefits (or advantages and disadvantages) involved in different approaches to the solution or mitigation of a serious problem or set of problems over time. A variety of approaches would normally have to be analyzed in order to determine the preferred approach, including consideration of:

1. Investment in built elements (that is, developmental expenditures).
2. Changes in rules of the game (for example, in regulations and other controls).
3. Reallocation of resources (for example, through subsidies and income supports).
4. Changes in service delivery.
5. Changes in selected values and/or behavior (for example, trying to change certain driving habits or certain kinds of prejudice).

Policy analyses by planning agencies should provide useful guidance to the municipal officials and the general public toward the most cost-effective approach that can be used and the degree of probability that the problem can be substantially mitigated over a given period of time through one or another of the possible approaches.

As with all planning problems, the attack on special problems and difficulties must be people conscious, place conscious, money conscious and time conscious. The capacity to deal with all of these concerns must be strengthened in most planning agencies around the country, but it is the last of these, time consciousness, that needs the most work. What is particularly missing in most cases is a consciousness of the length of time needed for a problem and its solution. This kind of consciousness is essential both to avoid stopping before a reasonable effort has been made toward solution or mitigation of the problem and to avoid waste by continuing too long on a given path.

Many uncertainties are involved, of course. One of these uncertainties in the past has been the lack of this kind of time consciousness on the part of the federal government's housing and urban development programs. For example, the federal government launched both the model cities program to aid neighborhoods with unusually high proportions of disadvantaged persons and the new-town-in-town program for major physical reconstruction in cities, but in each case support for the program was stopped only a short time after initiation. Not only city planning but all levels of government must learn to cope with this time issue in tackling urban problems.

Another feature that deserves attention is the anticipation of new problems, that is, difficulties that are not seen as serious problems at the present time but which can be expected to increase in scale and/or intensity over time. For example, a set of problems can be anticipated to stem from the ever-increasing proportion of women entering the labor force (that is, problems of child care, housing, and transportation requirements). Other problems can be expected to emerge in the future as a result of identifiable forces at work today. Examples here are the implications for demands made on urban services and facilities (and city planning) of the widespread use of flextime, part-time work, and footlooseness of work places (Bell, 1973; Garn et al., 1975). The capacity of planning to carry out sound analyses on such issues and to suggest policy and programs geared to such analyses will no doubt determine the extent to which municipal officials and the general public look to planning operations for guidance on difficult policy and program decisions.

OPPORTUNITIES AND POSSIBILITIES

An urban information system should also be able to provide the raw materials for analyses of future conditions, opportunities, and possibilities either not in existence today or not yet being exploited. Because this topic is of central importance to considerations of the long-run future, or "the future component of the future," it is treated in some detail in Chapters 20–23.

Information that serves the need for analyses of the most current issues well is essentially the same as that needed for policy and program analyses when long-range considerations are involved. In each case, the view must encompass a complex urban system evolving through time, generating some severe urban problems at the same time that it satisfies many human and organizational needs. Sound analyses of such problems can be made, as of future opportunities and possibilities, only if the informational base is adequate to treat the urban system in terms of its major elements and interconnections in a time-conscious manner. A good test of the adequacy of a city's information base is whether it permits an analytical probing in some depth of the urban transformation underway, the asking of the right questions.

HIGHLIGHTS OF THE EMERGING PLANNING PARADIGM

The discussion of information needed in urban planning has provided the opportunity to also discuss the new paradigm that is emerging in urban planning. The earlier paradigm focused almost exclusively on considerations of land-use planning and transportation interconnections with economic, social, and other considerations providing essentially a background for the mapped proposals on land uses and physical development in the municipality for the near-term and long-range future. By contrast, the newer paradigm has these features:

1. It starts with the conception of the subject of urban planning as a municipality made up of several interrelated elements (an urban system).
2. These elements encompass economic, social, political/governmental, and physical/environmental sectors.
3. The various sectors must be considered in trying to understand and to influence the functioning of the municipality within its region.
4. An understanding of how the community (the municipality) evolves over time—from the past, through the present, into the future—is essential to coping with present and anticipated problems and creating new conditions, opportunities, and possibilities in the future. The

achievement of both near-term and long-range goals involves the need to accomplish certain systemwide improvements since both problems and future possibilities are products of the functioning urban system.

5. Plans for the future (whether aimed at the mitigation of present problems or creating new conditions and opportunities in the future) can be evolved and presented most effectively and flexibly in terms of policy and strategy. Mapped land-use plans—formerly the main tool to guide municipal decisionmaking—should be expected to serve only certain limited purposes, often giving way to the use of standards and prescribed procedures to guide future actions. Policy planning should be the main concern, while mapped land-use planning is subordinate.

The last of these and related aspects of the new paradigm will be discussed more fully in Chapters 26 to 28.

PART 5
THE FUTURE ASPECTS OF THE FUTURE

Chapter 20
Reaching for Future Possibilities

The discussion of the **past** (inheritance) and **present** aspects of the future, in Parts 3 and 4 of this volume, focused attention on elements of the future that are not normally thought of in connection with the question of how to deal with the future in urban planning. To round out the discussion, Part 5 will touch on the **future** aspects of the future. Combined, Parts 3, 4, and 5 demonstrate the multidimensionality of the future concept.

THE FUTURE ASPECTS

All city planning decisions (and, in fact, most public and private decisions) involve two aspects concerning the future: (1) some assumption(s)—implicit or explicit—about what the future will be like and (2) some ideas of what is desired for the future. On the first count, assumptions are hard to avoid about such matters as the numbers and characteristics of the people who will reside in the municipality, about the rate of inflation and its impact on the cost of housing, and about local economic trends. Similarly, some ideas about the possibilities and opportunities of the future on the one side and about new kinds of problems that might appear on the other cannot help but be involved when major decisions—and particularly developmental decisions—are made. Everyone involved in making the decisions is certain to have some ideas about what he/she would like to see happen in the future.

The issue for urban planning is whether it is helpful in decisionmaking to have many of these assumptions and wishes-for-the-future set out explicitly and whether decisionmaking and action can be strengthened by introducing information about the long-range future as well as the more immediate future. The answer given here is *yes* to both questions.

This *information* about the possibilities and problems of the future can be used by the political and technical decisionmakers as they use all other types of information—as factors to be weighed in making decisions *currently*. Even specific end-state plans for the future, for example, a specific design for a given part of town is a type of information. Legislators will want to review periodically whether the plans are still appropriate as circumstances change, and they will still want to control the application of resources to the given project. But a plan normally provides information of a special type, because of the political commitment involved, which no other type of information can duplicate.

Information about the possibilities of the future is particularly valuable to municipal governments in the face of the major transformations our cities are facing. The great urban transformations underway in the industrialized countries involve significant changes in both outlook and values (see Chapter 1). People in these countries no longer feel—as they did earlier—that they can automatically rely on continuous progress through technological innovation. A price must be paid for material progress in the destruction of irreplaceable natural resources, in air, water, and noise pollution; in millions of disadvantaged individuals and families who are left behind; and in cities that are also left behind with large sections in decay and poverty. The concept of progress itself requires thoughtful definition and redefinition. Conscious trade-off decisions cannot be avoided. Some of the things people want as individuals must be given up in order to achieve high-priority social goals. We must not only conserve our material resources but must also develop them and create entirely new ones. Planning can contribute usefully to these difficult tasks and, to some extent, is already doing so. What is not yet widely accepted is that it is difficult to do these tasks well without learning how to "bring the future forward," that is, learning how to realize the possibilities of the future.

TWO APPROACHES: OPEN OPTIONS AND END STATE

Two different ways exist for realizing the possibilities of the future and various ways in which these two approaches can be combined. The *open-options* approach attempts to position the society or municipality so as to be able to take advantage of any possibilities that may appear in the future. The *end-state* approach involves defining the desired future specifically. The first approach would be comparable to an individual going back to school for advanced training so that he or she would be in a position to acquire more of the things desired in the future. The second is similar to a family saving specific amounts each year in order to acquire a home in ten years.

The End-State Approach

Planning has a built-in conflict dealing with future possibilities: how to reconcile the desirable features of leaving options open as against taking actions to achieve certain desired end states? (The latter, incidentally, can encompass seeking to prevent an undesirable future or something worse than the present.)

The traditional end-state city master plan aims at achieving a specific, better future. In the present context, it can be seen to have several major shortcomings:

1. It normally does not concern itself with new possibilities in the future (those in the technological, economic, social, cultural, and political realms).
2. It normally does not provide any contingency planning; that is, any means for dealing with surprises.
3. It tends to rely almost entirely on essentially abstract physical features, such as broad land-use concepts which have only limited meaning and appeal to most people. It does not adequately indicate how many of the things that people care about strongly (jobs and income, the value of their homes, the taxes they will have to pay, and the ability of their children to get a good education) are to be achieved through the plan.

On the other hand, traditional end-state planning does have significant advantages in aiming to provide a strong image of or for the future and in providing a framework within which short-term and quite specific decisions and actions can be taken. An important question becomes can the advantages of the traditional approach somehow be retained while the disadvantages are removed or mitigated? The essence of what should be retained is the desirability of projecting a strong image or images of the future which can give people a greater sense of assurance about their own futures and of providing a useful framework for short-term, more specific decisions and actions.

What can be substituted for a physically oriented master or general plan, while retaining its good features? A critical issue is whether physical specifications (that is, specific land uses, transportation lines, open space, and so on) are essential as a framework for decisions and as images of the future or whether more appropriate features can be used.

Keeping Options Open

Before attempting to answer this question, refer back to the alternative approach to the future mentioned earlier—keeping options open, that is, trying to be in a position to take advantage of new opportunities that may arise in the future. In asking how a community might conceivably be put in such a position, steps such as the following come to mind.

The institutions of the community might become more flexible and more open to new opportunities. This subject has concerned people for a very long period of time, but it has not become a matter of official planning concern. Yet, it should be, if advantage is to be taken of the possibilities of the open-options approach. Since it is the planners in a municipal government who have particular responsibilities for relating policies and programs to the long-run future, planners should logically be concerned with the flexibility and adaptability of the government itself in being able to cope with the unexpected as well as the expected features of the future. If the municipal government has little capability in dealing with broad problems and possibilities of the future, then it should be the responsibility of the planners to make this fact well known and to make recommendations for improvement (Susskind, 1975). The flexibility and adaptability of institutions which impact strongly the subjects with which urban planning deals (for example, the construction industry within the community) would also be of concern to urban planning under the approach considered here. It is appropriate for urban planners to suggest governmental measures that might be taken to enhance flexibility and adaptability of such institutions where that is appropriate (and politically sound), as well as provide information to such institutions about what is ahead and how they may need to adapt to new situations.

The open-options approach depends not only on flexible institutions, but equally on individuals who are prepared to meet new challenges and to grasp new opportunities. Both formal and informal education can be important in helping individuals in the community become more open to new possibilities. Again, this is something that has long been recognized as of great importance, but it has not been an official concern of urban planning. While educational planning itself is often the responsibility of those not involved in comprehensive urban planning, the latter group of planners can do much to put the subject in proper priority order in the municipal scheme of things. They can also point to informal (nonschool) educational possibilities that fit the particular community, provide useful information on expected changes in ethnic composition and in lifestyles and the implications for education of such changes, and show how residents can learn about changing urban life by being involved in a wide variety of urban activities. The last of these is a special component of the citizen participation idea and deserves attention as important to the learning society—which, in turn, is a key to helping individuals become open to future possibilities.

A municipality can also sponsor research and development in areas of particular importance to its well-being (for example, in the realms of building and managing public facilities and other life-support systems) so that it can better meet new situations as they arise. Some municipalities have been involved in these kinds of R & D efforts—often in attempting to reach higher productivity levels in public activities—so that there is experience on which to proceed. The very existence of muncipal R & D suggests being open to new possibilities in the future just as industry-sponsored R & D is suggestive of the search for new products and improved processes in the private sector. In the same light, municipalities can foster social experiments aimed at opening new opportunities—for example, in creating jobs and providing public services in poor neighborhoods through cooperative and self-help methods. Conscious experimentation (which involves detailed continuous evaluation) with various forms of urban design in neighborhoods to improve accessibility and parking with minimum costs could conceivably provide valuable guidelines to future city form. The same would hold for all sorts of experimentation with variable pricing to increase accessibility and limit the amount of space needed for parking. Experimentation is needed in all phases of urban development including zoning, subdivision control, encouragement of high quality private development, and savings on the provision of services and facilities.

Used in order to understand the possibilities of the future, both R & D and social experimentation are logical arms of urban planning. Planning would itself not necessarily carry out such experiments, but it should be able to suggest the appropriate areas of research and experimentation, evaluate the results, and build the findings into its future decisions. Even modest programs in R & D and social experimentation would help set an appropriate tone for municipalities in their approach to an uncertain future.

While the potentials for fostering flexibility and adaptability within municipalities are both attractive and important, the open-options approach poses some serious problems and has some obvious disadvantages. First, in its most basic form of simply keeping options open, it is not evident what the options are for (what opportunities are being sought). This suggests that the definition of goals and objectives is crucial. Without such, it would not be clear when an opportunity was being realized or what should be done in the face of endless options. The community might conceivably be in the position of the dog in Aesop's fable who dropped his bone into the pool in attempting to grab the bone in the pool's reflection. The reality is not evident on the surface.

Second, without specifications of desired priorities, higher-order achievements can be foreclosed by taking advantage of earlier or lower-order end results. This would be the case, for example, in deciding on an already available technology for movement of persons and foreclosing on a much better technology that might deliberately be developed through a targeted effort. Sending a man to the moon was, of course, the prime example of such a targeted effort in recent decades. More limited, but important, results might well be sought in municipalities by joining forces to pressure the national government and private groups to meet the municipal requirements for movement of persons.

Third, unless resources are being set aside for the future (something that is not necessarily built into the open-options approach), the community may not be in a position to actually take advantage of the opportunities that arise. Such financial reserves are normally politically feasible only when there is a clear-cut plan for their use.

Still another problem is that highly flexible institutions, which might indeed be equipped to take advantage of new opportunities, could also be highly opportunistic. There could be a constant drive to get credit for accepting or creating something *new* without much concern for the long-run impacts on the community as a whole. Flexibility is fine if it leads to a desired end result, but it is not necessarily good for its own sake.

Combining the Two Approaches

It is not self-evident that the advantages of the two approaches (open options and end state) can be retained and combined into a broad, future-oriented framework for current decisions, but that is a worthwhile objective.

It is encouraging to note that the traditionally specified physical form of the general plan (essentially land-use form) is already giving way to a more generalized set of images and proposals with rather substantial nonphysical content to add to the more traditional physical content (such as Boston's planning thrust toward economic development). Can the urban general plan evolve further as an instrumentality to encompass at least some of the valuable advantages of the open-options approach without losing its value as a future-oriented framework? It can and should.

Such a development would call for substantial improvements in urban planning in two directions. The first of these is in the futurecasting realm and involves the ability to forecast elements of the future, such as population, to image alternative better (preferred) futures, to be comfortable with the uncertainties and ambiguities of the future, and, in general, to deal effectively and comfortably with what lies ahead. The other direction is a sharpening and bolstering of the key phases of the planning process: the definition and establishment of goals and objectives, the laying out of alternative paths to their achievement including resources needed (and available), and the choosing of preferred specific strategies, policies, programs, and other instrumentalities of implementation. These are inevitably intertwined. The forecasting of elements of the future and the imaging of a better future (or futures) often interconnect, and the various elements of "futurecasting" are useful in carrying out the different phases of the planning process. Thus, none of these can be discussed in isolation since the interrelationships are themselves important. However, for convenience in what follows, the focus will first be on futurecasting and then on the planning process. In each case, possibilities of making improvements are discussed.

Chapter 21
Approaches to Forecasting in Time-Conscious Planning

Planning or acting without making assumptions about the future is impossible. When these assumptions are conscious, they take the form of forecasts (for example, of population), or more general statements about the anticipated future, such as the expected continuation of certain trends (for example, continued increases in demand for single-family housing). Even the most narrowly conceived urban planning, such as planning which is limited to a set of specifications for zoning and subdivision control, involves assumptions about the continuation of certain patterns of building, living, and working, even if such assumptions are not recorded anywhere.

Recorded assumptions about the future can prove to be wrong and, under certain circumstances, embarrassing. Consequently there has been an incentive for planners (and politicians) to avoid recording assumptions about future conditions upon which decisions are made. A wider acceptance of planning as a basic part of societal learning would remove some of this incentive to hide assumptions about the future. In turn, the more general consciousness there is about the assumptions that underlie decisions and actions, the easier it becomes to monitor actual developments and to learn something about the nature of the errors that have been made. As a result of such learning, planning can become more accomplished at making the assumptions that are needed in carrying out its activities.

STATEMENTS ABOUT THE FUTURE

Various kinds of statements (and decisions) can be made about the future.

These often tend to be combined or used interchangeably and often result in confusion and a lack of precision. A common example would be a population forecast which is a blend of extended projections from the past and a politically motivated interest in having the population figures either higher or lower (for example, because certain grants depend on the size of population). The motivation may be readily understandable, but if decisions are later based on the forecast, the forecast itself may be misleading.

In preparing a forecast, the first distinction that should be made is between "will be" and "might be." A "will be" statement is a prediction of a definite event in the future (for example, the largest growth in the next decade will be along Route 100 rather than along Route 200 or 300; population will increase in the city by 100,000 over the next ten years). By contrast, a "might be" statement specifically accepts the uncertainties involved and normally attaches probabilities to several alternatives (for example, the highest probability is that growth will be along Route 100 and lowest along Route 300; population is expected to increase somewhere between 50,000 and 150,000 with the highest probability attaching to the higher number). While normally, the words "prediction" and "forecast" are used interchangeably, a useful distinction in technical literature is sometimes made between the word "prediction" (limited to "will be" statements) and "forecast" ("might be" statements). Regardless of the words used, the concepts should be distinguished.

Another distinction that must be made is between each of these and the "should be" (or normative) statement. The latter refers to the desired changes or outcomes. Urban planning has traditionally emphasized the "should be" statement. That is one of the reasons why forecasting in planning operations often contains elements of the "should be" kind. If planners are not cautious, they can easily slip into the "should be" mode. There is another very practical reason for this type of blending. Desired outcomes that are risky or disturbing in the present context or form can be put into a futures context to achieve a greater impact in a policy debate. The scare tactic is a common form (for example, environmental controls will definitely cause severe unemployment in the 1980s). Even if one accepts the need to play the political-psychological game in planning, where there is need for precision, distinctions among statements about the future simply must be made.

Yet a fourth kind of statement can be made about the future; the "could be" statement involves a feasibility judgment. It can be made in association with either the "might be" (forecast) or the "should be" (normative) statement. Feasibility is a key factor in determining the probability of a future condition or trend, but it is also important in judging receptiveness of the existing socioeconomic-political system to alternative policy proposals or specific plans for the future.

There is no great precision about the concepts discussed here, but the commonsense logic which differentiates them must be kept in mind when contemplating and planning the future.

DIFFERENT FORECASTING TECHNIQUES

Techniques for and approaches to forecasting have been invented, developed, and used in a variety of fields including military, business, and economic planning. Scholars have also played a role in developing methods of forecasting. With experience, more is learned about the fit between the methods used and forecasting problems encountered in the various fields. However, since forecasting is still in a very early stage of development, the basic approach continues to be trial and error.

Urban planning has limited its reliance on forecasting and has been slow in incorporating newly conceived methods of forecasting. This has probably been due in large part to the special history of urban planning with its earlier heavy emphasis on the normative master plan and its later emphasis on immediate problems.

One particular forecasting method, extrapolation of trends as in population forecasting has been most heavily relied on. More recently, with the strong emphasis on impact analysis (in many cases, a mandated emphasis as in the requirements for environmental impact statements), some methods associated with forecasting, such as cost/benefit analysis, have come into wider use.

If urban planning is to develop more of a time-conscious, future-oriented posture, it must begin to employ some of the newer methods of forecasting. However, in examining the rather large array of forecasting methods available, one might find little that seems relevant, because most of the methods are associated with a specialized literature (for example, on technology forecasting) or a special set of activities (for example, military or business planning). Yet, potentially there is substantial relevance. The relevance for urban planning lies in learning how to think about the future more effectively, to encompass a much larger spectrum than at present. This requires covering more of the practical considerations of the short term (including feasibility considerations) and more of the open possibilities of the long term (that is, learning to forecast possibilities other than the commonly accepted or "surprise-free" kind).

Forecasting Techniques Related to Planning Processes

One useful way of considering forecasting methods and approaches that might be incorporated into urban planning is to relate available techniques to key planning processes. Robert U. Ayres (1969) has provided some valuable leads. His various suggestions are brought together in Table 21–1.

Since Ayres is concerned largely with newer methods, he does not include certain established techniques, such as extrapolation of trends, simulation modeling, and input-output analysis. Some new techniques, such as cross-impact analysis, have been developed since his book was published and naturally are not mentioned. (For useful discussions of the major forecasting techniques, see Ascher, 1978; Bell, 1966; Blohm and Steinbuck, 1973; Brockhaus and Mickelsen, 1977; Chishom, Frey, and Haggett, 1971; De Jouvenel, 1967; Encel, Marstrand, and Page, 1975; Jantsch, 1972; Kahn and Weiner, 1967; Martino, 1972). For our purposes, it is the approach that is pertinent rather than the specific methods mentioned.

Sound logic can be found in associating methods of forecasting to the different stages in or levels of planning, since each has its own requirements. Forecasting methods are normally treated in isolation, or in relation to a specific field of interest as in technological forecasting. This is true of the valuable volumes referenced earlier, with the exception of Ayres, who introduces the concept of appropriate *fit* of a given method to a given phase of the planning process. The planning he considers is generalized and not specifically related to *urban* planning. He suggests the logical idea of going from basically intuitive methods in goal setting such as brainstorming, gaming, and scenario-writing, to methods useful for rank ordering in broad strategic planning, such as morphological analysis, and on to the most quantitative and systems-related methods in getting down to specific programs and projects in "tactical" planning, including cost/benefit analysis. While the logic is impeccable, it will take a substantial amount of experimentation with various forecasting methods in the different phases of the urban planning process before there is a sense of appropriate fit in specific circumstances.

Table 21–1. Forecasting Techniques Applicable to Different Levels of Planning

	Goal Setting	Strategic Planning	Tactical Planning
Largely concerned with	Future environment[1]	Rank ordering of the possibilities	Suboptimization (of certain indexes of performance)
Techniques	Intuitive judgment, strengthened by: brainstorming gaming Delphi scenario writing	Morphological analysis intuitive methods: Delphi man-machine games cost/effectiveness linear programming PPBS[2]	Operation research/systems analysis network analysis cost/effectiveness benefit/cost analysis PPBS

Source: Adapted from Robert U. Ayres, *Technological Forecasting and Long-Range Planning* (New York: McGraw-Hill, 1969), pp. 160-202.

[1] Goals arrived at in consideration of (1) broad technological trends, (2) perceived social needs and wants, and (3) characteristics of socio-political-economic structure and institutions.
[2] Planning, Programming, Budgeting System

Forecasting Techniques Related to Planning Capability

Other considerations are involved in contemplating the use of given forecasting methods in meeting the tasks faced by urban planning. An important one is the capacity of the local planning agency to use a given technique. Other considerations are the relative usefulness of forecasting techniques for involving citizen groups at various stages in the planning process and the ability of a local (neighborhood) group to use a given technique in making its mark on planning decisions.

One approach is suggested by Dean Runyan (1977) in evaluating various forecasting tools for what he calls "community-managed impact assessment," that is, the relative usefulness to neighborhood groups of such tools in weighing local impacts of contemplated planning actions. "Impact assessment forecasts consequences of specific proposed actions; it is a particular form of predicting the future" (Runyan, 1977: 126). He applies three criteria: (1) the technique should be simple; it should not require complex procedures, extensive preparation, or a large commitment; (2) the technique should not rely on an extensive data base; and (3) use of the technique should bring new insight and information. Runyan has evaluated a number of forecasting techniques on the basis of these criteria, several of which are shown in Table 21–2. As an example of Runyan's evaluation, the need to rely on sophisticated methodology and computers make simulation modeling and input-output analysis inappropriate for use by local groups. Naturally, it is conceivable that local groups might be provided with technical assistance so that certain of the more complicated methods could become appropriate. However, Runyan's

Table 21–2. Usefulness to Local Groups of Certain Forecasting Techniques

Techniques	Simple to Use	Does Not Rely on Data Base	Provides New Insights
Delphi	Medium	High[1]	High[1]
Scenarios-surveys	Medium	Medium	Medium
Trend extrapolation	Medium	Medium	Low
Cost/effectiveness	Low	Low	High[1]
Cross-impact	Low	High[1]	Medium
Simulation-modeling	Low	Low	Medium
Cost/benefit	Low	Medium	Low
Input-output	Low	Low	Low

Source: Dean Runyan, "Tools for Community-Managed Impact Assignment," *Journal of the American Institute of Planners* 43:2 (April 1977): 131.

[1] High is the best ranking with regard to the criteria employed.

criteria are basically sound and could also be applied in evaluating forecasting methods appropriate to a well-staffed planning agency in a large city. The main point is that not only are different forecasting techniques less or more appropriate to different stages of the planning process, but they are also less or more appropriate depending on the capacity and interests of the agency or group using them.

Adapting Forecasting Techniques for Use in Urban Planning

As indicated earlier, all of the forecasting techniques have been developed either as general-purpose tools or for specific purposes, such as technological forecasting, which have only peripheral connection to urban planning. Thus, one would not expect most of these techniques to be readily applicable to urban planning. That does not mean, however, that they cannot be used in city planning. What it does suggest is that the methods would not necessarily be appropriate in their original forms; they may have to be adapted to the requirements of city planning. The Delphi technique, which has been used in many fields to establish the views of experts on the future, provides a good example. It can readily be used in urban planning, but some special adaptations would be appropriate to make it particularly useful in a city planning context.

This use of expert opinion to construct long-range forecasts (with little or no face-to-face contact in order to avoid the influence of strong personalities on other participants or too quick a group convergence effect) was first developed in the early 60s at the Rand Corporation, which at the time concentrated on military matters. The initial design and applications were focused on technological forecasting in the defense and aerospace fields. Later applications broadened the scope of the Delphi approach, and some of these applications provide some hints as to ways in which the Delphi approach might be usefully employed in urban planning for forecasting—and other—purposes.

The Delphi technique is based on carefully questioning and requestioning *experts* in the field pertinent to the inquiry. These selected experts interact anonymously through answering questionnaires prepared by a special team brought together for this purpose. A typical initial questionnaire going out to the selected panel of experts might ask the panelists to identify future developments that might affect the operating environment of the subject matter involved (for example, transportation or energy) over some selected period of the future (of maybe 10 to 50 years). The panelists might be given a list of topic areas and asked to identify specific events (for example, technological breakthroughs or introduction of free rapid transit) and significant trends (for example, population growth and reversal of the decline of central cities). The items mentioned by the experts might then be reduced by the managing group, and a second questionnaire sent out to elicit specific forecasts. The panelist would now be asked to indicate the earliest, most likely, and latest time periods in which a given event would occur. The experts might also be asked to estimate trend values for given years in the future. A later questionnaire would indicate the voting by the experts, who, in turn, would be asked if they wanted to change their minds about certain items if their answers were substantially different from other experts. In this way, the convergence effect can be measured.

Later users of the Delphi technique began to experiment with policy issues. Such issues, of course, vary greatly from technological ones, particularly since "expertness" is of a different nature and trade-offs are invariably involved. One of these uses of Delphi was particularly suggestive.

The National Alternative Inner City Futures Project, managed by the Bureau of Social Science Research in Washington, D.C., used the Delphi technique to arrive at an understanding of how much of a concensus there was for future national urban policy in the middle 1970s. First, the Delphi dealt entirely with urban policy issues and only those aspects of the future that most directly influenced such policy. Second, the panel was comprised of 237 experts with widely ranging economic and political philosophies, including federal, state, and local officials, big city mayors, city planning directors, leaders of urban-oriented organizations, interest group and political party leaders, religious and civil right leaders, lawyers, judges, leaders in the business community, academics in many fields, futurists, writers, and media leaders. Because the residents of inner cities are disproportionately black and Hispanic, half of the leaders and experts on the panel were recruited from these groups (Curtis, 1977).

Not only were a wide range of policy options to be considered, but panelists were asked to identify funding sources and to estimate necessary levels of funding to support the initiatives they suggested. Participants were also asked to develop a budget policy for the period between 1978 and 1992 indicating where the money for the inner city was to come from. This project provided the panelists with basic information on current policy and budget expenditure and revenue patterns. The leaders and experts were not assumed to be actually expert on everything involved. Other features of this use of the Delphi technique are intriguing, but need not be detailed here. However, a substantial adjustment has been made in the technique, compared to its earlier uses, in order to make it applicable to an urban policy interest (though here largely at the federal level).

Urban planning deals extensively with policy questions, so that the use of the Delphi technique in planning must adapt to the special nature of such questions. A strong case can be made for the fact that ultimately "a policy question is one for which there are no experts, only advocates and referrees" (Turoff, 1970: 151). Urban experts can supply data or analyses of probable cause and effect, but policy choices are, in the end, value questions. The rise of citizen participation in urban planning decisionmaking underscores the importance of giving full consideration to competing values and competing assumptions as well as to what constitutes an acceptable trade-off.

Policy Delphi is one method for enhancing the ability of municipal governments to forecast the acceptance of given policy positions and to account for conflicting values and priorities. The complexity of most urban issues argues for such a broad-based understanding of group positions and anticipated impacts on diverse interest groups. Turoff (1970: 153) suggests a possible use of policy Delphi appropriate to city planning:

> A policy Delphi can be given to anywhere from ten to fifty people as a precursor to committee activity. Its goal in this function is not so much to obtain a consensus as it is to establish all the differing positions advocated and the principal pro and con arguments for these positions. It allows the utilization of larger numbers of people that can effectively be employed by the committee approach. In many policy areas, a large number of respondents . . . is commensurate with the number of differing interests that must often be considered in the increasingly complex issues facing government.

Other purposes, through other forms, could readily be served by the Delphi technique in urban planning. In each case, Delphi's effectiveness is a measure of the representativeness and qualifications of its participants as much as it is a measure of the clarity with which questions are posed, responses evaluated, and the biases of the management team are accounted for and corrected.

Similar adaptations of forecasting techniques to urban planning seem possible and called for. This includes such techniques as cross-impact analysis and scenario writing. Just as cost/benefit analysis and cost/effectiveness analysis had to be adapted to the special requirements of urban planning, and planners had to learn new skills in order to use these techniques productively, so can the newer forecasting methods be adapted to advantage. Which of the techniques will be most useful under what circumstances will not be known until there is a certain amount of experimentation. Urban planning must pay the price of experimenting with these methods since it urgently needs better forecasting approaches as frameworks for bringing the future forward in current decisions.

Chapter 22
Forecasting Accuracy

Forecasting like everything else in urban planning is a political as well as a technical matter. The developers and users of forecasts must themselves be politically sensitive as well as technically able.

Population forecasting provides a useful framework for viewing the questions of political interests in, and accuracy of, forecasting. Population forecasts have long played an important role in most urban planning activities. One of the more widely used manuals on urban planning states:

> Analysis and projection of population are at the base of almost all major planning decisions. As measures of the size and density of the various groups within the urban or regional population, they determine the level of demand for future facilities and serve as indices of most urban and regional problems (Goodman and Freund, 1968: 51).

Estimates of future population greatly affect decisions on public investments and policies toward existing or anticipated problems, such as traffic congestion, air pollution, unemployment, and social development. Anticipated population growth or decline also affects expectations about future resources. An area anticipating relatively strong growth will probably be more aggressive in its approaches to problems and more willing to experiment than an area anticipating slow or no growth.

The difficulties involved in making population forecasts for given areas have long been appreciated. Two of the three factors involved (births and migration) can be quite volatile, and census information is made available only once in ten years. Furthermore, census data can contain some substantial errors, particularly in accounting for minority populations (Lee, 1966; Schweder, 1971; Shaw, 1975; Siegel, 1972). Because of the difficulty of estimating migration, local population forecasts are often grossly erroneous. Figure 22–1 exhibits a set of population forecasts made for the Southern California region at various times, together with actual population growth. The major

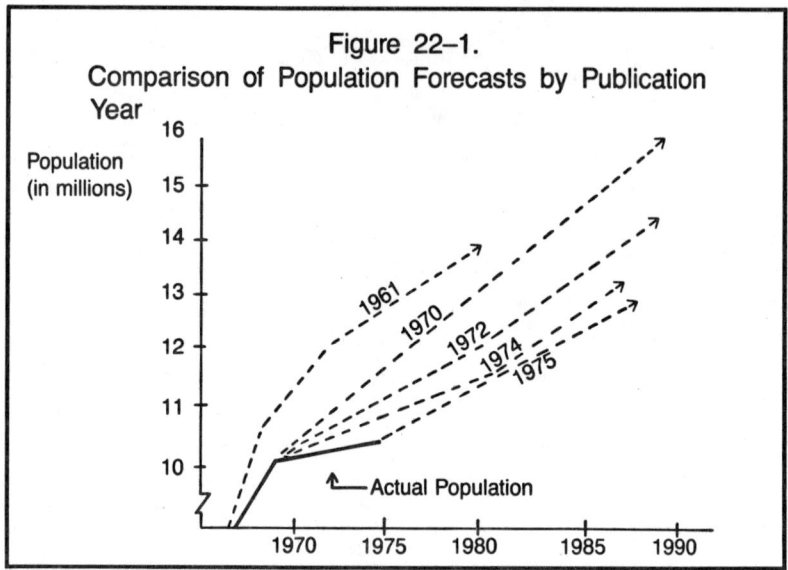

Source: Southern California Association of Governments, "SCAG-76, Growth Forecast Policy," 1976:7.

contributor to the differences between actual and projected population figures was the assumed rate of migration.

If population forecasts are not necessarily accurate, and if they are needed for so many of the planning and political decisions, what is the sensible approach to population forecasts? Forecasters have supplied one answer. Instead of making one forecast they make several, varying significant parameters within reasonable bounds to develop a range of estimates within which the actual future population is likely to fall. But the range is often quite substantial, and individual planners are left with the problem of selecting the figure they feel is most likely. Attempts are being made to put such an alternative forecasting approach on a formal probabilistic basis, but this has encountered great difficulties.

From the standpoint of time-conscious planning, another approach might draw on decision theory. Decision theory suggests that actions based on uncertain information should be made by considering the *risks* of being wrong in a given direction. If forecasted population growth underestimates actual growth, many of the problems (and benefits) associated with population growth will be more extreme. Similarly, if the orecast overestimates actual growth, a number of anticipated problems may fail to materialize or be reduced in severity, while problems associated with low growth may be worse. One might conceive this in terms of the accounting format shown in Table 22–1.

Table 22–1. Evaluating Impacts of High Versus Low Forecasts

	Positive Impacts	Negative Impacts	Net
Forecast High			
Forecast Low			

Although such an approach is conceptually pleasing, given the present state of knowledge, it can only provide a framework for developing awareness and sensitivity to the nature of the issues involved for all those who share in urban decisionmaking.

Many problems and benefits have been attributed to population stability or decline on very limited empirical evidence. For example, growth is commonly viewed as an aid to reducing unemployment and raising levels of living within a city, yet a review of the statistics suggests that the connections are often tenuous. Population growth in some cases attracts many unemployed persons and many poor families so that the problems remain or are exacerbated.

A partial list of problems attributable to population growth would include pollution, the depletion of locally unique resources, more complicated social interactions, greater restrictions on individual behavior, and greater demands for public services. Problems associated with population stability or decline include pressures on governmental finances, increased social service costs per capita, and economic decline. Our present information and understanding do not permit a *precise* evaluation of the risks of being wrong when making population forecasts. However, the very exercise of coping with these uncertainties makes for better understanding and can provide useful information. Focusing on one aspect of the problem is often suggestive.

Decisions on capital investments for future public facilities are an important part of urban planning which involve the use of population forecasts. Certain conclusions may be made about the risks of employing inaccurate forecasts in such decisions.

Small forecasting errors in either direction may not mean very much at all. Certain types of public facilities, such as public buildings and streets, contain a degree of flexibility which allows for some increase in utilization if demand is higher than expected due to population growth. Alternatively, lower utilization because growth is lower than anticipated can often mean improved service. This is demonstrated graphically in Figure 22–2.

Figure 22–2. Benefits and Costs of Small Errors in Estimation

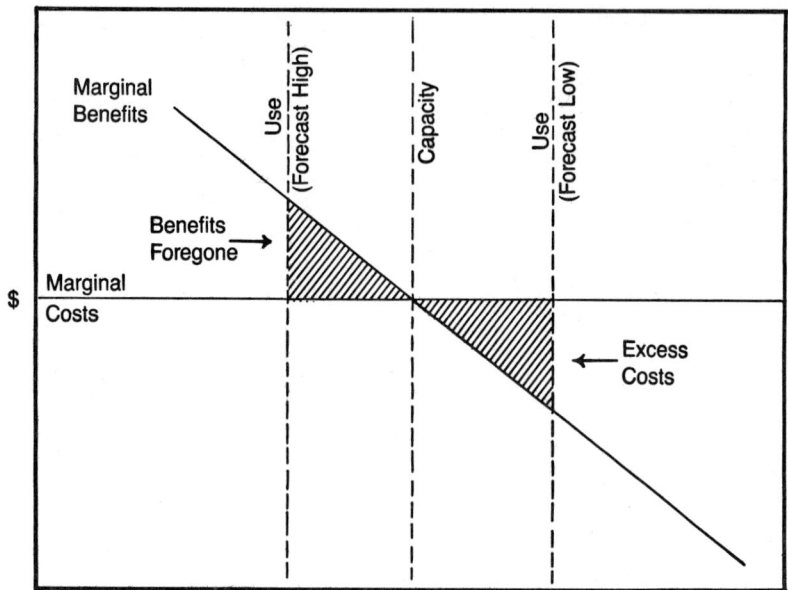

The capacity of a public facility is originally estimated on the basis of an expected future population. If actual use is less than constructed capacity, a relatively small amount of the net benefits that would accrue under optimum conditions is foregone. Likewise, if actual use is more than anticipated, relatively small excess costs are imposed if marginal costs do not increase drastically. In both cases, the net benefits can be quite high.

For some types of public facilities, such as freeways and sewers, marginal costs do increase drastically if expansion is needed after the facility is constructed. However, even for these types of facilities, *modest* increases in capacity can be obtained with relatively minor effort and cost, as demonstrated in Figure 22–3.

Under these conditions, large errors in estimating future population have different implications, depending upon their direction. Serious underestimation of future population results in a significant increase in costs if expansion of the facility or the construction of a larger one is necessitated. Quite conceivably, these additional costs could exceed the benefits of the facility. Conversely, serious overestimation of future population leads to significant loss of net benefits. Yet, total benefits may still exceed total costs so the decision to build the larger facility remains economically justifiable. The overbuilding of

Figure 22-3. Benefits and Costs Resulting From Large Errors in Forecasting

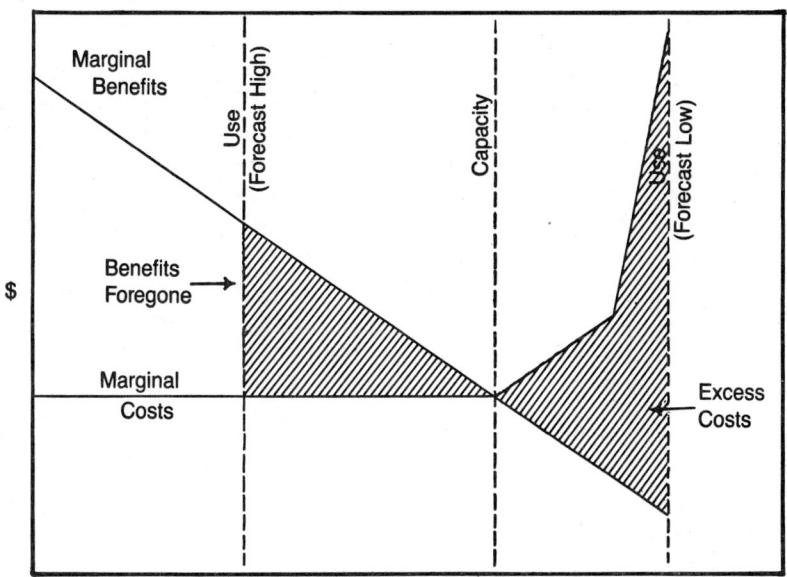

public facilities in anticipation of unrealized growth can be counteracted to some extent at a later time through a period of underbuilding. A major underestimation of population growth is likely to be more serious because of the high costs associated with the planning and construction of additional capacity.

On the basis of the preceeding analysis, it might be concluded, that population forecasts should always be adjusted upward. But such a conclusion is too hasty. What the analysis does suggest is that an estimate of the maximum possible increase in population might be a useful part of the forecasting effort. It implies that this estimate might well be done independently of the demographic model, allowing for a comprehensive analysis not only of the demand side of the equation (natural increase and migration), but of the supply side as well (the carrying capacity of the area). Most of all, it suggests that the planning operation must treat population forecasts (and other kinds of forecasts) as part of the realistic range of possibilities in dealing with the evident uncertainty faced by planning. One should not simply focus nervously on the actual accuracy of a single projection.

Planning must clearly seek to make the forecasting effort a usefully integral element of the political process of decisionmaking. The epilogue of a recent forecasting publication suggests that some forecasters at least are beginning to appreciate the necessity of this approach.

> On a cynical note, the question of who takes notice of forecasts anyway was linked with the cloak of secrecy which often obscures the assumptions behind such forecasts. It was generally agreed that disclosure of assumptions would encourage much greater public participation—too often, it was remarked, the label "confidential" meant either that the figures were so unreliable as to be useless or else that the policy decisions built into the projection were highly controversial . . .
>
> The discussion was brought full circle . . . it was inescapable for forecasters to become involved with the goals and hence with policy. Forecasting as such was thus not only an academic process but inevitably social and political process (Chisholm, Frey, and Haggett, 1971: 460).

Participatory approaches to population forecasting are already starting to evolve. One example can be drawn from the approach used by the Southern California Association of Governments (SCAG). SCAG is responsible for population forecasts for the six-country region containing Los Angeles. The association relies on the examination of historic and recent trends in births, deaths, migration, and projections of expected changes in these basic components of population. However, SCAG (1976: 4) has added an important refinement to the process, recognizing that population forecasting is a political as well as technical process that cannot be done in isolation:

> The process for developing the growth forecast has been built on local and state governments and private institutions and groups to the extent they were able to contribute. The process was open to those who wanted to comment during the development of the forecast and before the final adoption. The existence of such a process has encouraged more local governments to participate and to refine their own approaches to growth forecasts. . . .

Only through such a process can individuals and organizations with particular information or perspectives help refine projections and add insights that might be lost in a more cloistered technical environment. It allows the people who will actually use the forecasts in their planning to be involved from the beginning and to develop some sense of the validity, limitations, and usefulness of the forecasts. Such a process allows for a broad-based questioning of assumptions and may help insure that the important question of "What if we're wrong?" is asked.

Still needed are some inventive commonsense approaches and techniques to fit forecasting in general (and not population forecasting alone) into the requirements of time-conscious planning. Among other things, this calls for the invention of methods to identify the more politically motivated changes in assumptions and final outcomes so that, for certain uses of the forecasts, these assumptions and outcomes can be accounted for (to prevent misleading decisions based on the forecasts). Methods are also needed that will permit decisionmakers to get the maximum value from testing the implications of errors in different directions.

Chapter 23
The Time Horizon in Forecasting

Time is, of course, necessary to all forecasting. The concept of passage through time raises the issue of how to deal with an uninterrupted flow of time that extends indefinitely into the past and on into the future. In a literal sense, the future starts in the fleeting split-second of the present and never stops. But a planning operation needs stopping or reference points in time for both forecasting purposes and for operational convenience.

In forecasting, all change is necessarily associated with a given time horizon, since it is the coming together of various forces and elements at a given point in time (population, jobs, housing, land use, and so on) that is of primary concern. More specifically, the matching of demand and supply (for example, population and housing), the matching of costs and benefits, and similar balances (and trade-offs) in urban planning require specific time horizons if they are to be calculated. The costs and other impacts of building something or bringing about a major change in behavior patterns (as in driving arrangements) are very different if the task is to be accomplished in a brief period rather than a longer span of time. Generally, the issue of feasibility is closely associated with time horizons.

Different time horizons tend to reveal different kinds of information and require different kinds of questions. Quite limited questions have to be asked of a one year or even a five year view into the future because there are so many "givens" for planning in the near term. Only when the view is extended further into the future can questions be raised about changes in the basic urban systems—and in the transformations that are taking place in cities. Repeatedly developing knowledge for just one year ahead, year after year for 20 years, is not the same as a 20 year view.

Operational convenience, as well as forecasting, raises issues about time horizons. The two are, in fact, interrelated. Many forecasts have to match the time horizons established by the requirements of planning operations. Political elections, budget cycles, departmental traditions and requirements, and many other factors tend to create decision points which, in turn, determine time horizons for forecasting.

Against this background, the question arises as to whether there is some built-in logic in establishing time horizons for forecasting and the related processes of planning.

A useful analysis is provided by Platt (1971: 36) who suggests three time scales for dealing with the future in terms of the degree of *scope* for collective action and the approaches that can be employed. The periods he proposes are:

1. An "inertia period," 2–10 years ahead, in which mechanistic projections are feasible and useful.
2. A "choice period," up to 20–40 years ahead, in which interactive models (man-environment-man) can be revealing.
3. An "uncertainty period," beyond 20–40 years ahead, in which our present choices can be treated only by ". . . some very general heuristics of values or moral rules that have worked in the past, or by some kind of *Sitzgefuhl* as in chess."

The critical boundary in this concept seems to be the end of the "choice period," since it is here that shifts in values become the dominant feature. (Of course, some shifts in values are continuously taking place, but growing in importance over time.) Other treatments of the time-scale problem also suggest that there is some middle level choice period in which there is a particularly significant interaction between value systems of the members of the community and the constraints and opportunities which are set by the external environment. Since each works on the other, the planning operation should seek to reveal the conflicts, the coincidences, and the trade-offs between the values on the one side and the constraints and opportunities on the other. This suggests the chief time components for planning as the *near term* of 2–10 years (as largely locked in to various givens in the external environment) and a *long-range* horizon of up to 20–40 years with critical choices to be made.

Platt's first (near-term) category has some counterpart in administrative experience and usage. The near-term "inertia" period has its parallel in the established budget period and fiscal plans. Programs and projects are projected on a stable (everything-else-being-equal) course. The almost ubiquitous use of a 4, 5, or 6 year capital budget time frame in every part of the world suggests that there is probably a strong operational logic to this length of time as the initial time horizon in planning. Two capital budget periods would cover about 10 years, extending to the outer limit of Platt's inertia period where mechanistic projections still apply in many instances.

The same is not as true of Platt's second (or "choice") period. While there are some 20 and 25 year long-range general plans in cities and metropolitan regions (for example, the citywide plan and the various local community plans in Los Angeles extend over 20 years), in many other cities, (for example, Boston and Cleveland) neither the general plans nor the specific programs for public facilities extend beyond 10 years. In yet other cities, the only long-range operating plans are for transportation, water conservation, solid waste collection and disposal, and waste water management. Some of these specific plans extend over 25 years. A strong implicit logic can be found in the longer time horizon for these infrastructure items—their longevity. But the reasons for the different time horizons are not explicit in any of the plans.

Forecasting and other planning operations would be strengthened if the logic behind the time-horizon selections was explicit and provided a framework for such activities. Here considerations revolving around the reconciliation of the demand of an open-options approach and an end-state approach, as discussed earlier, must come to the forefront. It is a matter of reconciling the relative advantages and disadvantages of a longer or shorter "choice period." On the one hand, there are the advantages of taking as long range a view of the future as possible, since more and more options open up in the future. This has to be set against the disadvantage of facing a set of possibilities that is too open, the ever-increasing uncertainties that accrue with time. With time, however, there is also the loss of political and popular interest and the loss of an operating base for calculations (which inevitably draws on past experience and past relationships and which, increasingly, loses relevance with time). In the end-state approach, quite similar considerations are involved, with the disadvantages compounded by the fact that the longer the time horizon, the greater the certainty that the values of today would be outmoded and the plans of today provide a constraint on the urbanities of the future.

One of the noteworthy attempts to rationalize the planning process in time horizons is by Boyce, Day, and MacDonald (1970: 106) who advocate a continuing planning approach for metropolitan areas containing five components:

1. A 20 year regional development framework.
2. A detailed 20 year plan for each facility and service system.
3. A 10 year multifunctional program of capital improvements.
4. Studies of generalized regional alternatives for a 20 to 50 year time horizon.
5. Studies of submetropolitan organization and development for varied time horizons.

They recommend that the regional development framework and the facility-service-system plans be revised every five years and that the system plans be coordinated with the regional framework. The linkage between the capital improvements program and the short-term capital programming and budgeting process of state and local governments necessitates the annual update and revision of both these components. While they suggest that the long-range regional studies of alternatives undergo a comprehensive review every ten years, they refrain from suggesting time horizons for the subregional studies.

They anticipate Platt's analysis of appropriate time horizons for dealing with the future by distinguishing between studies over a "choice period" (which in their case involves studies of regional alternatives over a 20 to 50 year time horizon) and the short-range operating plans (covering 10 and 20 year time horizons). The former is missing in current city plans. There are very few in-depth analyses of alternative city and/or regional patterns of development over a period extending beyond 20 years.

Platt's 20 to 40 year span and the Boyce/Day/MacDonald 20 to 50 year time horizon for the "choice period" reflects the difficulty of estimating this period, so the spans are appropriately broad. When it is felt that a specific time horizon is preferable to a range in treating the "choice period," a valuable dimension can be added by specifying 25 years, putting the "choice period" into *generational* terms (with 25 years taken as a generation). Some technical and political/psychological advantages can be found in such a selection. The technical reasons relate to the importance of population forecasts in urban planning. Age patterns are the central point of information in many of the more critical urban decisions. Age patterns are vital components of statistics for jobs, migration, education, health, crime, housing demand, recreation, and other features of urban life. This suggests that 25 years, the normal length of a generation, lends itself particularly well both to operational information and forecasts. Even more significant, however, is the symbolic value of treating the future (as well as the past) specifically in generational terms, since the logic of the forward look (as well as the backward) is apparent in the very concept of generation. A two-generational view for the outer length of the "choice period" is strengthened by the fact that a common estimate of the longevity of buildings is 50 years, which again makes the case for a long-term view seem apparent.

A city planning operation which took the long-term urban-system transitions which cities have been experiencing seriously and the even longer period over which the transitions toward a postindustrial society will play themselves out might well establish a framework which:

1. Analyzes developments over the past generation to highlight current and future problems and possibilities (to ensure an appreciation of the long swings involved and to get at the origins of the current difficulties).
2. Speculates on the implications for the community of possible developments over the *next* generation for most urban features and over the next two generations for a few trends of special long-range interest.
3. Designs (with other members of the community) a small number of alternative futures based on compelling images of the future (for example, a conservation ethic as contrasted with a rapid-growth pattern) and forecasts the impacts of each.
4. Creates ultimately an operational framework within which short-, medium-, and long-term implementing instrumentalities (that is, plans and programs ranging from 1 to 25 years) might be prepared through the political process for local communities within the city and for facility and service systems, as well as for capital improvements involved in both.

Recognizing the inevitability of rapid change in all of the urban sectors, a sound city planning operation would have to provide for periodic revisions in all of these features. Even the longest range forecasts and plans might well be revised every five years, while ten year investment plans and five year capital programs and budgets should be revised every year. Revisions are appropriately carried out in a societal learning stance. Forecasting mistakes are to be expected, but the important thing is that the search for the reasons behind the mistakes is seen as an opportunity to learn more and more about the nature of the urban developments so that our ability to achieve desired situations in the future is continually enhanced. This is particularly important in the face of the powerful urban transformations presently being experienced. Without speeding up the understanding of what is behind such transformations—and the capacity to guide them in desired directions—the result might be an urban future nobody wants.

PART 6
BOLSTERING THE PLANNING PROCESS

Chapter 24
Introduction to Planning-Process Considerations

If the best features of both the open-options approach and of the end-state approach to urban planning were to be realized together, substantial improvements would be found in key phases of the planning process. Such improvements in the processes of planning are discussed in this chapter and in the chapters that follow.

City planning is best characterized and best understood by the processes through which municipal developmental decisions are made and carried out. If both long- and short-range considerations are to play appropriate roles in decisionmaking and execution in city planning, the basic processes involved must be appropriate to the task. To consider the improvements that are both needed and feasible, the planning processes must be viewed as a whole. Such an overview must logically encompass the substantive materials already covered but in a different framework. Thus, some of the materials already covered in earlier chapters will be reintroduced, but in a different context and in a different form. An attempt is made to avoid repetition even while reaching for a comprehensive view.

A comprehensive view is best provided by interrelating in the same framework the substantive matters with which city planning must deal (the environmental, economic, social, and governmental/administrative subjects of city planning) with its key processes (the establishment of goals, the development of strategies and policies, and the development of implementing plans and programs). Figure 24–1 suggests such a framework as a guide to the many—and complex—issues with which the remainder of this volume deals.

Many appropriate ways can be found which encompass the various substantive matters and process elements involved in city planning. Figure

24–1, one of them, is largely a convenience for purposes of the present discussion but has no particular merit beyond that.

The framework suggested here treats both processes and subject-matter sectors in separate categories, rather than as integrated wholes. The only integrating element indicated is the "overarching images and philosophies that characterize the municipal planning." This assumes that there can be such "overarching images and philosophies," but, clearly, planning can proceed without such an integrating element. An official land-use plan for the city as a whole can no longer be regarded as an appropriate integrating element. It is simply one of several tools used to achieve more ultimate goals. "Overarching images and philosophies" in the current stage of planning could appropriately be such integrating ideas as "a conservation ethic," "the encouragement of economic growth" (as is actually the case in Boston), "the reinvigoration of the neighborhoods of the city," or "the provision of additional choices to residents who have few choices" (as is the case in Cleveland).

Figure 24–1 also suggests that each of the major process elements in the city planning (the establishment of goals, the development of strategies and policies, and the creation of implementing plans and programs) take their substantive form through the major planning sectors (the environmental, economic, social, and governmental/administrative). These sectors can provide—and should provide—the backbone or structure of the urban planning activities. While the major sectors are closely interrelated (as suggested by Figure 19–2), urban planning can not necessarily treat them in a comprehensive, unified manner through giant computer models or through other such means. Our capacity in model-building and use is limited, although models can be used to strengthen understanding of interrelationships among components of the urban system. While comprehensive models are beyond our capacity at this stage, it is possible—and necessary—continuously to be concerned with interrelationships among the various sections and to study these by whatever means are at hand. It would be nice if one could press a computer button and immediately learn what the impact on jobs and income of various income groups would be of certain proposed major changes in land uses, but even if this cannot be done, such probable impacts can be studied through whatever rough-and-ready social science tools are available to us. At least such land-use proposals would not be adopted, as they have been so often in the past, without trying to understand important impacts in various sectors of the urban system.

The key point here is that each of the major sectors described earlier can furnish a significant focal point not only for analyzing the functioning of the urban system as a whole but for all the other tasks of urban planning as well. This is what is suggested in Figure 24–1. Thus, the establishment of planning goals—one would assume ultimately aimed at increasing individual and household welfare—would have to be translated into goals for the local and regional economy, for the natural and built environment, for social and cultural matters, as well as goals for service delivery and other activities of government. The use of these focal points for establishing goals (and later, alternative futures) is both a convenience and a desirable way of checking for possible conflicts and/or mutual reinforcement.

Resources (including institutions) that may be drawn on in attempting to achieve the community goals and desired futures can also be usefully analyzed (and forecasted) in terms of the various sectors. Without this type of approach, overlooking the human resources can be easy, particularly the issue of the quality of human resources that would be available in the future under different planning strategies. Without serious reliance on the human resources, material municipal resources can always be expected to be inadequate for even reasonably ambitious urban futures. In the same light, a careful review of the economic resources and institutions of the community, the social institutions, the natural resources and capital assets, and, of course, the fiscal and other governmental resources and instrumentalities is essential to a sound planning approach.

Strategies, policies, and action programs lend themselves equally well to breakdowns into sectoral components, again more as a way of checking for conflicts and mutual support rather than a concern for proper categorizing of such strategies, policies, and programs. Actually, strategies, policies, and programs need not carry any of the sectoral titles (economic, social, and so on) for this sectoral approach to be useful.

Finally, the information (including forecasts) needed to enlighten all of these planning tasks is quite readily encompassed along sectoral lines, as suggested earlier in Figure 19–2. The main point is that the various sectors and their major components (the substantive concerns of city planning) must be comprehended by urban planning to understand the workings of the urban system; and that they, in turn, are essential in seeking to establish and carry out urban goals. Urban planning, under the new paradigm for its effective functioning, must have the capacity, the will—and the authority—to deal with all four major sectors—the economic, the social, the broad environ-

Fig
Plann
(As R

Local and Regional Economy

Information on local and regional economy within a national context (including problem and malfunctioning); also forecasts

Strategies, policies, and programs for local and regional econon

Economic resources and institutions

Goals for local economy

Goals for natural and made environment

Amenity resources and capital assets

Strategies, policies, and programs for natural and man-made ment

Information on environment (including problems and malfunctioning); also foreca

Natural and Man-Made Environment

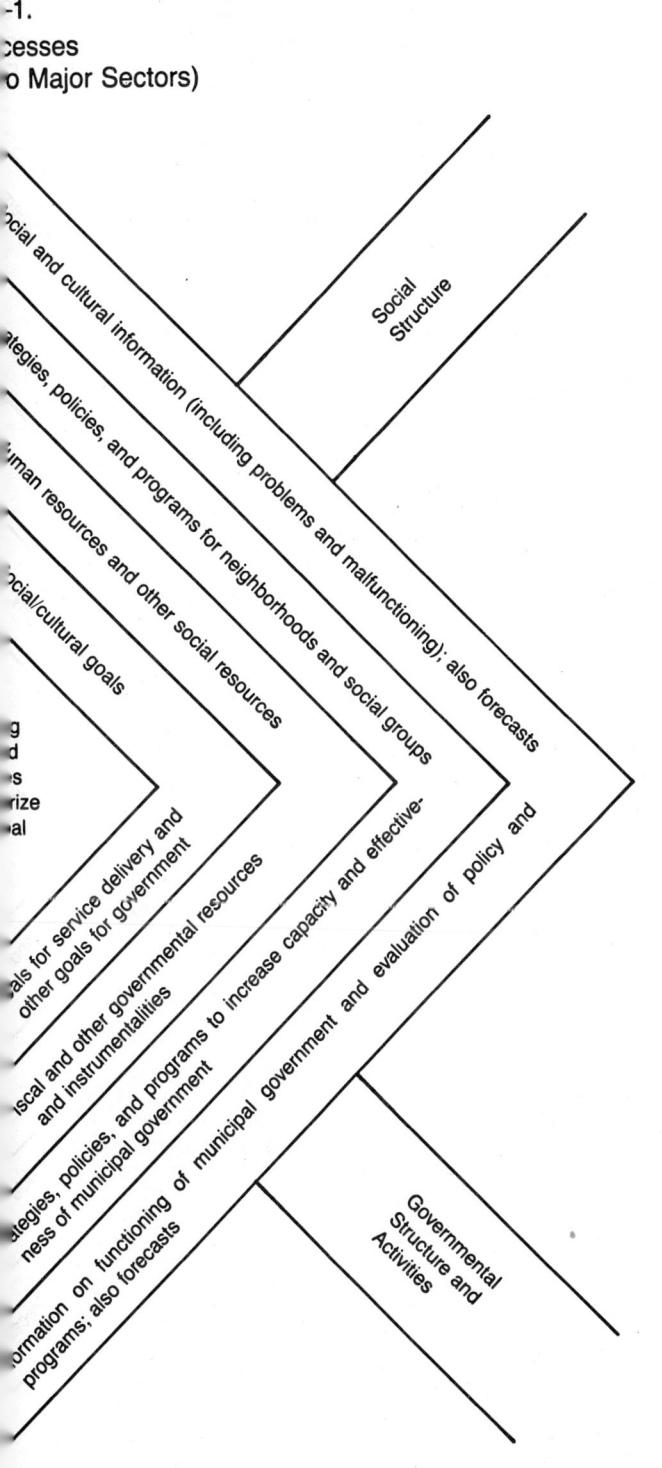

mental, and the political/governmental—and not just the environmental alone as in the past. And, equally important, the various planning processes must be adjusted to a new world of strategy-and-policies planning as a substitute for the older, more limited physical master planning.

Chapter 25
The Definition and Establishment of Goals

Goals can be thought of as the first phase of the planning process even though the process is essentially circular and each phase influences the other. Urban-planning goals can easily slip from view entirely in the heat of political debate on specific current issues and in the fights for personal advantage when specific decisions are being made on such matters as land use, zoning, and subdivision control. Yet, without goals at the center of the planning operation, planning simply becomes a near-term management tool to help the political leaders reconcile and pacify the contending pressure groups. Political reconciliation is certainly of critical importance in the governing of a municipality, but urban planning achieves its reason-for-being through the *added dimension* of helping to guide current decisions so as to increase the possibilities of defining and achieving community goals. This feature gives goals their importance.

DIFFERENT TYPES OF GOALS

The forms that a city's goals take, as well as the manner in which they are formulated and carried out, influence the degree of future orientation and the time consciousness of its planning. Goals can be of a here-and-now nature and largely instrumental in character, or they may be more ultimate in nature and future oriented to an important degree. In considering how urban planning may be strengthened, it is helpful to clarify the nature of the different kinds of goals and to determine how each may be best used.

The Hierarchy and Variety of Goals

No matter how determined, goals for urban planning and development inevitably form a hierarchy. Some are more ultimate in nature, and others more instrumental. However, it tends to be difficult to disentangle them. This difficulty is compounded by the traditions in urban planning which have made physical form a dominant concern. Specific forms have often become the key goals. Yet, it is obvious that the various land-use forms (concentric, linear, star-shaped, multicentered, and so on) as well as density levels, transportation modes, zoning separations, and other matters that have comprised city planning goals have more general goals behind them. In dealing with the short- or long-run future, distinct advantages exist for clarifying just how basic the goals should be. Such clarification may be accomplished by separating goals into the following three divisions, categorized by their functions or what they are intended to achieve.

1. *Urban-system goals* are concerned with the outcome of the urban system as a whole. They are similar to the overriding concerns in other fields (for example, of law for justice, of medicine for health, and of economics and management for efficiency). Such urban-system goals have relevance for all cities and over very long periods of time; thus, they are the most general and most long-lasting goals of all. Conscious concern with urban-system goals would serve to put urban planning and development into a future-regarding mode.

2. *General-plan goals* are the higher-level, operational goals established to provide guidelines for general plans. These will vary from city to city and over time as conditions change, power shifts, and ideas evolve. Such goals are integral elements in planning in various cities discussed in the first part of this volume, goals such as trying to maintain the economic importance of the downtown area (a goal in each of the cities covered), to increase low- and moderate-income housing, or to reduce air and water pollution.

3. *Instrumental goals* are all the goals not encompassed by the first two categories. They comprise the means of getting at the more general goals. They might include such endeavors as increasing or decreasing density levels, reducing scatteration in urban settlement, constructing a mass transit system, or providing adequate financing for housing improvement.

From the standpoint of long-range planning, the urban-system goals are of particular importance. They are directed at the functioning of the basic urban system of the city and the metropolitan region and in that sense differ from the other two categories (which focus more on specific problems and approaches). The specific testing of proposed lower-order goals and of means against the basic functioning of the urban system is critically important for long-run planning.

Drawing on the signals provided by the history of urban planning and urban policy from the turn of the century, the logical urban-system goals can be taken as efficiency, equity, and quality of life (or, more specifically, a healthy and satisfactory environment).

In historical terms, these goals have been gradually coming to the forefront of planning activities during the whole period of the modern planning movement. Thus the dominant concern of the earliest period, the "city beautiful" era, was for order and beauty or a quality-of-life objective. The second period, coincident with the era of municipal reform, introduced the efficiency goal. It was actually entitled the "city efficient" period, but efficiency considerations were more of an engineering nature than an economic one (the latter becoming more important in a later period). Equity considerations came to be of more significance in the New Deal period and again in the mid-1960s with the Great Society programs, but they did not permeate urban planning very deeply. More recently, with the growing importance of the environmental movement, the quality-of-life goal was broadened to encompass concern for the natural environment.

Even with this historical background, urban planning did not fully establish these urban-system goals as the overriding principles of the field (as medicine did health and law, justice). They remained more as background than as the foundation for specific plans and actions. Specific physical forms and concepts (as in the separation of uses in zoning) somehow had more appeal and dominated planning work and thinking.

Substantial gains for planning could be made if the importance and power of the urban-system goals were recognized. This calls for consideration of the content of the basic urban-system goals—as well as of the general plan and instrumental goals which follow.

THE URBAN-SYSTEM GOALS
Efficiency

Most cities came into being for reasons of efficiency, that is, the achievement of necessary functions with the minimum resources. Economic activities in the production of goods and services have to be close to other economic activities with which they interact (summed up in the economic concepts of agglomeration and scale economies). Because business enterprises need a labor force, residences of workers must be within commuting distance of the work places. Energy shortages and the high prices of gasoline have brought this efficiency feature to every urbanite's attention in recent years.

From the standpoint of both city government and of urban planning, two levels of efficiency need to be considered—the system level and the public-program level.

System Level Considerations

Conceptually, the system level consideration involves arriving at a net figure of all gains and losses of an actual or contemplated action for everyone residing in, working in, or affected by the city. In practice, of course, the netting-out cannot be as complete as would be desirable. This is the kind of calculation that must be made when a proposal for building a rail mass transit system or for increasing building density allowances throughout the city is offered. Conceptually, the final net figure is calculated by weighing the gains to be realized against the losses suffered by various groups to be affected. Thus, in this kind of calculation, when more than averages are involved, equity and political considerations will come into play together with the efficiency considerations. Of course, benefits and costs change over time as conditions change. Thus, efficiency calculations (and those related to the other goals) depend on assumptions about the future. The importance of the exercise stems mainly from the political value of bringing the efficiency considerations to the forefront.

Urban planning must recognize that it is a guardian of system efficiency, the city's main reason for being. (Cities begin to die when they no longer are efficient.) No matter how firmly ingrained, specific land-use forms, transportation modes, density configurations, and other factors that have loomed so large in urban planning must, first and foremost, meet the efficiency test. A political decision may be made to give higher priority to another basic goal (or value) in a given situation, equity or quality of life, but that does not remove the need to at least consider system efficiency.

Since system-efficiency thinking has not been widespread in urban planning in the United States, views as to what should be included in the concept have not been agreed upon. Nevertheless, it seems obvious that several factors should come into play. One is *the balance between labor supply and job availability.* In some cases, where there is an usually high and persistent unemployment of local residents or of some particular group of them (such as minority youths), considerations of this particular factor might well justify weighing heavily the economic impacts in urban planning proposals. In the same light, it would be appropriate to weigh proposed developmental projects on the efficiency scale in terms of the extent to which they increase or decrease the real costs of doing business and of living in a city compared to the past and to similar cities.

The use of the efficiency goal requires that the concept of urban efficiency itself receive continual study and attention. Of particular significance to the long run is continuity in system efficiency, including considerations of system adaptability. A critically important, yet frequently overlooked, feature of urban planning should be the search for signs of system nonadaptability. In a crisis, nonadaptability becomes a major concern, but then the problems are often overwhelming. This was true of New York City when, as a result of the fiscal crisis of the mid-1970s, several developments were found to be causing the urban system's problems. One was the burden on the city's budget of meeting the wage demands of municipal unions that had become politically and economically very powerful. Another was the imbalance which occurred as a result of the out-migration of tax-paying families and businesses and the in-migration of poor families requiring substantial social services. (The comparatively high level of such local services was a factor in bringing such families to New York.) Other problems arose because of the inappropriate fiscal procedures employed, procedures which were evolved by politicians to gain immediate political advantage. These imbalances had been accumulating over a long period of time. If urban planning is to be depended upon to provide a unique, long-range point of view, it should be in a position to point out such system imbalances and weaknesses long before crisis conditions are reached—and in a fashion compelling enough to strongly influence political decisions. This is not to suggest that urban planning can take on and necessarily win tough political battles. But urban planning *can* approach municipal system health in the same spirit as public health officials approach biosystem health hazards: making the dangers known early in a forceful manner.

The Public Program Level

Efficiency, which is also an issue at the public-program level, involves calculations of how close a proposed government program is to the goal of achieving a specified end with the least resources. This goal must play an important role in all rational human activities. The efficiency consideration is involved in cost/benefit analysis in urban planning, but generally the most important decisions made in urban planning—for example, a proposed basic pattern of land uses (separated versus mixed) in a given community or a general zoning proposal in a specific area (such as broad-scale downzoning)—is a matter of advocacy rather than neutral calculation in a resource-allocation framework. Planners often propose a preferred set of governmental programs without full consideration of the efficiency goal. In recent years, efficiency considerations have begun to receive more attention in urban planning due largely to the pressures exerted on local governments by taxpayers to hold down public expenditures and taxes.

As a general principle, given the inherent interest of planning in resource allocation, both public-program and systemwide efficiency should logically be continuous goals of urban planning.

Equity

National urban legislation first contained equity elements in 1936 when public housing for poor families was legislated. Over the years, the concept of equity has been broadened and extended to encompass (1) greater equality in public services and facilities, (2) fairer distribution of access to opportunity, resources, and political power; and (3) freedom of location. Equity considerations at the local level and within urban planning have occurred largely within the context of federal legislation and funds. Planning in Cleveland in the 70s, which had a strong equity and advocacy focus, was an exception to the rule of cities merely following the federal lead.

Equity is firmly enough established politically in urban development to justify treating it as an overriding urban-system goal in urban planning, parallel to efficiency. This is not to suggest that planners can by themselves bring about a more equitable situation in urban communities than the members of the community are ready to accept. They *can* keep the equity goal in front of the community as a built-in feature of planning activities, as a top-priority goal against which proposed policies and programs are always to be tested.

More specifically, urban planning, in the interest of the equity goal, should be centrally concerned with the following:

1. The strength of representation of disadvantaged groups in the establishment and execution of standards (or rules of the game) in urban development and services delivery.

2. The nature of the institutions given roles in urban development and services delivery (whether public, private or mixed, and whether socially oriented or not).
3. The appropriateness and strength of the incentives available to encourage behavior in line with equity-oriented legislation (such as the incentives to achieve an open-housing situation).

Learning to meet these kinds of concerns effectively can only come with continuing efforts and monitoring of results achieved. If equity is to be a major goal of planning, urban planning operations need to develop approaches, tools, and data to make it possible to monitor continuously the impact of urban developments and services delivery on different income and ethnic groups and to weigh equity considerations in decisions on specific plans and programs. Having the necessary data and tools of analysis and monitoring does not, of course, automatically resolve the many difficult human and political issues involved in equity. The trade-offs among the three basic goals—efficiency, equity, and quality of life—pose some of the most difficult problems for both municipal government and urban planning, and these must ultimately be resolved in the political arena. Urban planning ought to provide the decisionmakers and the general public with the information required to weigh the equity considerations and the trade-off considerations when urban development plans, policies, and programs are being contemplated.

Unfortunately, even the most basic local data associated with the equity goal—data on income, employment, use of public services, proportion of income spent on housing, use of public and private transport, and the like, broken down by income and ethnic groups—are not available in many cities in a form that can be used for equity analysis. Officially acknowledging equity as one of the overriding goals for urban planning may help speed the development of the information needed to weigh this factor properly in urban decisions. More strenuous efforts in the political realm (something along the lines of planning in Cleveland during the 1970s) would be called for if equity is to have an equal footing with the other basic community goals.

Quality of Life

Since the traditions of urban planning reveal a deep-rooted concern for the urban environment, the quality-of-life goal is often assumed to be highly developed. For several reasons, this is not the case. First, natural resources were not a primary concern in urban planning until the modern environmental movement took hold in the United States at the end of the 60s. Therefore, such issues as air and water pollution were discussed little in urban planning until the 70s. Second, even the man-made environment has been conceived rather narrowly in terms of land-use considerations and zoning controls, transportation, and a few features of the downtown environment (malls, public buildings, and the like), the redevelopment of already blighted areas and small enclaves of public housing.

Full-bodied treatment of the important environmental dimensions of the many communities in a city—including the relationship of individual communities to the urban region as a whole—is to be found only in rare instances. And even in these cases, there is a tendency to treat the most important factor in the picture—the relationships of the people of these communities to their environments—only in every general terms (essentially as income or racial averages, or even more simply as population numbers). Differing lifestyles and lifestyle groups rarely receive consideration at all, even though it is evident that the environment has varying meanings for them. A satisfactory environment for older individuals and/or childless couples who may strongly prefer an exciting, urbane environment is obviously very different from an environment that is satisfactory for child-oriented couples.

The task of providing basic standards for setting and judging environment and quality-of-life goals has begun in earnest, in order to evaluate existing conditions and specific proposals in a more or less objective manner. A variety of environmental indicators have been developed and are being applied. (Those related to air and water pollution are more advanced than those related to visual and noise considerations.) Thus, the basic technical requirements for using broad quality-of-life goals in urban planning are beginning to be met. The problem now is effectively to incorporate such standards and measures in ongoing planning processes.

Several key requirements exist for the three urban-system goals discussed here. The basic nature of the goals must be appreciated and understood. They should be thought of as permeating all planning activities, so that the processes of arriving at trade-offs among them are seen as almost defining the very meaning of urban planning. There is a need for better standards and measures than now exist for evaluating proposed policies and actions in terms of these broad goals. And it is necessary to find ways of relating effectively the general-plan goals and the instrumental goals to these high-order goals.

COMBINING NONPHYSICAL WITH PHYSICAL OBJECTIVES

To move down the hierarchy of goals from the urban-system goals to the instrumental goals is necessarily to move further into localized conditions and special local political considerations. There are, however, several general principles that apply to the lower-order goals. Some of the most important of these are related to the question of the appropriate linking of physical and nonphysical objectives in the evolution of a general plan and related instrumental goals. Economic and social/cultural goals have to be combined with physical/environmental goals so that the physical development of the city and region is consistent (coherent) with the nonphysical goals. This calls for merging into a single planning operation some of the approaches now central to some cities, such as Boston's economic focus in its planning and Cleveland's social approach, with the more established and more common physical/environmental approaches of other cities.

Boston has established goals for increases in jobs and income in its general plan and has attempted to relate these goals to the physical development of the city, including quite specific targets for capital investment (for example, in downtown redevelopment, transportation, housing, and commercial construction). Boston's planning, which is relatively sophisticated, addresses several of the broad urban-system goals, with at least some references to the efficiency, equity, and quality-of-life implications of both the goals and the strategies proposed.

However, it has two limitations from the standpoint of the criteria for future-oriented planning. The first is the time horizon. Being concerned as it is with the economic aspects of urban life and with the use of the investment tool, it concentrates on the middle-run future (essentially the ten year horizon with the time-scope of the investment program dominating the view of the future. Thus, only limited attention is given to the broad implications of the shift in the nature of Boston's economy (as in other central city economies) from the formerly heavy reliance on the manufacturing sector for jobs and income to the future reliance on the service sector. But which service industries are to provide the economic base of the future? How should a city put itself in a position to exploit the service opportunities that may arise in the future (such opportunities as in tourism, in nutrition, health spas, psychological, and other newer health-related services, in conferencing; in specialized training services; or in private security services)? Over a substantial period of time, a city may well have to develop institutions and physical forms appropriate to an urban economy largely dependent on newly evolving services. Here the end-state and the open-options approaches can logically come together in the form of plans to cope with a long-range structural change that poses new problems and opens new possibilities.

The other limitation of Boston's planning is its "thin" treatment of social considerations (although this aspect has been strengthened in the more recent neighborhood plans). One has to turn to Cleveland to observe substantial planning interest in the social aspects of urban life. Planning's concern with the unhappy condition of that city's poor draws the city toward an even shorter planning horizon than Boston's, essentially focusing attention on steps that can be taken in the near- and middle-term future to try to improve the lot of those who are currently the most disadvantaged.

Trying to speed improvement is logical in the situation of those who are disadvantaged, but such an approach does cut off possibilities that the long-run future offers. In the Cleveland case, possibilities in the realm of human development over time are not deeply analyzed even though the planning focus is on human opportunity. While such issues as transportation and physical accessibility to jobs and other human needs are clearly important for the poor of Cleveland (or of any city), social accessibility to many kinds of training opportunities and to various kinds of human-development opportunities (as in self-help programs and new forms of cooperative living) are probably even more important. Faludi (1973) significantly places human development at the very center of the planning concept. Human development is clearly a long-range matter. Yet, the contribution that planning can uniquely make to urban life (as compared to other problem-solving approaches) is precisely in introducing the long-run dimension in current decisionmaking. This potential contribution is hampered by an overly foreshortened view of human problems and human welfare.

Yet, the efforts of planning in Cleveland to improve *physical* access of the poor to a wide range of opportunities is clearly of major importance. Many kinds of human-development opportunities depend on physical access as well as other environmental considerations. Because they need both physical and nonphysical kinds of support, it is hard for children growing up in crumbling, filthy, dangerous homes and neighborhoods to develop into psychologically sound, productive, and self-motivated persons. In the present context—which seeks to combine the advantage of both end-state and open-options kinds of planning—open options seem particularly important in looking toward the optimizing of opportunities for human development, but social and cultural changes to meet human requirements also need the support of appropriate end-state physical forms.

Having noted some important interrelationships, it is also well to note that physical forms are not necessarily *means* to accommodate higher-order economic and social/cultural goals. They may themselves be among a community's higher-order *goals,* and economic and social/cultural means may have to be found to realize these goals. Thus a community—as part of its quality-of-life goal—may put great emphasis on the protection and extension of its natural amenity resources (for example, seashore, lakes, mountains, woods, greenbelts, and other open space), want to preserve cherished historic districts, protect existing residential neighborhoods or add beauty and drama to its major activity (employment) centers so that the community has a strong physical image. What is required, however, is that such physically oriented general plan and, to some extent, instrumental goals must consciously be related to the economic and social/cultural goals so that any potential conflicts or symbiotic ties are openly recognized.

An effort must be made concomitantly to look for ways of achieving the designated environmental goals while foreclosing the fewest possible future options and opportunities. In this light the relationship of the physical goals to the maintenance of a strong economic base in the long-run future must be a matter of constant concern for urban planners. Actually the growing importance of services, particularly tourism, makes many of the traditional physical/environmental goals of urban planning a key factor in strengthening the local economy *for the future.* The issue of foreclosing the fewest possible future options and opportunities also arises with regard to decisions about the conservation of existing community assets. If such assets are preserved for as long as it is economically advantageous to do so (on a long-range cost/benefit calculation), how are options at the same time to be kept open? Such a reconciliation may materialize if physical-form goals are posed whenever possible in terms of spatial relationships rather than in terms of specific locations. For example, goals for activity (employment) centers as a class would be more open to accommodating future options and opportunities as they arise than would goals specifically for the central business district and other existing centers (for example, industrial districts). Such general goals might relate to achieving certain environmental (such as pollution) outcomes; achieving certain standards of mobility and parking; achieving certain desirable relationships to work and residence in and around the activity centers. Plans for the preservation of assets would then be consciously related to the changing situation with regard to employment and other activity clusters.

Even goals for open space can be in terms of spatial relationship so that the city can provide for changing sizes, shapes, and location of open space without giving up the total amount of open space (or providing for an increase in the total over time). In this way, the flexibility needed to provide for new human needs and new opportunities is retained. In fact, the creation of new open space and the conservation of existing open space is a key feature needed to retain flexibility in city building. A significant problem in urban planning is how large such open spaces need to be in order to permit new patterns of urban development to emerge. Building in large units (such as planned unit developments) has the advantage of providing the possibility of clearing the whole unit at one time when it is appropriate to do so. Very little work has been done to date on how large new building units should be in order to permit urban renewal—in the basic sense of the term—in a later period. But it is a topic that deserves serious attention.

FORMULATING COMMUNITY GOALS

The goals of urban planning must reflect the will of the people living and working within a given municipality. There have been highly significant efforts in various cities in recent decades to involve community residents in goal setting. Thousands of individuals were involved in goals efforts in cities such as Los Angeles, Dallas, Seattle, and New York. Citizen committees worked conscientiously for months on end, and the products of such efforts have greatly influenced planning in the cities involved. In Los Angeles, for example, the emphasis on the maintenance of the residential neighborhoods and the funneling of new growth into dense activity centers (so as to protect the residential areas) evolved from the citizen goal-setting effort.

Several comments can be made about such efforts against the background of the principles discussed earlier. They should logically be carried out on a periodic basis, possibly every ten years. As far as this author knows, none of the cities mentioned have had a second round of community goal setting. The idea of periodic review of community goals is important in view of the reality of a rapidly changing urban situation. Members of the community need to be conscious of the urban changes underway and for professional planners to have to face openly the changing values of the community.

The differences as well as the commonalities among the various income, ethnic, and age groups in the community must be a matter of conscious planning concern. Previous goal efforts have been largely self-selective, with the typical middle-aged, middle-class concerned citizen as the backbone of the activity. As all planners know, it takes an enormous effort to involve either the people from the poorer neighborhoods or the youth. Yet, both groups are obviously important in laying out the goals for urban planning, and no goals effort is really meaningful without involving them in a major way. This suggests the importance of using newer methods of dialogue, including TV, classroom projects, computer gaming, and similar methods. Also, planning needs to be able to deal with a variety of goals for different neighborhoods, different lifestyles, and different ways of viewing the community, the city, and the region. The priority order of residents in poor neighborhoods and in various ethnic neighborhoods differs substantially, and this must be reflected in planning if it is to be truly democratic. In a study of priorities in Los Angeles (geared to questions about what government expenditures should concentrate on), the importance of education in black neighborhoods came out very forcefully, while the wealthiest neighborhoods (which are also the safest in fact) put safety from crime at the top of their priority list (Grigsby, Perloff, and Shapiro, 1973). Substantial evidence was found in the study that individuals in a large part of the city were little concerned with the pure residential character of neighborhoods (the issue of the intrusion of mixed uses) as compared to the bread-and-butter issues of crime and education, which were all-important. Few cities have yet elabroated goals which reflect the true diversity of city life and city residents.

Members of the community can be expected to react differently to the various categories of goals. Directly involving the community with the very general urban-system goals can be very difficult. Such goals, as suggested earlier, are actually standards that must *permeate* everything that is done in urban planning. Thus, when a goals effort is being undertaken, information on outcomes over the past decades should provide a *background* to the discussion of general-plan and related instrumental goals. Those involved with a goals effort should be informed about the changing economic viability of the municipality-within-the-region, results obtained from municipal investments (the efficiency element), and what implications this has upon investments that can be undertaken by the community in the future, on the relative employment and income standing of various groups (the equity element), and on the condition of the community's environment—measured against quality-of-life standards. A fuller appreciation of the role of the urban-system goals by the community can be a significant factor in the politics of urban planning within a municipality over time. Increasing understanding of and concern for the municipalwide and regionwide goals of efficiency, equity, and quality of life are necessary offsets against the built-in interest of neighborhood residents in their immediate environments and situations.

In the formulation of the more specific general plan and related instrumental goals, the contribution of community residents can be direct and determining. However, to ensure that the municipalwide and regionwide factors are fully considered in goals efforts (for example, regional transportation and communications requirements and possibilities), care needs to be taken that organizations and interest groups reflecting such considerations be involved in the effort. Since expert knowledge about these broad matters (as in economic development, pollution, energy conservation and so on) is needed—as is representation of municipalwide and regional interests—use can be made of the Delphi tool in the formulation of goals. The very purpose of a Delphi exercise is the establishment of an expert view of a given subject. Thus, the use of questionnaires asking about the preferred goals of a variety of expert groups can be a valuable supplement to the typical neighborhood-oriented goals effort. This would help ensure that certain considerations important in goal setting, such as changing technology and changes in population structure, were brought to bear in the goals effort.

Such a combined use of both community-based, nonexpert, and expert opinion is needed not only in goals setting, but in the creation of plans for the future and of instrumentalities for the execution of these plans. This combination is essential to all facets of urban planning.

Chapter 26
Development of "Strategies-and-Policies" General Plans

For many years, urban planning has been moving in the direction of replacing the traditional mapped land-use general plan as the main tool for guiding municipal decisionmaking with a policies or strategy general plan. Such a shift is at the very center of a new paradigm for urban planning. If the new paradigm is to provide a way of combining the best features of the open-options and end-state approaches, and if it is to bring the past, present, and future aspects of the future into a coherent whole, it can only do so by speeding the transition to a "strategies-and-policies" general plan as the main focus of planning activities.

THE SLOW TRANSITION TO POLICIES PLANNING

The transition from the mapped land-use general plan to the strategies-and-policies general plan is by no means complete. The legitimacy of focusing on broad policy planning rather than on the creation of a specific design of future land uses is not yet established. One of the reasons is that the legitimacy of urban planning to deal with matters other than land use and physical development—matters of economic, social/cultural, political, and fiscal impact—has not yet been fully accepted. Such legitimacy must be established, and one of the main purposes of this volume is to make the case for such an increase in the scope of urban planning.

Another reason for the slow transition to policies planning is the difficulty of determining exactly when policy plans are adequate for decisionmaking by the municipal government and by special agencies concerned with development (for example, the zoning body) and when specific land-use designations are needed—particularly when legal issues are also involved. As long as the specific designations on a map continue to be important in the guidance and control of land use, planning agencies find it difficult to put great store in policy proposals. Most important of all, the logic of guiding decisions of a developmental nature (mainly how the city should grow and change) through policy planning has not yet been fully absorbed in the field of urban planning or by political officials. This point requires particular attention.

The specific mapping traditions in urban planning are very strong. They have been reinforced not only by all the factors mentioned previously but also by the persistent adherence by practicing urban planners to certain beliefs about city development. These include such fundamental assumptions as the overriding desirability of spatially separating the major urban functions, the desirability of maintaining the dominance of the downtown area, and the desirability of rail mass transit over other forms of personal transportation. Some of these beliefs—particularly the separation of land uses—have essentially given urban planning its very reason for being. Thus, the transition from mapped land-use planning to policy planning has been delayed by a specific belief structure.

Some of these assumptions of planners—which are, in operating terms, actually general plan and related instrumental goals—might well be the correct ones in certain municipalities at a given period of time. They are not, however, ideals under *all* circumstances, but are matters to be decided by various kinds of calculations and continual testing of community preferences. It is useful, in this regard, to appreciate the fact that these values (or beliefs) were the result of the conditions in American cities when the modern planning movement came into being early in the 20th century: generally an unpleasant and unhealthy jumble of land whose urban patterns made personal movement difficult and costly. The beliefs were carried forward into the present by the assumption that they had made important contributions to the maintenance of property values and to the strength of the urban economy.

It is useful to be openly conscious of this belief structure. It is essential to a full appreciation of the fact that concepts of good urban development must necessarily change over time as conditions and values change. Appreciating this becomes easier as one contemplates the implications for land use of energy shortages and high prices for gasoline, because then the uniqueness (rather than generality) of the traditional goals becomes apparent. Mixed land uses may well become a necessity in energy-shortfall situations. Chapter 25 made the case for viewing the goals of urban planning primarily in very general terms of efficiency, equity, and quality-of-life objectives and for setting rather broad standards even at the general plan level. Contrasted with the standard assumptions, all sorts of mixtures of land uses can be permitted and still retain a high quality of life; many activity centers can be encouraged which compete with the downtown and still maintain efficiency and economic viability; and buses and other forms of mass transit can under certain circumstances provide more efficient, equitable, and high-quality services than rail mass transit. The tendency for the mapped land-use approach to be tied to a specific belief structure is itself one of the disadvantages of such an approach.

These considerations argue for the advantages of working within a more general framework, a strategy-and-policies framework. The evolution of a developmental *strategy*, by its very nature, demands great clarity in those goals the community wants to achieve. And such clarity in goals is particularly important if advantage is to be taken of working through several possible alternative routes in achieving goals before specific policies, programs, and other tools of implementation are finally decided upon. The benefits of such an approach must be appreciated by urban planners and public officials before the transition from the traditional mapped land-use approach to the broader and more flexible strategies-and-policies general planning approach will be complete.

THE SUBJECTS OF A STRATEGIES-AND-POLICIES GENERAL PLAN

The urban transformation through which American cities are passing provides a rather compelling framework for urban planning in the latter part of this century. Dealing with the present and anticipated problems and with the possibilities of the future, urban planning will have to encompass concerns in the economic, social/cultural, and political/governmental realms as well as the more traditional environmental realm. But what should be included in the general plan for a major city, say, one with a population of 50,000 or more?

In the economic realm, strategic considerations might well include the following:

1. The intensity of the effort to retain existing manufacturing plants and/or to attract new ones and the relative emphasis to be given to the service industries compared to the manufacturing industries and to the newly evolving service industries compared to the established ones.
2. The types of incentives to be employed in each case and the relative emphasis to be given such methods as easing land acquisition, helping with mobility and parking problems, helping with manpower training, and providing loans and/or tax exemptions or reductions.
3. The kind of emphasis to be given to the economic strengthening of the downtown as compared to that of other activity centers.
4. The emphasis given to encourage tourism and the kinds of physical and nonphysical attractions to be developed in any planned expansion of tourist income.
5. The particular efforts that might be effective in trying to overcome high unemployment rates among various groups, particularly minority youths.
6. The principles and standards used to guide municipal investments.

In the social/cultural realm, strategic considerations might cover subjects such as the following:

1. The intensity of municipal efforts at improving neighborhoods of various kinds (those in the poorest condition, those on the decline but with some strength, those already making some efforts at self-improvement, and so on).
2. The efforts made to encourage self-help measures in neighborhoods, institutions, and/or various population groups.
3. The measures taken to ease the adjustment of newcomers and to discourage intergroup conflicts.
4. The most effective approach to encourage the expansion of cultural activities and to support the role such activities play in achieving human development goals.

Strategic considerations in the physical/environmental realm might include the following:

1. The growth or decline of the downtown area compared to other activity centers—particularly in the face of energy shortages—whether any

specialization should be encouraged in the different centers and the nature of the transportation ties between the various centers.
2. The balance of employment, housing, cultural, and other activities to be encouraged in the various centers and how to achieve those balances.
3. The nature of the physical and nonphysical measures employed to improve the condition of neighborhoods; how to create unique neighborhood identity and community pride; and ways of meeting mobility and parking needs of different kinds of neighborhoods.
4. The processes, regulations, and controls employed in evaluating the condition of public facilities and private plants of various kinds, and approaches employed in deciding on special conservation measures, rehabilitation, adaptive uses, or demolition.
5. The approaches used in establishing green areas and other open space throughout the municipality and region.
6. The approaches used in bringing about improvements in air, water, visual, and noise pollution.

Strategic considerations in the political/governmental realm would cover the political, organizational, managerial, and fiscal approaches employed to carry out the strategies projected in the other sectors as well as:

1. Ways to strengthen the capacity of the municipal and regional governments to adequately perform the anticipated tasks of the next decades.
2. Approaches to informing the federal and state governments of anticipated problems and needs of the municipality and region and to enlarging the possibilities of receiving the financial and policy assistance required.
3. Approaches to achieving truer and stronger representation of all groups in the municipality in planning and other governmental decisions and greater and more effective community involvement in such decisions.

These are examples; the actual subjects covered within a given strategies-and-policies general plan would, of course, be geared to the special conditions, problems, and possibilities of that municipality. But the examples do demonstrate the breadth of the subjects with which planning must deal in the last part of the 20th century. What remains the same is the need for planners to be genuinely creative in designing approaches to the achievement of community goals. No matter how much information is available for analytical purposes, no matter how much effective input there may be from other governmental departments and from the community, there still remains the need for a creative general plan design which provides the community and governmental officials with an understanding of where choices lie as they move into the future. The task is particularly demanding when alternative futures are considered—as they should be—since it takes great skill to make strategy and policy alternatives manageable and effective in decisionmaking. The difficulty is compounded when the alternatives contain elements of both the end-state and open-options possibilities in logical and feasible combinations. But all this makes up the very art of planning. Unless planning can help a municipality choose preferred paths to the future among the real possibilities open to it, it is not providing to the community what it can uniquely provide.

ALTERNATIVE PATHS TO THE FUTURE

There is only one future at any point in the future, but it is not preordained. It is a result of many specific decisions and actions within a given evolving context. The whole point of planning is to try to guide the decisions and actions within a given sphere of power and policy space toward agreed upon goals.

From the present into the future, there are alternatives. Many possible goals exist as do many ways of achieving those goals. Planning for the future involves the selection of preferred goals which reflect particular values and assumptions and are then expressed in particular strategies-and-policy packages. The act of choosing one set of these involves rejecting others.

Planning inevitably involves imposing certain values upon the future. These will be present values, but only some values of the present will be imposed while others will not. How can we determine the extent to which our values correspond to those of the next generation? What are the implications of a radical change of future values over current ones? Edwin A. Bock (1979: 291) poses this dilemma when he writes:

> The permeation, not to say domination, of our future-oriented efforts by underlying present needs would not of itself establish, between those living in the present and those living in the future, a self-serving, exploitive, colonial relationship of doubtful rightness, if it could be shown that the essential interests of the present coincide with the essential interests of the future. We yearn to believe that such a coincidence of interests exists.

Sensitivity to the problem of our own values changing over time and the high probability that a different set of values will be held by future generations is an important starting point in trying not to be "exploitive" of the future. Planners might also try to forecast value changes, as some writers have suggested (Iklé, 1971:146; Toffler, 1969:2). But most important of all, the development of alternative paths to the future can permit the evaluation of each alternative in terms of the extent to which it forecloses options in the future. An example is furnished by the development of alternative energy sources ranging from highly centralized nuclear energy plants at one extreme and a wide variety of "soft" energy sources at the other. Clearly, heavy dependence on nuclear energy provides far fewer options in the future than does the latter. The same is true of a decision to concentrate most new economic activities in the downtown area as against opting for the development of a large variety of activity centers; the former offers fewer openings in future periods.

The degree of flexibility provided future generations by choices made in the present is only one of many considerations involved in choosing among alternative possibilities, but it is important. In general, the alternative futures approach permits a much more effective balancing of present values and needs as against future values and needs than does the traditional single intuitive conception of the best path to the future. As has been noted, the traditional approach has permitted planners to hold on to values and ideas inherited from the past which are of doubtful applicability to the present, much less the future. The alternative futures approach is needed to make planners themselves, as well as municipal politicians and the general public, more future oriented.

While the alternative futures approach offers extremely valuable advantages, it also poses difficult problems. Significant alternatives can be found at every stage of the planning process and within each of the sectors with which planning must deal. Thus, the permutations and combinations of alternatives can easily be overwhelming. The concept of scenarios has been developed (importantly through the work of Herman Kahn) to help make the alternative futures approach manageable (Encel, Marstrand, and Page, 1975: 63-64, Wiener 86-89; Kahn and Wiener, 1967).

An example of how scenarios can be used to define alternative paths to the future is furnished by the issues urban planning faces in addressing a significant energy shortfall in the future and its implications for the urban form. John Van Til (1979: 318-29) takes three scenarios of future energy supply for the United States developed by the Energy Policy Project of the Ford Foundation and adds two additional images of energy supply so that there are five scenarios ranging from an alternative which contemplates continued growth in energy use of 3.5 percent per year to one which assumes a decline to 75 percent of 1973 levels (The energy amounts involved range from 187 to 56 quadrillion BTUs). For various reasons, he posits the conclusion that, should there be less energy available, the most drastic cuts will be made in transportation rather than in household, commercial, and industrial uses. The most drastic curtailment would be in gasoline available for private automobiles. He then considers the probable impact of the required reductions in auto usage on spatial form and structure employing a typology developed by Catherine Wurster. This is constructed from an analysis of two dimensions: (1) concentration to dispersion and (2) regionwide specialization to subregional integration (the last of these involving regional nodes spread across the landscape but with employment and housing concentration in each of the nodes). Van Til (1979) indicates that this last alternative provides the preferred form in an energy shortfall situation, but even it would require the encouragement of more concentration inside the regional nodes. The alternative spatial forms are also presented in scenario style. Van Til (1979: 327) concludes by suggesting that even though a fully "rational" approach to the problems involved is not to be expected, "Planners should at least . . . begin to construct plans for an energy-short future as one option in every city or regional plan, extending the time lines of these plans well into the 21st century and beyond. . . ."

This exercise is complicated by the fact that planners must consider total energy supply alternatives, urban energy reductions by sector (likely private transportation), and alternative spatial forms and structures. But it also points to significant choices and invites fuller consideration of their implications, and it may reveal the costs of doing nothing, since that is a real choice.

In certain choices in any alternative futures approach, values and assumptions as well as goals are centrally involved. The more explicit these are, the easier it is to make the choices. One of the values to be considered and tested is the provision of maximum possible flexibility for future generations, as suggested earlier. (Van Til does not consider this feature in his various scenarios, but it should be a built-in feature of official urban planning.)

It requires great imagination to devise scenario forms which provide meaningful choices for political decisionmakers and the general public, always remembering that only a small number of alternative futures can be considered in a political context. There are no formulas or cookbooks for designing politically effective scenarios representing alternative futures. As a general principle, however, the most politically compelling scenarios are those focused on dominant values rather than on technical considerations. Thus, people can understand even a complex set of goals and strategies if they are brought together in an alternative labeled "resource conservation." This is then compared to an alternative set of goals and strategies aimed at "growth accommodation" or at maximizing jobs and income." Different groups in the city can grasp the implications for their welfare if impacts are spelled out and they can react accordingly. Decisionmakers are thus likely to choose mixes rather than pure total sets (such as a resource conservation scenario) to accommodate the people mixes that make up the municipality. Effectively devised packages of goals and strategies sharpen implications and permit choices reflective of different preferences and values. The scenarios should seek to ease the process of arriving at effective trade-offs.

There are certain tools that can help in this process. W. K. Tabb (1972: 25-26) suggests:

> ... Distributional cost-benefit analysis that stresses program diffusion effects and estimates needed compensatory side payments can help the planner avoid overly conjectural abstract planning. By focusing on the effects of particular plans on particular groups, distributional cost-benefit analysis continuously raises (and answers) the questions: Who pays? Who benefits? Used in combination with the more speculative alternative futures approach, such analysis is an important corrective.

The search for the general welfare or *net* social benefit is enhanced when distributional effects are made evident and efforts at equalization (including compensation) are provided for.

The time in which the general plan is going through its periodic revision (updating) within a municipality can and should be a time of intense political debate over goals and strategies, with the politicians and professional planners seeking as much convergence as possible. The use of alternatives is simply a way of making the implications of different paths as clear as possible to the officials and people of the municipality. A single path must ultimately be decided upon, however. A relatively consistent set of goals and strategies is essential if the next stage in the planning process is to be manageable—the design of policies and programs which follow the preferred strategies to achieve the chosen goals.

If it is assumed that the general plan is revised every ten years, it doesn't follow that questions about goals and strategies are put to rest for a decade and everything from that point is simply implementation. Given the pace of change in today's world and the appearance of such critically important developments, as a worldwide energy shortage or a drastic change in birthrates, questions about goals and strategies always remain politically pertinent. The more thorough the analysis of alternative goals and strategies in the general plan, the more information will be available on the relation of the goals and strategies chosen to the situation then existing, as well as greater clarity and understanding about why they may have to change with changed conditions. But granting some revisions in goals and strategies on a continuing basis, some policy and program changes must be relied on to meet changed conditions. Policies and programs are among the most important tools of the urban planner.

Chapter 27
The Art of Creating Policies, Plans, and Programs

Solomon Encel and his colleagues, in *The Art of Anticipation* (Encel, Marstrand, and Page, 1975:33) point out:

> If one believes that the central task is the tracing of alternative ways to alternative goals and that the choice between various paths can be influenced by purposeful action, that we are not totally at the mercy of uncontrollable forces, then a preoccupation with policies is inevitable.

Policies are the link between goals and general strategies on the one side and implementing specific plans and programs on the other. They express commitment to a course of action to meet the goals. There is a tendency to mix goals, strategies, and policies in many policy statements in urban planning (and in other activities).

How can statements such as "maintain and conserve sound existing development" or "revitalize declining parts of existing urban development" be appropriately classified? These are listed in the "policies" section of a general plan (in a western urban county). Are they really goals, strategies, or policies? The classification itself is not of great importance. But what is inadequate about these general statements as policy in this instance is the fact that the general plan itself contains no concrete directives to guide governmental agencies or private investors. At a minimum, some definitions of terms such as what is "sound existing development" and "declining parts of existing urban development" should be included. Priorities should be indicated in some way (since everything cannot be done at once). And there should be an indication of implementation tools preferred, for example, tax exemptions, subsidies, special land-use provisions, and/or special zoning arrangements. It is not enough to go directly from general statements of this type to specific mapped land-use allocations and assume—as is often done—that thereby a policies plan has been created. The general issue of policy implementation has to be addressed, and the land-use designations seen as only one of the implementing tools.

The policies section of a general plan should ideally propose a specific legislative agenda for action and an agenda for administrative regulations and other forms of guidance to administrative bodies. The legislative body will be receiving proposals from many groups. If the planning work is properly done, the decisionmakers should see the planning agenda as providing an unusually valuable reference point for its consideration of new legislation and amendments. For it would be the product of a careful process of discerning community goals and preferred approaches to achieving them, specifically developed to provide an appropriate framework for legislation. Although an ideal, it should be seen as a goal to which municipal planning departments should aspire if urban development is indeed to be guided by planning considerations.

The policies section of the general plan as well as policies recommended by the planning department in between general plan revisions should be the product of choices among alternative paths. Even after specific strategies for achieving goals are chosen, there is normally a range of policy options along the pathway suggested by the strategies. A strategy that calls for "revitalizing declining parts of existing urban development" can be met by policies that call for emphasizing either private or governmental development (or certain combinations of both), and which require subsidies or strongly enforced regulations. The most attractive of the possibilities have to be evaluated and tested for responses through detailed interactions with builders, developers, various governmental officials, and a cross-section of citizens in various affected neighborhoods. The use of alternative policy packages or policy scenarios is needed to make the exercise manageable in the face of the usual large number of choices. The process should also achieve as broad a concensus as possible on preferred packages of policies. This consensus is as necessary in designing programs and other implementing tools as it is necessary to converge on preferred goals and strategies to lay the basis for decision on policies.

THE DESIGN OF IMPLEMENTING PLANS AND PROGRAMS

In plans and programs, as in policies, terminology is not fixed. Policies are sometimes considered part of plans and programs, and sometimes it is the other way around. There can be reference to renewal plans and programs which involve policies aimed at revitalizing sections of the city as well as other activities aimed at such revitalization. Within the context of the present discussion, the preference is for the use of the terms plans and programs as arrangements to carry out agreed upon policies.

Land-use policies can set general standards to guide development by private interests, thus giving the developer choices among the geographic areas in which development may take place. This can be a substitute for specific land-use designations on the city map (or the standards might apply within designated areas). A strategy that calls for minimizing municipal government costs for facilities and services in new developments in outlying areas can be accomplished by policies that require the internalizing of all facilities and services costs resulting from each development project over a specified period into the future. The developer can proceed once guarantees are made to cover the associated costs by providing the specified services and facilities. This amounts to achieving a community goal through an agreed upon strategy without the need for specific land-use designations.

Similarly, amenity resources of all sorts can have generous boundaries around them on the city map and prohibition of all development within such boundaries, or the strategy can provide for differentiation and for policies which set standards under which some development is possible. The latter can call for the establishment of a permit system with appropriate criteria. While the differentiation approach may have certain risks attached, it may also permit more areas to be designated as amenity resources or as "Significant Ecological Areas" (SEAs) than would be possible on the more rigid boundary-setting approach. Under any circumstances, by not having to rely solely on mapped land-use designations, the decisionmakers and the community generally are given more choices and more ways in which trade-offs can be considered.

A permit arrangement, a municipal land-buying program, a program which calls for the drafting of specific ordinances on developments in specific areas or in specified situations, and general plan land-use designations on the city map can all be thought of as plans and programs that can be used to control developments in outlying areas.

If it is appropriate to go beyond mapped land-use designations in carrying out policies in the realm of land use, it is even more so when an urban planning operation considers how to carry out strategies and policies in the economic, social/cultural, and political/governmental realms. Economic policies for strengthening the downtown area and/or other activity centers may involve tax and other subsidy programs, manpower training programs, and programs to strengthen tourism through encouraging the arts without requiring any land-use designations or changes in such designations. Policies that call for the conservation of historic buildings may not involve land-use designations to any important extent. Even plans and programs of neighborhood improvement may be only minimally concerned with land use. Thus, to put everything into a land-use framework is largely to put the cart before the horse. Land-use designations and changes in land uses should appear only when they are significant elements in realizing the goals that have been set for the city.

Planning through land-use maps does have certain highly important advantages. It permits a comprehensive view of the whole municipality, and in some cases the whole region as well, through a single lens. It not only permits comprehensiveness but consistency as well. Everything is of a piece. Unfortunately, it is also unidimensional when a multidimensional view is needed; it does not cover all the important sectors that need to be covered or all the important levers (other than land-use plans) that need to be used in achieving municipal goals. However, the other approach, a general plan that does not provide for coverage along any consistent and comprehensive lines, also has its disadvantages. For it would then be hard to have a systemic view along any dimension—only a miscellany of plans, programs, and other implementation tools.

AN IMPLEMENTATION AGENDA

The best approach is probably to evolve a specially designated *implementation agenda,* which would contain the official land-use map and plan but would also contain other accounts and plans directed at carrying out the strategies and policies for urban development established by the municipal government.

The land-use map, in its record-keeping characteristic, is often viewed as an account of land uses in the same way that gross national product (GNP) is deemed to be a total coverage account of national economic activities. However, other municipalwide accounts are also needed.

A review of possibilities in this regard suggests that there are four such accounts and plans that can provide a municipalwide framework for urban planning appropriate to the needs of city governments in the decades ahead. These are based on the major resources of a municipality as the appropriate foundation for planning in the remaining years of the 20th century. Land-use planning, the traditional base for urban planning, is, in effect, an effort to optimize the use of the scarce and important land resources of the municipality. The proposed accounts and plans carry this basic concept to a logical next step of encompassing the other basic resources important to the people of a municipality.

The four proposed accounts and plans are:

An Asset Account and Plan

The need for such an account in urban planning has already been discussed at length in Part 3. At this point, it need only be added that by permitting total coverage of the municipal plant, actions to be taken over a substantial period into the future—such as 20 or 25 years—can be designated in both time and financial terms and any other terms that are thought to be needed. This account and plan would provide the same advantages for the "third dimension" of the municipality as land-use planning offers on the ground.

A Land-Use/Natural Resources Account and Plan

These would contain the present types of land-use record-keeping and plans but would be expanded to cover air and water also—including all natural amenity resources. Air and water carrying capacity as well as land capacity would be considered, as would use characteristics in all of them. Special plans for all amenity resources should be included. Many municipal planning agencies have already expanded beyond the traditional land-use planning, so that what remains is a strengthening of the techniques for record-keeping and planning of all the natural resources of the municipality (and of the region as a whole).

A Manpower Account and Plan

Such an account and plan—which is comprehensive in terms of the human resources of the city—could be expected to focus on skills needed to provide for the present jobs and anticipated employment within the municipality, for the necessary skill training, and for the expansion of employment within the city as a whole and within its various subareas. Such an account and plan would be concerned with industrial trends and occupational characteristics, including the shifts to service industries, and with the investment requirements to meet the employment objectives. The plan would indicate the segments of the population at which various programs were being directed.

The expansion from traditional land-use planning through the proposed accounts and plans would mean coverage of all the natural, capital, and human resources of the municipality (and region if possible). All these resources are precious to the community and are impacted by urban life, not just land. All should be accounted for and plans made and carried through where the municipality directly wants to achieve improvements and provide for the future.

An Investment Plan and a Fiscal Plan

Yet, a fourth set of comprehensive accounts and plans is needed, one encompassing the financial consideration of the other three and covering all public services and revenues, as well as investments. The investment plan (following the lead of Boston) might include estimates of anticipated private investments as well as planned public investments to try to achieve a comprehensive investment picture. These might well be encompassed in a long-range fiscal plan with five-year segments to display the financial problems and possibilities of the municipality in the future.

The fiscal plan deserves special attention. Given the increasing resistance of taxpayers to larger governmental budgets, fiscal planning will become an important tool both in designing programs that advance municipal goals in a cost-effective manner and in carrying them out. Planning agencies have traditionally advocated physical development programs that emerged from planning studies with little attention to fiscal priorities or even to the availability of budgetary resources in the city. If planning is to play a meaningful role in municipal affairs in the future, it will have to become centrally involved in every phase of fiscal planning and management.

Fiscal planning is quite different from the usual municipal budgeting operation, since it has to provide the fiscal dimension for long-term developmental plans and programs. *Feasibility* has to be introduced into the implementation processes.

What should fiscal planning encompass? Table 27–1 suggests the major components that might be included in fiscal planning to meet these requirements. Both the revenue and expenditure components of the required kind of fiscal planning are uniquely geared to achievement of the developmental goals of the city. Note that in the revenue section, the ability to make reasonable estimates based on sources of revenue generation depends on the kinds of information already suggested as important for comprehending the workings of the urban system, including analyses of the economic base of the city and region. Asset accounting also comes into play. The expenditure

Table 27–1. Components of a Fiscal Plan

Revenues (Past, Present, and Future)[1]

Bases of Revenue Generation	**Actual Projected Revenues**
1. Analyses of economic base of city and region, to arrive at income flows (earnings from jobs, transfers, and other sources); to be used in calculating bases for nonproperty tax revenues.	1. Nonproperty Tax Revenues
2. Asset accounts analyses to arrive at bases for property tax assessments and value of nontaxed property.	2. Property Taxes
3. Analyses of laws, regulations and traditions influencing intergovernmental transfers.	3. Intergovernmental Transfers a. General and special funds from the federal government b. General and special funds from the state

Expenditures (Past, Present, and Future)[1]

Investments	**Expenditures**	**Estimated Investment and Expenditures Related to Goal Achievement and Shortfalls**
Public capital items 1. Maintenance 2. Rehabilitation and preservation 3. Replacement 4. Urban renewal 5. Other developmental outlays	1. General government 2. Service delivery 3. Income supports 4. Controls	Referenced to standards used in judging efficiency, equity, and quality of life, as well as specified goals.

[1]Five years back and five years forward.

component significantly distinguishes between investment and noninvestment outlays and summarizes expenditures according to the implementing tools to be employed in realizing the community goals and strategies. It also provides for estimates of projected shortfalls.

The approach to estimating shortfalls would be by way of cost/benefit analysis, measuring anticipated outcomes against established goals. Such calculations and projections involve difficult problems of estimation (Mancur Olson, 1973). However, if approached with appropriate humility, making the limitations clear to everyone, such estimations can be valuable inputs into municipal decisionmaking processes. To an important extent, they might be encompassed in fiscal-impact analyses which have become an increasingly accepted tool of urban planning.

Even more difficult and tenuous would be an attempt to relate new opportunities to revenue, investment, and expenditure alternatives. Any projections in this realm would be purely conjectural (given the limitations of existing forecasting methods and social science knowledge), but would, if undertaken with imagination, provide interesting and often provocative possibilities to be considered by municipal officials and the general public in making budgetary and fiscal decisions. At the very least, such calculations would get people thinking about the opportunities of the future as well as about the problems and fiscal burdens.

The availability of this kind of information would give the planning operation significant advantages over the normal budgetary operation by enabling it to relate projections to ongoing and proposed developments within the community.

The four types of accounts and plans discussed previously would provide urban planning with powerful tools for implementation. These are needed not only because they provide base information, but because they provide necessary frameworks for the establishment of concrete plans and programs to achieve the goals of the municipality.

PLANS AND PROGRAMS FOR "ELEMENTS" AND FOR NEIGHBORHOODS

One of the most important developments in urban planning in the last two decades has been the concept of evolving plans and programs for various elements. These usually encompass housing, transportation, land use and natural environment, economic development, downtown and other activity centers, recreation, urban design, safety (covering various hazards), and so on. In some states, the elements are mandated by the state government, and in some cases, the plans and programs are carefully designed and demonstrate substantial imagination and political sophistication. Often, the various elements not only provide the building blocks of the citywide plans but also of the plans for the individual neighborhoods or communities of the municipality.

The most common problem, as far as providing tools of implementation is concerned, is that the "should be" and the "will be" tend to be mixed. On examination, the plans and programs often turn out to be wish lists, things "that ought to be done." Very rarely are they geared to a stated time horizon, to planned expenditures and investments from the municipal budget, and to detailed agreed upon actions by the various operating agencies of the municipal government and of private investors.

Thus, while the concept of plans and programs for specified elements in the municipality and in the communities or neighborhoods of the city is a powerful one and has been moving planning closer to the world of reality, certain features are still missing. Most noticeable is the lack of implementing levers other than land-use plans, subdivision controls, zoning, and building controls. That is why the four sets of accounts and plans have been stressed as urgently important. By subsuming the elements under the four sets of accounts and plans (for example, in a matrix form), a checklist for comprehensive coverage could be provided. Thus, the housing element for instance could be viewed in terms of the assets account and plan which would be concerned with existing and projected condition of existing housing, maintenance requirements, whether included in a rehabilitation program or in a redevelopment program, present and projected prices, and the like. Under the manpower account and plan, such issues as the availability of labor for construction, the possibility of increasing minority employment through construction activities, and the training requirements could be considered. Under the land-use/natural resources account and plan, the locational issues would be faced including such questions as the availability of nearby open space and recreational areas. Under the investment plan and fiscal plan, the specific investments in housing and the methods of financing would be spelled out.

This is not to suggest that all of these "boxes" could be filled with actual plans and municipal decisions. But, then, at least it would be evident as to which elements and which features of which elements are actually provided for, and which are part of a wish list. Urban planning urgently needs this kind of reality structure, rather than the present mixed bag of plan specificity and wishful thinking.

In the case of the individual neighborhoods of the city, specific time-related plans for infrastructure and other capital assets of the community, for land use, for manpower training and employment, for public and private investments, and for public services and facilities financing are needed to help mitigate the difficult neighborhood problems of the present and to provide significant improvements for the future.

There is in all this a substantial proliferation of information and implementation tools. This is not a development to be particularly welcomed, but it is an inevitable concomitant of the complexity of the modern city and metropolis and of the urban transformations that are taking place. Fortunately, the evolution of the functional elements and neighborhood plans by planning agencies has begun to give them the understanding of tough urban issues needed to cope effectively with the kinds of implementing tools discussed earlier. Furthermore, the development of these tools is not a task for urban planning agencies alone. Asset accounts and plans can only be created in a municipality if all the operating agencies, and particularly the public works and the financial units, are fully involved. Nor can the manpower accounts and plans be prepared without the full cooperation of the various human resources agencies, the school system, and the office of economic development. Fiscal planning quite obviously depends on the complete cooperation of the fiscal agencies of the municipality. As suggested earlier, none of these agencies are likely to invite the planning department to enter their realms. The suggested implementing tools will come into being only if the planning agency can make a compelling case for such an expansion to the chief executive and city council, as well as to the operating officials, by demonstrating that they are needed to meet the challenges faced by the municipal government. And that will take a bit of doing in most cities.

Chapter 28
Requirements of Implementation: Working with Many Actors

The ideal for urban planning has been defined as an approach which combines the best features of both open-option and end-state planning. The main content of this approach has been discussed earlier. Now the discussion will focus on the organizational and operational elements of such an approach.

THE HINGE FUNCTION OF URBAN PLANNING

Given a developmental focus for urban planning, it should provide an important hinge function—that is, relate the governmental to the nongovernmental or private development activities. Planners must seek to involve all the major institutions as well as the citizenry in the various phases of the planning and development processes.

To take a specific example, suppose that the major governmental and private institutions have agreed that it is essential for the future health of the local economy and society for a planned changeover from a manufacturing-oriented city to a largely services-oriented one. The urban planning agency would not only have to involve many of the municipal agencies in planning for and implementing such a changeover, but many of the private and nonprofit institutions as well (including the labor unions, the banking community and other financial institutions, various service industries, and a host of others). All of these would have to contribute to the desired end result through their own policies and actions. Since the form that a more mature services economy is likely to take is still uncertain, the participating institutions would have to be highly flexible in encouraging the desired development of the service industries.

Planning's task, in cooperation with the municipal office of economic development and other public agencies, should be to carry out studies of the evolving nature of service activities and of their requirements for municipal infrastructure and public services; forecast probable lines of development and analyze implications of different lines of development for city form and public and private investments; discuss with educational institutions the implications for education and manpower training; and consider with private and public economic agencies how they might contribute to citywide goals for strengthening the local economy. In the latter activity, the planning agency would be helping the private organizations to better understand the nature of the evolving challenges and possibilities and the implications of the government's plans for their own future plans.

That urban planning is required to cooperate with many actors on the urban scene is also illustrated by following through a city's decision to concentrate new growth in many activity centers (for example, something along the line of the goals of Los Angeles, as was noted in Chapter 2). The full cooperation of most municipal departments would be required, as would the cooperation of many elements of the private sector. If each activity center is to be capable of retaining most existing firms and drawing in new ones and is to make possible a broad mix of activities, attention would have to be directed to improving accessibility, parking, preparation of sites for industry, commerce and high-density housing, and the redevelopment of sections that have outlived their usefulness. Every city department that deals with building would thus have to be involved. And the private sector would have to become aware of the city's goals, forecasts, and plans. Its cooperation would be sought in every phase of the development of the various centers.

Urban planning must also be able to give individuals and families a useful foundation for their own plans. It can do this by spelling out the implications of the community's plans in terms that are meaningful to different groups in the community, including both the anticipated opportunities and the kinds of uncertainties that are seen ahead. These include the education of their children, opportunities for different lifestyles that will be available over time, recreational and cultural opportunities that can be anticipated, housing availability and prices, probable tax burdens, and so on. Such an exposition of implications must be totally credible, an honest presentation of what is known and what is not known, what is highly probable, and what is largely uncertain.

Citizen participation in urban planning and governmental policymaking can have little meaning and substance unless, at every stage in the planning and decision process, the implications of broad planning goals and strategies and of specific plans and programs are translated into terms that are real to the various groups in the community. City planning cannot be effective unless the plans and actions of individuals and families, as well as of various businesses and other institutions, are themselves congruent with the city plans. To refer to the earlier illustrations, city plans for the development of a services-based local economy and the encouragement of balanced residences and jobs in activity centers would be paper exercises unless businesses and individuals made investment, education, and home-choice plans in congruence with city plans (the latter hopefully reflecting a substantial communitywide agreement on the goals and approaches selected). Moreover, flexibility in city goals and planning strategy in the face of an uncertain future must be matched by similar flexibility on the part of individuals and businesses in their own plans and their own outlook on the future.

An essential part of the societal learning that has been shown to be critical in all urban planning focuses on this point—learning how urban planning can be an increasingly useful tool for individuals and institutions who also want to meet the future with the necessary flexibility in the face of built-in uncertainties—but within a generally accepted and understood strategy of urban development.

INCREMENTAL ACTIVITIES

The more firmly established the goals and planning strategy in a city, the more flexible and open can the execution phase be. When the city's planning effort is evident, there can be substantial scope for incremental, ad hoc private activities.

If there was agreement that the various activity centers and not the downtown alone would be strengthened and a full range of housing opportunities encouraged in the vicinity of the centers to reduce the need for worker commuting, then a wide variety of private construction and reconstruction could be allowed without worrying about zoning details. In such a case, the planning directives might provide outcome standards only (that is, standards dealing with the end results wanted). Private developmental proposals would be analyzed by a centralized permit office in terms of the likelihood of achieving desired outcomes. The highest quality proposals could then be chosen, with the first test of quality being adherence to the plan objectives. In many cases, such an approach would be more effective than trying to specify land uses controlled by detailed zoning.

Another requirement is essential if the dynamism of individual incremental decisions and actions is to be brought into the service of the city's goals and planning strategies: the need for firm and broadly understood municipal policies and programs for development. Such programs are needed to provide a specific foundation (of governmental actions and expenditures) for the desired private actions. But municipal actions and expenditures must first be brought into the service of the city's goals and planning strategy. Thus, to continue with the example used earlier, the strategy for strengthening the activity centers would require a coordinated set of actions on the part of several municipal departments, including those responsible for parking, streets, highways, economic development, community development, urban renewal, and police, as well as planning and zoning. The capital program and budget ought to provide for the required facilities for the planned development. The operating budget ought to provide for the necessary services, if the desired private activities are to be forthcoming.

The present weakness of many city planning agencies in achieving coordination among municipal departments in developmental activities stands out as a barrier to these objectives. In some cities, a strong mayor or planning-oriented city manager can bring about the desired coordination. Whatever the approach, coordination in achieving the public-sector part of the overall plan is essential if the necessary private incremental actions are to be in line with what is generally desired.

The ability to guide private actions in line with the planning strategy is critical. Most cities are severely constrained at this phase. Either they lack the appropriate resources with which to induce desired private actions or the categorical nature of the governmental incentives has rendered them unattractive to the private sector.

The judgment that cities often do not have enough incentives to induce the desired private actions is based on a study of urban renewal, model cities and new-towns-in-town (Perloff et al., 1975). These various urban activities, because they were encouraged by the federal government, actually had an unusual amount of support. Yet, in most cases, they fell far short of the municipal planning goals that had been set. More federal and state support for urban needs would have helped, of course.

But even more to the point, municipal goals and strategies should be realistic, given the funds that can be relied upon. The incentives themselves must be carefully chosen, again in line with the resources available. Thus tax exemptions, mortgage and other forms of insurance, the use of public powers such as eminent domain, tax-increment financing, and similar approaches can often provide strong leverages on private actions yet use far less public resources than direct subsidies and public investments. Relatively little study has been done of what it takes to achieve given levels of goals in urban planning or what benefits and costs there are in using various kinds of incentives. Knowledge of these matters becomes a key tool in the implementation phase.

Controls on private actions are very tempting to municipal politicians and bureaucrats as a way of trying to achieve the planning goals. Through specific controls, they can at least avoid undesirable outcomes that are politically damaging and threatening to their positions. Controls are an inevitable concomitant of urban planning, but their ability to induce private actions is limited. This is particularly true for most of the large central cities today when business and middle-class flight is both a continual reality and a constant threat.

City planning agencies have often been quite aware of the discouraging impact on development and redevelopment of the tangled regulations on private activities but have rarely taken a leadership role in reducing and untangling such regulations in order to create the appropriate environment for inducing the desired private activities. The ongoing study of the impacts of controls should be a high-priority feature of the implementation phase, as should efforts to simplify such controls (as in the creation of one-stop building permit centers).

INVOLVING ALL OF MUNICIPAL GOVERNMENT

Urban goals and strategies can be realized only if all of municipal government is involved in every phase of the planning process. In many cities, the long tradition of planning in isolation has still not been overcome. While urban planning everywhere is much closer to the operations of municipal governments and to the political arena than in past decades, a disturbing distance can still be found between the technical work that goes on in central planning agencies and the ongoing administrative and political processes of the municipal government.

In spite of a substantial literature in political science, public administration, and planning, which views planning as an integral part of ongoing municipal government, the central planning operation in many cities tends to be removed from the other parts of municipal administration. A major reason for the distance of urban planning from other municipal operations is the failure of the central planning activity to translate all of its plans and program proposals into terms that are operationally meaningful for other municipal agencies. Plans that focus on relatively abstract provisions for land uses cannot accomplish this. Only plans designed in terms of people and resources (particularly fiscal resources), places, and along clearly delineated time dimensions can serve as a bridge to other political and administrative operations.

The weaknesses, however, are not only in terms of the central planning activities themselves. The planning that goes on inside municipal operating agencies is generally confined to issues of immediate operating significance. This is as true of the agencies concerned with physical development as of the others. Redevelopment, transportation, public works, and water and sewerage agencies rarely develop citywide, time-conscious plans for their activities but, rather, tend to function on an ad hoc, project-by-project (and almost timeless) basis.

Effective city planning does not depend solely on the quality of the central planning operation. It depends in large measure on the caliber of the planning carried out by the operating agencies—particularly those with developmental and financial responsibilities. The current interest in strengthening management capabilities in municipal governments often entails an approach which has little or nothing to do with planning. This misses a critically important aspect of current municipal government responsibility. If the municipalities are to meet the problems and challenges of the significant urban transformations now underway, they must be equipped to relate not only their central planning activities but also the activities of the developmental and financial operating agencies to the requirements of these transformations. That means, among other things, developing a capacity for long-range planning among their key administrative agencies alongside the central planning agency. Only a strongly linked set of planning operations, interrelating the work of the major operating agencies with that of the central planning agency, can hope to meet the demands of the rapid changes underway.

If it is important to provide strong operating relationships between central planning's technical work and the technical work of the municipal operating agencies, then it is even more important to bring city planning significantly into the political arena. The mayor and the members of the city council cannot be expected to express much interest in abstract issues, such as conservation and preservation or housing improvement, but even the most abstract issues of city planning have real counterparts. These are in terms of jobs, income, housing availability, housing costs, housing values, neighborhood maintenance and decay, neighborhood services, taxes and governmental expenditures, and all the other questions that are the bread-and-butter of debates in the city council and decisions in the office of the mayor or city manager.

It is widely assumed that people in the neighborhoods care only about the most immediate problems and that active citizen participation in planning depends on bringing only current, narrow, neighborhood issues to the members of the community, and that urban politics necessarily reflects this limited view. But people do care about the quality of their neighborhoods and the value of their homes (or about the rents they must pay), the services they receive, and the taxes they pay. They care about the amenities (such as parks, playgrounds, and civic centers) as well as buildings of particular importance (such as schools and churches), and they have ties to various groups and (sometimes) even to the city as a whole. The fact is that what is done about the city and region's future will influence all these matters that concern residents, and somehow this must come across to the citizens as well as to the politicians.

From this, it becomes evident that the quality of communication (as well as of the plans, policies, and programs themselves) has a great deal to do with the extent to which urban planning really matters to the residents and political leaders of the city. The longer the time horizon being treated, the more critical the question of communication becomes. Maps and even three-dimensional models communicate only to a relatively small number of people, and the various planning reports that are the product of technical planning work can only be appreciated by other professionals and bureaucrats. Against this background, a good case can be made for the idea that popular participation in planning should be interpreted to include the involvement in planning (particularly in long-range planning) of a wide variety of talented communicators: poets, fiction writers, artists, actors, moviemakers, architects, educators, humanists, social scientists, and many others. One can begin to appreciate how many different areas of knowledge and talent need to be brought to bear on the great problems of urban development. Those with responsibility for city planning operations should be at the forefront in encouraging these beginnings and in making use of the diverse talents that are so urgently needed, particularly talents in the field of communication. The great art in city planning is to make members of the community—and their leaders—feel that what is involved is their future and that they must be a part of it.

IMPLEMENTATION OF PLANS

The individual urban community, as part of a vast interdependent national system of cities, has just so much control over its future development. It is subject to the dominant national socioeconomic trends as well as to the movement of people and firms within the individual metropolitan region. Given the existing arrangements in a federal system, financial assistance is needed from higher levels of government. This suggests that, in trying to achieve its goals and chosen strategies, it can optimize its chances of being successful by fully recognizing that implementation happens within an intergovernmental framework. This, in turn, has several ramifications. (1) The urban community needs good current information on what is happening "out there" and what others are planning. (2) It needs to join forces with other cities to negotiate shifts in responsibility for public services, such as welfare, education, and health among the various levels of government. (3) It should join forces with other cities to influence federal and state policies and expenditures toward long-run issues.

A municipality's planning can be realistic only if its goals and developmental strategies take into consideration the plans and policies of the other jurisdictions around it, such as federal, state, regional, and the neighboring local. A municipal strategy that specifically aims at coping with the vagaries of federal policies and programs is particularly important. In the past, most urban plans were removed from the specifics of federal policies and programs, while the municipal executive departments tied their actions to the ups and downs of specific federal grants. Municipalities have carried out public housing programs, urban redevelopment programs, highway building programs, model city programs, and others with volume, scale, and timing principally dictated by the ad hoc approach of grabbing for federal grants.

Municipal developmental strategy must be so designed that progress can be made in desired directions in spite of the ups and downs of federal and state funding. Scope and timing will certainly be influenced by such fluctuations, but the capacity to absorb these changes without giving up higher-order goals is a mark of sound planning. Under certain circumstances, cities might pass up federal grants to advantage (particularly where there are requirements for continued local expenditures over a period of time) in order to maintain their own priorities and not overburden their tax structure.

In the cities studied most closely, it was found that the municipal planning agency had little if any contact with the city agencies that handle federal and state grants. This type of isolation tends to be reflected in planning that is largely removed from the contextual considerations. The planning agency must have a detailed understanding of what is happening in intergovernmental fiscal relationships so that its planning can reflect the potentialities as well as limitations of such relationships.

City plans which show the extent to which urban development strategies can be carried out with anticipated local revenues and the extent to which they depend on outside funding and policies would provide significant information for municipal government in its negotiation with the federal and state governments. Today, federal policy is designed with little regard for what is contained in local plans—and for good reason. Such city plans do not show exactly what kinds of federal policies and programs would be most helpful or harmful to the city's overall urban strategy.

Similar considerations apply to state government. Urban planning agencies should be at the forefront of the local effort to bring about needed changes in state policies and programs (for example, in land-use regulations, formulas for the financing of social services, and housing finance programs). The goals and developmental strategy of city planning should not only encompass consideration of existing state policies and programs, but they should also show how the projected city programs would be influenced over the next decades by variations in state policies and programs. The need for given types of state laws and actions to assist the goals of the city should be spelled out in the city's plans and the anticipated impact of different types and volumes of state assistance made explicit. Ideally such plans should provide the mayor and local representatives to the state legislature with guidelines for influencing state laws, policies, and programs.

In comparable fashion, municipal planning should provide a base of information for the city's relationships with the surrounding communities. Some of these relationships are inevitably competitive; many others can be cooperative. The long-range plans of the city should show ways in which the cooperative relationships among the communities of the metropolitan region can be enlarged and deepened to mutual advantage (for example, in regionwide transportation, policies for the protection of amenity resources and open space, the reduction of air and water pollution, the provision for low- and moderate-cost housing, and the strengthening of the region's economy).

Municipal governments have joined forces in organizations such as the National League of Cities and the Conference of Mayors in part to pressure the federal and state governments for changes in policies, programs, and financial assistance favorable to the cities. There is very little flow of information from the municipal planning agencies that is directly helpful in these efforts. The mayors should be able to negotiate with federal and state officials based on solid knowledge of what it would take (in federal and state policies, programs, and financial assistance) to carry out the municipal plans. This is a very different matter from the kind of negotiation that takes place when a city applies for a federal or state grant and tries to demonstrate that the city projects to be financed by the federal or state grants fit the general plan. Urban planning should be an important tool in this kind of intergovernmental negotiations. If the plans of the northeastern cities had shown year after year, beginning in the late 1950s, exactly what was happening to these cities under the force of socioeconomic trends toward decentralization, the changes in federal urban policy might possibly not have been a full decade out of phase with the needs of these cities.

Only when urban planning addresses the critically important issues in all the key sectors—economic, social, and governmental, as well as physical—and the quality of the planning is such as to be fully credible in intergovernmental negotiations will the potential for implementation of relatively ambitious municipal goals and strategies be high.

Chapter 29
Implementation: Organization of Planning and the Recruitment and Education of Planners

The new paradigm for urban planning with which this volume has been concerned could be realized in a variety of organizational contexts. The ideal organizational setting for urban planning is an important subject in its own right. Two issues deserve mention here.

One is the very old issue of whether planning should become essentially a management function directly within the office of the mayor or city manager. This concept goes back more than a generation to the classic volume of Robert Walker, *The Planning Function in Urban Government* (1941). Within the past decade, the British have developed the concept of *corporate planning*—planning at the executive center for all matters that are within the purview of the municipal government—which closely resembles the Walker concept of planning (Cowan, 1973; Friend and Jessop, 1969). In this concept, planning joins the other staff functions of budgeting, personnel, and finance as a direct arm of the chief executive and is concerned with all municipal subjects, no matter how short or long range, that come before that chief executive.

In some U.S. cities, the mayor does rely on a planning agency for all sorts of management assistance. This has been true at various times in New York, Philadelphia, New Haven, and Boston, for example. But this has been a sometimes thing based on personal relationships between a mayor and the planning director. Usually, after a relatively brief period of management involvement, the planning agency reverts to its traditional functions in the developmental realms.

The trade-off here is obvious. As a purely staff function, planning would be close to the chief executive, be directly involved in matters of political importance, and have a substantial amount of clout. On the other side, it would undoubtedly have to devote its major attention to the more immediate issues and get around to the long-range developmental issues only when time allowed for them. The developmental issues would probably suffer. The author is inclined at this stage in the maturation of planning in the United States to favor a setting which emphasizes the urban *developmental* problems and possibilities, but the matter is too important and too complex to resolve without an in-depth study.

Another issue centers on the organizational capacity of planning to carry out needed developmental activities. The individual municipal departments—organized as they are along functional lines—cannot readily negotiate and work effectively with private developers and private business in general. The exception is the redevelopment agency which does have the necessary organization and power to be effective in this regard. Boston's experience in combining the planning and redevelopment agencies into one to ensure the implementation of the city's development plans deserves the attention of cities everywhere. But the traditional approach of redevelopment agencies is limited, focusing on already blighted areas and not encompassing important developmental problems in the city as a whole, for example, in helping to bring about the transition from manufacturing to a services economy. Areas around the nation have experimented with economic or industrial development agencies. In many cities, particularly in the manufacturing belt, such agencies have been organized as citywide or regionwide economic development corporation, often with mixed private and government ownership and direction. Such agencies may purchase land for sale or lease to businesses they are trying to attract, build industrial estates, and assist with the financing of new businesses. There has also been much experimentation with subcity community development corporations (CDCs). Some of these (such as the East Los Angeles Community Union) have a broad scope of planning and development activities, including the building of housing, running of supermarkets and other retail activities, and the training of minority workers.

The creation of a development agency with powers in all aspects of physical and economic development might well be needed in cities with difficult development problems. Such an agency might be strongly associated with the planning agency (or combined with it as in the Boston model). The issues involved are too complex to be resolved without further study. Greater effectiveness in the implementation phase of urban planning is urgently needed, and probably some significant changes in the organization of municipal government will be required.

THE RECRUITMENT AND EDUCATION OF PLANNERS

What kind or kinds of persons should be brought into the planning operation if it is to fit the specifications of the new paradigm proposed in this volume? The answer about planners in general has long been that since urban planning is a team activity, a wide variety of talents and personalities is needed. This is particularly the case for the kind of planning described in this volume as needed in the coming decades. In a close look, the problems of recruitment and education become extremely complex.

Let us begin with the chief planners: the mayor and the members of the city council. Starting with the assumptions that American cities (and cities in other industrialized countries) will be making a thorough-going transformation and that unusual leadership characteristics (marked by forwardlookingness and flexibility will be needed), how does a city ensure that such persons come into office? A continuing educational campaign through the public and private school system and through the media on the nature of the problems that urban communities face in the decades ahead would probably help to clarify leadership characteristics needed and may help to some degree to bring the right people into office. The establishment of a program to provide intensive training of newly elected officials, as is done in the Eagelton Foundation program in New Jersey and in the training program at the Kennedy Center of Harvard University would address this need more directly. The Eagelton program is especially appropriate since it focuses on local officials. Not too much can be included on any one subject, such as urban planning, but the training can alert them to the kinds of problems they will face and the kinds of assistance they should expect to receive. An important kind of training goes on in meetings of organizations that mayors attend, such as the Conference of Mayors and the National League of Cities.

The quality of the key staff officeholders in a municipal government and their sensitivity to and understanding of the long-range problems and possibilities of the city are also vital to the effective functioning of urban planning. Planning in a city cannot function well unless the city manager (if there is one), the chief administrative officer, and budgetary, financial, auditing and personnel officers are themselves planning minded and carry out their operations in close cooperation with the city planning department. The importance of the city manager and of the chief administrative officer to the planning that is done in the city is self-evident. The critical role of the various officials dealing with fiscal matters has been spelled out in previous chapters.

A more subtle connection arises in the case of personnel, but it is equally important to the requirements of long-range planning. This was described vividly by Daniel E. Berry, of the Kettering Foundation:[1]

> I think it is important to have a . . . municipal staffing plan for each department and/or agency which is integrated with the . . . speculation of alternative futures. Unless this is undertaken, it is extremely difficult to shift the bureaucracy to meet changing conditions because of public employee unions and the tendency of bureaucracies to become self-serving and perpetuate themselves. [An example] from my survey work with city managers in major world cities make(s) this point: . . . In London shifting the bureaucracy to meet new city needs is traumatic in the short run because of vested interests on the part of those who are directly employed by the service. The point is made by one respondent to my survey as follows:
>
> "In manpower terms you cannot just cut off programs in the sense that there is built-in resistance on the part of, shall we say the architects, who have been trying to build 6,000 units of housing per annum when future needs require only 2,000 units per annum. It is of little consolation to them that more technicians may be required to build roads and other infrastructure."

The importance of a municipal staffing plan to be able to understand the manpower requirements dictated by developmental and service proposals made by a planning department is symbolic of the interconnection of urban planning with the staff activities of a municipal government. The difficulties of executing such manpower plans also impact the possibilities of meeting plan goals and should be of concern to all parts of municipal government in times when financial cutbacks are prevalent.

Similar considerations arise in the case of the top officials of municipal departments and agencies who must clearly be involved in urban planning if it is to be effective. Without their cooperation, sensible municipal plans can neither be prepared nor carried out. The central role of a public works department in dealing with long-lasting municipal assets was spelled out in Part 3 of this volume and is symbolic of the role of all departments involved in developmental, infrastructure, and public service matters.

That there is understanding of the importance of these interconnections on the part of administrative officials is attested to by the fact that the most

[1] Personal communication: May 4, 1979.

substantial text in urban planning is brought out and revised periodically by the International City Managers' Association (It appears as part of a "Municipal Management Series" which also covers such topics as municipal finance administration and municipal public works administration). Still, persons who tend to rise to the top administrative posts in municipal government are more apt to be interested in and good at dealing with urgent current matters of administration than with long-range developmental issues. Only with a greater understanding of the long-run problems of the city can a greater emphasis on developmental interests and skills in the recruitment and promotion of administrative officers be developed. Here, too, the "public interest groups" can play a valuable role in training, including the provision of training materials.

The federal government can also play a highly significant role in bringing urban planning and the various aspects of administration into intimate juxtaposition. If the federal agencies could stop bouncing back and forth between a total emphasis on planning (as in the peak of the "701" period) to an overriding emphasis on management and could settle down on supporting the improvement of both in an interconnected manner, municipal governments would find it in their interest to think through how best to combine the immediate aspects of both planning and management with the long-run aspects of both planning and management. The art of combining these two is critical in the governing of municipalities who have to shift over consciously from an industrial to a postindustrial structure.

Finally, there is the question of the recruitment and education of professional planners and of other professionals who do planning. This issue has been researched and discussed at length over the whole period of the existence of the modern planning movement.

Urban planning needs individuals who can prepare strategies, policies, plans, and programs in the economic, social, physical, and fiscal realms, as well as to carry out economic, social, fiscal, and environmental analyses. The former, which might be referred to as the policy design skills, call for uniquely creative talents. The preparation of programs of economic development, of medium-range fiscal plans, or of large-scale redevelopment plans, for example, involve different kinds of wisdom and talents (including the talent for negotiation) from those involved in making analytical studies. The persons who are to prepare such strategies, policies, plans, and programs—working closely with the political leaders, the administrative officials, and the general public—must not only be well grounded in the subjects with which they deal but must have a deep understanding of how the political system works and how best to bring contending groups together while aiming at substantial improvements and new visions of the future. These are subtle and probably rare skills, but they are needed in a successful urban planning operation.

Urban planning, in seeking to meet present needs and future possibilities and images in a coherent manner, still needs the physical design skills. It is hard to conceive a better future which does not provide elements of physical beauty, drama, excitement, and compelling physical symbols of our culture. Physical improvements may not solve all sorts of social problems as has been assumed in the past, but satisfying architecture, urban design, and land-use arrangements are appropriate values and goals in their own right. They are important elements in reaching for high quality life in the future.

The analytical skills needed in urban planning of the type described in this volume are broader and deeper than those that have been typical in city planning departments in the past. Thus, following the time-related aspects of the future discussed earlier, some of the skills needed can be characterized as skills in:

- Asset-accounting analyses and capital-program and budget analyses (under the past aspects of the future).
- Analyses of urban system change and policy analyses—particularly the analyses of the impacts on the present of alternative choices for the future (centering on the present aspects of the future).
- Forecasting, model-building, and analyses of anticipated impacts of alternative futures (under the future aspects of the future).

There are beginnings in all of these areas in the better-endowed and more forward-looking planning agencies, but vast improvements are still needed in analytical abilities everywhere.

Much discussion has been held in recent years as to which of these skills the planner needs most urgently. This does not seem to be the best way of looking at skill needs. Urban planning, because of its unusual breadth and complexity, will inevitably draw on a variety of skills. Every large planning department has on its staff individuals with backgrounds in law, economics, architecture and urban design, geography, statistics, policy science, sociology, and/or other fields. This is likely to be the pattern of the future as well. Individuals who enter the urban planning field through training in planning itself should be expected to bring with them some generalist skills and some specialist skills through education in both process elements as well as substantive knowledge (including the workings of the urban system). Their specialist skills, as well as innate talent and personality, will determine where in the planning operation they can best function.

That, however, leaves the question of recruitment and education of the nonplanner specialist (the specialists brought in from outside the profession). This is an especially important question. The narrow specialist can be useless or even damaging to the urban planning operation. For example, the demographer who does not appreciate the relative costs and benefits of under- and over-estimations (as discussed in Part 5 of this volume) or the model-builder who cleverly proves that by discouraging low-cost housing the city can save all sorts of costs of services (thus implying the appropriateness of a beggar-thy-neighbor approach) will not be very helpful in dealing with the problems and possibilities of the postindustrial city. The various specialists are needed, but they will be functioning in a unique environment—the planning environment. They must, therefore, have—or acquire through additional training—an understanding and appreciation of the special problems involved in dealing with an operation that seeks to cope with present urban problems while trying to shape the future.

Chapter 30
Summing Up

URBAN TRANSFORMATION UNDERWAY

During the last two decades of the 20th century, urban planning will be functioning under special conditions. Its problems and potentials will derive from a special urban setting—a changeover from industrial to postindustrial status of cities.

Most of our major cities (unlike the big European cities) developed in the industrial age, during the latter half of the 19th century and the first half of the 20th. This was a time when manufacturing was the foundation of the economy, in employment as in output, and transportation technology required a clustering of economic activities as well as workers' homes. They either became industrial cities—such as Pittsburgh, Detroit, Cleveland, St. Louis, Buffalo, and Atlanta—or were strongly influenced by industrial-age ideas of city building—seeing the city as essentially a workshop. The city as a workshop was practical and brought workers and jobs together, but it was also basically ugly, with very few amenities, and little to make neighborhoods vital and livable. Even cities that developed in recent times, such as Los Angeles, Dallas, and Houston, borrowed city-building ideas from the industrial age. Only cities that were essentially resorts or service cities, such as university or government centers, did not follow the typical industrial urban pattern.

After the midpoint of the 20th century, it became increasingly evident that American cities were going through a major transformation, which scholars have labeled the move to a postindustrial society. The major features of this transformation have deeply impacted cities and give every sign of continuing to do so during the next two decades. Manufacturing has been diminishing in relative importance and has become increasingly footloose, that is, not tied to specific resources and transportation lines but able to move in response to markets and locational preferences of owners, managers, and workers. By midcentury, and increasingly since then, industry began to realize that it did not like what it had created. There were new industrial needs and new industrial styles, and the industrial city had been built with little scope for change and flexibility. So industry has simply been moving away from the city and has set up shop in the suburbs and in the outlying areas of the metropolitan region, leaving behind a mess, euphemistically called our urban problems. The seriousness of the urban problems is directly correlated with the extent to which a city had become a manufacturing city, with the Detroits and Clevelands in the greatest trouble and with those that are less manufacturing-oriented in less trouble.

The question becomes what do we do with our industrial cities and our industrial-style cities? How do we get them to adjust to the postindustrial age? City planning should, conceivably, be in an ideal position to guide cities in making the necessary adjustments. City planning is centrally concerned with urban development and redevelopment, and the problems involved in the transformation are developmental in large measure. City planning is supposedly concerned with anticipating future developments, as well as with urgent immediate problems, and the issues of adjustment to a new age abundantly involve both immediate and long-range features. Planning has at its core the idea of imaging a better future, and the potentials of the postindustrial age seem remarkably bright against the grayer image of the industrial-age city. Is city planning, then, playing its appropriate guiding role?

CITY PLANNING IN PRACTICE

A close look at urban planning practice in major cities and regions across the country suggests that planning is trying seriously to cope with the problems posed by the current urban difficulties and the complexities of adjustment to a major societal transformation. Planners in various cities are trying new approaches, while not necessarily abandoning the traditional ones and are even entering upon new areas of activities.

Significantly, planners in Boston have been addressing the economic problems of the city, including the decline of manufacturing jobs, and have been evolving new planning tools, such as the use of investment plans and neighborhood economic development plans. Planning in Cleveland during the 1970s concentrated on the immediate problems of the low-income groups in a city that was especially hard hit by the changes in manufacturing, seeing this approach as the logical reaction to severe industrial city decline. Planners in other cities have been less prone to emphasize the economic issues, but almost all of them have been concerned at least in strengthening the downtown area, building on the greatly increased service functions attracted to downtown. Improvements in transportation (including the building of rail mass transit) and redevelopment have been major tools. Urban planning in San Francisco has also emphasized preservation, restoration, and adaptive reuse of buildings and spaces as a response to changes in its situation, turning the urban design element into a major planning tool. Planners in Los Angeles and Phoenix have devised long-range plans (as well as short-range ones) aimed at maintaining residential character (in Phoenix in the form of villages) as well as strong activity/employment centers that could absorb the main thrust of growth. Regional planners in Atlanta have equally been concerned with the traditional land-use issues, but they have devised noteworthy planning approaches to evolving and deciding on alternatives of land-use/transportation developmental possibilities.

Planners in various cities seem to be going their own way, with little borrowing from each other or little learning from experiments elsewhere. Yet, most of them face the same difficulties: those associated with the socioeconomic changes underway (only Phoenix of the cities studied does not have to cope with problems of urban stabilization or decline), those stemming from the isolation of planning from many of the key municipal operating activities, and those resulting from the lack of planning approaches, tools, and action leverages appropriate to the tasks facing them. City planning is departing from its traditional paradigm—the physical master plan, with specific designations of land uses, as the comprehensive framework for its activities—but has not yet absorbed the evolving new paradigm focused on policies planning. This volume addresses the question of what are the features of a planning framework appropriate to the task of guiding cities through a very difficult societal transformation on to a better future—an urban environment that is satisfying to the people who live, work, and play in it.

Such a framework encompasses several elements: (1) a set of principles that can guide future planning practice, (2) identification of the features that characterize the **past, present,** and **future** aspects of a multidimensional view of the future, (3) an understanding of the possibilities for city planning of the available forecasting tools, and (4) a bolstering of the planning process so that it can effectively combine an open-options approach with an end-state approach to the future and more effectively combine the long range with the more immediate concerns of urban planning.

PRINCIPLES OF TIME-CONSCIOUS PLANNING

In trying to conceive the appropriate framework for future urban planning, valuable leads can be had from recent developments in social science theory. Particularly suggestive are the developments in the concept of *societal learning*, already having an impact on writings in planning theory. The theory of societal learning holds that history does not repeat itself even if certain features in the present have some resemblance to the past. There is instead a constantly evolving process based on learned reactions by members of a community. The problem is not mainly one of learning how to do the old tasks better, but rather one of learning how to meet new situations effectively. One of the most important processes is discovering how to improve learning capacity. The theory starts with a commonsense notion, but its implications are complex—and important. There has been a tendency to view governmental institutions as inherently problem-solving machines. We do not distinguish between tasks we know how to do reasonably well (such as having a water agency lay pipes to new homes) and those that we do not (such as asking a police department to prevent crime). People find it difficult to conceive any public agency as essentially engaged in a learning situation. *Learning* to deliver a service calls for a different approach than being in an established mode of delivering a service in an accepted and approved manner.

Urban planning has much to learn in carrying out the tasks assigned to it. Thus, planning does not know nearly enough about how the urban system works within a local jurisdiction to be able to help it function efficiently nor how to safeguard the environment without putting some jobs in jeopardy. The needed learning suggests the necessity of building research strongly into the planning process itself. There is need for an open organizational recognition of the concept that we plan as we learn, and a legitimization of experimenting on a small scale before launching large-scale efforts.

There is also the problem of the troubling lag in the application in practice of what has been learned. Thus, substantial improvements are needed in the techniques of monitoring so that a firm basis is provided for follow-through. An intensive effort is also needed in learning from the future and not just from the past and present alone. Planning derives much of its value in permitting this learning from the future—its constraints and its alternative possibilities. Planning can use the activity of reaching out to the future to help a community develop a learning posture.

A second principle concerns the importance of *images of the future* in community, as well as personal, decisionmaking and action. One's image of the future determines to an important extent how one thinks and acts and the same is true for collectivities; whether with optimism or pessimism, in short- or long-range terms, and whether assuming that events are within or beyond human control. Planning has always been involved with images of the future in one way or another, but value can be found in greater awareness in city planning of the role that individual and group images of the future play, and should play, in arriving at the goals and general strategy intended to guide local decisionmaking and action. Beyond that, there is the issue of whether planning is properly a translator of images already held or more appropriately a creator of images that will have a future impact on such decisions and actions. Ideally, it could involve each of these. It is at the very heart of the urban planning concept to seek for survival *and* betterment, and the latter calls for positive images of the future.

A third prinicple, the use of cybernetic models in developing knowledge for action in urban planning, is closely linked to the principles already discussed. Cybernetic models—based on concepts developed by Norbert Weiner and others—have been extended into many areas of human affairs, providing a framework for dealing with the accumulation, storage, and communication of knowledge and its use in human activities, particularly in societal decisionmaking and societal guidance or *self-steering*.

Amatai Etzioni has usefully examined the nature of a societal guidance system which can enable a community to act effectively in attempting to solve its problems and achieve the aspirations of its members. He sees this as involving the sound use of three elements: knowledge units, decisionmaking, and power, integrated in such a way as to bring about change in desired directions. A key feature is to get away from the disadvantages of both a pure rational-comprehensive approach and of a pure incrementalist approach to decisionmaking. To do this, he proposes a mix-scanning strategy which uses the best elements of each and avoids the disadvantages. *Mixed-scanning* involves making long-range, fundamental decisions concerning the future (adaptable to changes in values and priorities) as the evaluative criteria for short term, more detailed decisions. In a sense, this involves using two cameras: a broad-angle camera that would cover all parts of the sky but not in great detail, and a second one which would zero in on those areas revealed by the first camera to require more in-depth examination. The traditional physical master plan approach was actually based on a similar concept, with the broadly conceived land-use designations providing the long-range, fundamental decisions as the criteria for the short-range, more detailed decisions. Etzioni appropriately generalized the concept to cover all the various kinds of decisions involved in a governmental operation.

Etzioni regards current planning and decisionmaking processes in American society as overly incremental. Little long-range and comprehensive planning is based on solid knowledge. Instead, the tendency is toward muddling through, making limited adjustments on the basis of limited knowledge. The effectiveness of something like a mixed-scanning approach depends on the scope and quality of knowledge available to decisionmakers and to the community as a whole as well as the quality of the communication of such knowledge. Only if urban planning has the capacity for both in-depth analyses of trends emerging from the past and the imaging of desirable futures that reflect converging and negotiated values among various groups can it hope to create "high-order, fundamental policymaking processes" which set basic directions for the more immediate, incremental decisions.

A fourth, and final, principle suggests that local planning must continuously *determine the appropriate sources of knowledge and of political power and legitimacy* across the local horizontal spectrum (including the citizens and municipal agencies) as well as the verticle spectrum of the different levels of government. A key question is how best to involve citizen views, concerns, and aspirations in the planning process, while incorporating what professional knowledge can bring to bear on the process. This calls for a style of planning that involves *mutual learning* between the expert and the client (citizen) groups. Its success, as John Friedmann has pointed out, depends on developing effective means for interrelating the "personal" knowledge upon which the lay person or nonexpert in community groups must inevitably rely with the "processed" knowledge of the expert. This style of planning involves complex questions even in preparing neighborhood plans touching on immediate concerns; more difficult is the question of who is the client for the consideration of issues that have a broader (citywide or regional) impact and can only be achieved in the more distant future.

Broad representation is important. Particular efforts must be made to involve a wide range of interest groups, lifestyle groups, and age groups in a dialogue on the future. Much of the knowledge needed in urban planning as well as much of the power to implement planning decisions must come from the action agencies of the local government. The expertise (and authority) of the entire municipal government must be involved in urban planning if it is to be something more than a peripheral activity.

The question of expertness extends to the vertical plane, particularly in regard to that important part of knowledge which covers the larger context within which local planning must function. Expertise on subjects of regional, state, and national import cannot normally be available within the local government; a well-established flow of information and knowledge from higher levels of government is needed. Unless planning goes much further than it has in the past in providing knowledge extending over the whole urban hierarchy, mutual learning in urban planning can only be among different kinds of amateurs.

Some of the principles touched on here have already been seriously discussed in the planning literature and some have not. What is important in the present context is that they have yet to be fully incorporated into planning practice. Together, these principles provide a platform on which to build a new planning paradigm.

THE PAST, PRESENT, AND FUTURE ASPECTS OF THE FUTURE

Among municipal government activities, urban planning is uniquely involved with concerns that extend over the future—the short-run, intermediate, and long-run future. It is, therefore, particularly important for planning to be consonant with its various dimensions. On a practical plane, it must find ways of dealing effectively with the **past** (inheritance), **present**, and **future** aspects of the future. Important insights can be gained into what might be done to plan for the future (so that the future is more to our liking) by probing these three different elements of the future and being aware that all of them will ultimately come together into a single future.

The normal view of the future, stressing the element of change (that is, the newness element), tends by its very nature to bring the uncertainty feature to the forefront. It generates a tendency to overlook certain subjects about which decisions need to be made and action taken—for example, specific decisions on how long various physical and nonphysical features of the city should last into the future.

In a broader context, it is important to appreciate the centrality of the task for urban planning of reconciling continuity and change, for then all three components of the future can be seen to be of major concern for such planning. Many of the cherished values and features of our lives are lost in the jumble of unplanned changes about us. Planning has not attended seriously enough to the problems involved in holding on to the things enjoyed. Defined in a narrow way, continuity and change would seem to be inevitably in opposition to each other. Yet, what looks like an impossible task of reconciling seemingly opposing forces becomes a logical possibility when one realizes that one can hold on to the things one wants *only* by making certain necessary changes—often requiring planned public action in the social, economic, political, and/or physical realms. Only such planned changes will allow us to preserve the desired features in the face of the many changes that are taking place.

Clearly major problems exist for politics and for planning in attempting to reconcile the wishes and demands of those who are essentially satisfied with their lot and seek continuity in most features of urban life with the aspirations of those who want to move up. Urban planning can contribute to this extremely difficult governmental task by highlighting the benefits and costs of retaining over time the capital-in-place and features of the natural environment within the municipality. It can also contribute by evaluating the impacts on different groups and the community as a whole of alternative policy proposals looking to changes in the future. Finally, urban planning can provide a helpful framework for decisions influencing continuity and change by holding out images of alternative futures which largely mirror the views of community members as to areas in which betterment is particularly desired by different groups. In all of these tasks, planning has to learn to deal effectively with all three components of the future—past, present, and future.

The Past Aspects of the Future

At any point in the future, say 10 or 25 years hence, a city will be made up of much that is already in place, in addition to the features added between now and then. This suggests the importance of *inheritance* when one thinks about and acts for the future; this is the **past** component of the future.

The endurance of capital and other urban features involves benefits and costs. There are significant benefits in the additional resources (assets) that longevity makes available for carrying out the city's functions and in the comfort given urbanites by the availability of familiar features. There are also costs of longevity which appear in the form of constraints on the introduction of new technologies. The endurance of urban capital and urban patterns means that major urban transformations of the kind discussed at the beginning of this volume can only be carried out over long periods of time, barring unrealistically large resources dedicated to such changes in only a few years. Downtowns are not reconstructed to meet the requirements of a postindustrial society in less than several decades, nor can cities' layouts and work-residence locational relationships be made more energy efficient in short order.

Unfortunately, planning is not presently equipped to deal effectively with the inheritance component of the future because only limited informational capability is found in American cities for long-range planning decisions about physical plant. While fixed-asset accounting (covering land, buildings, equipment, and so on) is a well-established fixture of many municipal governments, it is related specifically to the management of public assets by operating agencies and to fiscal management. The information provided does not extend to the larger picture of the capacity of the urban plant to meet new community needs and demands, changing economic forms, or the requirements of community betterment over time. Urban rehabilitation and renewal in many cities is undertaken in a haphazard, project-by-project basis, weakly related to the long-run functional needs or fiscal capacity of the city. The wearing down of the physical plant can take place while funds are channeled to new projects without the true situation coming to decision points in a compelling way. However, recent discussion of crisis in urban infrastructure ("Repairs Lag, N.Y. Called in Peril of 'Wearing out'") may have provided the atmosphere for serious attention to the inheritance component in the coming decades.

Three areas hold promise of major improvements over present practices, areas which deserve further study by researchers and some experimentation in local government. These are (1) planning-oriented asset accounting (which deals with both physical and functional obsolescence), (2) the introduction of long-run planning considerations into the capital programming and budgeting process, and (3) changes in local government structure and operations.

The development of asset accounting for planning purposes would go substantially beyond recording the current physical condition of assets. The information sought might well include estimates of the degree of underutilization or above normal pressures in use; considerations of alternative uses of the assets (including adaptive reuse); economic values of existing and alternative uses; and the interrelationships among assets as well as the relationship of assets to their support systems and the surrounding environment. An economically troubled city might well consider the use of the concept of liabilities as a counterpoint to assets, not only the usually recorded public debts but a recording of those elements of the physical plant which block the achievement of the planning goals.

Planning-oriented asset reporting would have to be done with some care to convey timely information about capital assets to decisionmakers and the general public without drowning them in details. Ideally such reporting should provide a firmer base for major decisions on the five or six year capital program and budget and for the operating decisions on assets so that maintenance, rehabilitation, demolition, and renewal have some sensible relationship to the developmental needs of the city over the ensuing decades.

Unfortunately, in most cities, there is little interaction between the urban planning agency and the operating departments with regard to the capital portion of the budget—the place where decisions are made that affect the physical form of the city directly, with all its long-range implications. Without pressure for a long-range view of public investment in most instances, only the first year of a five year capital plan is used as the starting point and ending point for decisions about what actually get implemented. The items allocated for later years in the program are normally not taken seriously. The lack of meaningful multiyear fiscal planning and of substantial provisions for contingencies is particularly damaging to a planned approach to city development and redevelopment. If there is no reliance on the availability of fiscal resources for a number of years beyond the next one, the approach to capital programming and budgeting is almost certain to be pro forma, a simple exercise not to be taken too seriously.

While looking ahead over a period of 10 to 25 years, a city's general plan is supposed to provide the basis for the 5 or 6 year capital improvement program. That program, in turn, is to provide the base for the capital budget, encompassing proposed capital outlays and the revenues to finance such outlays. But in only rare instances does that happen. What is normally missing is a long-range capital improvement strategy translated into specific standards for capital asset management, as well as locational and other guidelines for public capital investment. Such strategy, standards, and guidelines have to be specific enough to offer a basis for joint development of the 5 or 6 year capital improvement program by the planning and operating agencies.

The Present Component of the Future

Just as focusing on the **past** aspect of the future serves to emphasize the importance of planning the inheritance of capital assets and other features of continuity so focusing on the **present** component of the future serves to bring to the forefront the importance to city planning of a strong information or intelligence capability. Planners need to grasp how the present situation has come into being and is evolving into the future and how present decisions are likely to impact people and places in the future.

Because present problems dominate the political scene, there is a tendency to see the better future as a later present in which the difficulties have been removed. However, the things to be eliminated are generally tied in to the social structure itself. It is not easy to remove the unwanted features in isolation, that is, without making some necessary changes in the system itself. That requires an understanding on how the urban system is evolving. It is important to know how the difficulties originated, what kinds of efforts in the past succeeded or did not succeed, which of the community institutions were effective in dealing with which problems, and the like. And it is equally important to try to conceive how the future community's urban structure may evolve—what might be called future history.

To provide the appropriate intelligence function for city planning, such planning must be able to describe and analyze the municipality as made up of several closely interrelated sectors evolving over time. Because the political/territorial community (the municipality for which the planning and the political decisions are being made and actions carried out) does not fully encompass certain of the sectors with which planning must be concerned—such as the regional economy and the air and water basins—a systemic municipality-within-the-region base of information must be developed.

The sectors with which a municipality must cope (brought to the fore by urban studies made by both scholars and planning departments) are in the economic, social, environmental, and governmental realms—themselves functioning subsystems. These sectors are interrelated in ways that can be explained and graphically displayed. They include asset items (people and things), financial flow items, and major institutions within each of the subsystems. Importantly, these sectors are not only the key to understanding how the city functions, but they are central to the definition of city problems (where it does not function well), to the evaluation of resources available to deal with the problems and to achieve goals for the future, and to the creation of policy and program proposals. They are the dominant threads of the urban fabric and of the content of urban planning.

Viewed in this broad context (focused on what municipal governments are trying to achieve), land use and its planning can be seen to be an important but limited part of the larger whole. The economic, social, broad environmental, and political/governmental sectors are all integral parts of the total picture and must be of central concern to urban planning if the goals and objectives of the community are to be achieved or approximated. All of them must be encompassed not only to understand how the municipality-within-the-region (the urban system) is evolving over time, but also to be able to analyze how to improve the system and how to approach the problems and possibilities of the future. For the future, urban planners must become more skillful than in the past at policy and action-program analyses which encompass total system improvements.

It is not always possible or feasible to try to improve the basic urban system in order to solve (or mitigate) the more troublesome current problems within the time horizon that is realistic in political and human terms. Problems often have to be attacked directly because some people or groups are suffering too much to wait for an improvement in the basic system (for example, problems such as the inadequacy of housing that poorer families can afford to rent). A good municipal data base should be able to show the relationship of the perceived problems to the workings of the urban system. A capable municipal planning agency should be able to provide reasonable figures on the costs and benefits or advantages and disadvantages involved in different approaches to the solution or mitigation of a serious problem or set of problems over time. A variety of approaches would have to be analyzed to determine the preferred approach, including consideration of:

1. Investment in built elements (that is, developmental expenditures).
2. Changes in rules of the game (for example, in regulations and other controls).
3. Reallocation of resources (for example, through subsidies or income supports).
4. Changes in service delivery.
5. Changes in selected values and/or behavior (for example, trying to change certain driving habits or certain kinds of prejudice).

Policy analyses by planning agencies should provide useful guidance to the municipal officials and the general public toward the most cost-effective approach that could be used and the degree of probability that the problem can be substantially mitigated over a given period of time through one or another of the possible approaches. What is particularly missing in most cases today is a consciousness of the length of time over which to devote attention to a problem and its solution. This kind of consciousness is essential both to avoid stopping before a reasonable effort has been made toward mitigation of the problem and to avoid waste by continuing too long on a given path.

Also deserving attention is the anticipation of new problems, that is, difficulties that are not seen as serious problems at the present time but which can be expected to increase in scale and/or intensity over time (for example, the set of problems that can be anticipated to stem from the ever-increasing proportion of women in the labor force); also problems that can be expected to emerge in the future as a result of identifiable forces at work today (for example, implications for demands made on urban services and facilities of the widespread use of flextime and part-time work). The capacity of planning to carry out sound analyses of such issues and to suggest policies and programs geared to such analyses will no doubt determine the extent to which municipal officials and the general public look to planning operations for guidance on difficult policy and program decisions.

The Future Aspects

The discussion of **past** and **present** aspects of the future has served to focus attention on features that are not normally thought of in connection with the future, but even the **future** aspects of the future are not yet well attended to. This is particularly true of the *possibilities* of the future.

Two different approaches can be used in trying to realize the possibilities of the future. The *open-options* approach attempts to position the municipality so as to be able to take advantage of any possibility that may appear in the future. The *end-state* approach involves defining the desired future specifically. The traditional physical master plan aimed at achieving the advantages of the end-state approach, but it had three major shortcomings: (1) relying on essentially abstract physical features which had only limited meaning and appeal to most people; (2) not providing for any contingency planning (that is, any means for dealing with surprises); and (3) normally not concerning itself with new possibilities for the future (those in the technological, economic, social, cultural, and political realms). On the other hand, it had several significant advantages in aiming to provide a strong image for the future and in providing a framework within which specific decisions and actions could be taken. The advantages of the traditional approach can be retained, while the disadvantages are removed, by the move to a broadly conceived, multisectoral *policies* planning framework which still aims to project a strong image of and for the future.

This still leaves scope for absorbing the favorable features of the open-options approach to the future. The open-options approach requires efforts to make the institutions of the municipality more flexible and more open to new opportunities; including the sponsorship of R & D in areas of particular importance to its well-being (for example, in building and managing public facilities and other life-support systems), so that it can better meet new situations as they arise, and the fostering of social experiments aimed at opening new opportunities (for example, in creating jobs and providing public services in poor neighborhoods through cooperative and self-help methods). Used in order to understand the possibilities of the future, R & D and social experimentation are logical arms of city planning.

In order for the urban general plan to evolve further as an instrumentality to encompass advantages of both the end-state and open-options approaches, substantial improvement is needed in urban planning in two directions. the first of these is in the *futurecasting* realm: the ability to forecast elements of the future, to image alternative better futures, and, in general, to be able to deal effectively with what lies ahead. The other direction is a sharpening and bolstering of the key phases of the planning processes.

Planning or acting without making assumptions about the future is impossible. When these assumptions are conscious, they take the form of forecasts. The more specific the assumptions, the easier it becomes to monitor actual developments and to learn something about the nature of the errors that have been made.

Techniques of forecasting have been developed in various fields, including the military, business and economic planning, and in technology. Certain of these methods are potentially applicable to city planning, but there has to be consciousness about appropriate fit. A useful way of considering forecasting methods and approaches is to relate available techniques to key planning processes. Robert Ayres suggests the logical idea of going from basically intuitive methods in goal-setting, such as brainstorming, gaming, Delphi, and scenario writing, to methods useful for rank-ordering in broad strategic planning, such as morphological analysis, cost/effectiveness, and PPBS, and on to the most quantitative and systems-related methods in getting down to specific programs and projects in tactical planning, including, cost/benefit analysis. While the logic is impeccable, a substantial amount of experimentation will be needed with various forecasting methods in the different phases of the urban planning process before there is a sense of appropriate fit in specific circumstances.

A similar consideration is involved in evaluating given forecasting methods in terms of the capacity of a local planning agency (or a neighborhood group) to use such methods. Dean Runyan has evaluated certain of the more common techniques of forecasting in terms of whether it is simple to use, does or does not rely on a large data base, and whether or not it is likely to provide new insights and information. Thus, for example, he suggests that the need to rely on sophisticated methodology and computers makes simulation modeling and input-output analysis inappropriate for use by local citizen groups, for example, in weighing local impacts of contemplated planning actions. It is conceivable that local groups might be provided with technical assistance so that certain of the more complicated methods could become appropriate. However, since Runyan's criteria are basically sound, they would apply as well in evaluating forecasting methods appropriate to a well-staffed planning agency in a large city.

Since the various forecasting techniques have been developed either as general purpose tools or for specific purposes which have only peripheral connection to urban planning, most of the methods have to be adapted to the needs of city planning if they are to be employed effectively. A good example of this is provided by the Delphi technique which has been used in many fields to establish the view of experts on the future. In the case of policy issues with which city planning normally deals (where policy choices are, in the end, value questions) the choice of the "experts" requires special consideration, with appropriate representation of various points of view and group positions more important than possession of technical knowledge in a given field. Just as cost/benefit and cost/effectiveness analysis had to be adapted to the special requirements of urban planning, and planners had to learn new skills in order to use these techniques productively, so can the newer forecasting methods be adapted to advantage.

Forecasting accuracy also has to be evaluated in a special way in city planning, as in certain other fields. Drawing on decision theory, it can be said that actions based on uncertain information (for example, on population forecasts) should be made by considering the political, economic, and technical risks of being wrong in a given direction. Both overestimating and underestimating growth pose certain potential problems or negative impacts, as with regard to making decisions on the capacity of public facilities. The costs of being wrong in different directions vary and should be considered in making the forecasts originally. In the case of population forecasts, for example, estimating the maximum possible increase is useful in noting the possible costs and difficulties of underestimation. This estimate might well be done independently of the demographic model, allowing for a comprehensive analysis not only of the demand side of the equation (natural increase and migration), but of the supply side as well (the carrying capacity of the area). The planning operation should treat various kinds of forecasts as part of the realistic range of possibilities in dealing with the evident uncertainty that planning always faces. One should not simply focus nervously on the actual accuracy of a single projection. Also, planning must seek to make the forecasting effort a usefully integral element of the political process of decisionmaking, including participatory approaches to population and other kinds of forecasting.

Finally, there is the issue of the appropriate time horizons in city planning. A choice among time horizons involves, in effect, asking different kinds of questions about the future. Quite limited questions arise about a one year or even five year view into the future because there are so many "givens" for planning in the near term. Only when the view is extended further into the future can questions be raised about changes in the basic urban system—and the urban transformations that are taking place.

Operational convenience, as well as forecasting, raises issues about time horizons. Many forecasts have to match the time horizons established by the requirements of planning operations. Political elections, budget cycles, departmental traditions and requirements, and many other factors tend to create decision points which, in turn, determine time horizons for forecasting.

John Platt has suggested a built-in logic in establishing time horizons for forecasting in terms of how much freedom or scope for collective action is available. He suggests three time scales: (1) an "inertia period," 2–10 years ahead, in which mechanistic projections are feasible and useful; (2) a "choice period," up to 20–40 years ahead, in which interactive models (man-environment-man) can be revealing; and (3) an "uncertainty period," beyond 20–40 years ahead, in which our present choices can be treated only by "some very general heuristics of values or moral rules that have worked in the past." The critical boundary in this concept is the end of the "choice period," since it is here that shifts in values become the dominant feature. This suggests the chief time components for planning as the near term of 2–10 years (as largely locked in to the various "givens" in the external environment) and a long-range horizon of up to 20–40 years with critical choices to be made.

These have counterparts in administrative experience and usage. The near-term "inertia" period has its parallel in the established budget and capital program periods, and many cities and metropolitan regions have 20- and 25-year "long-range" general plans. While capital programs and fiscal plans are projected on stable, everything-else-being-equal, assumptions, the long-range plans do not as openly reflect an appreciation of the opening up of "choices" over time—that is, the significant interaction between value systems of the members of the community and the constraints and opportunities which are set by the external environment. Forecasting and other planning operations would be strengthened if the logic behind the time-horizon selections was explicit and provided a platform for such activities.

A city planning operation which took seriously the long-term urban system transitions which cities have been experiencing and the even longer period over which the transitions toward a postindustrial society will play themselves out might well establish a framework which:

1. Analyzes developments over the past generation to highlight current and future problems and possibilities (to ensure an appreciation of the long swings involved and to get at the origins of the current difficulties).
2. Speculates on the implications for the municipality of possible developments over the next generation for most urban features and over the next two generations for a few trends and possibilities of special long-range interest.
3. Designs (with members of the community) a small number of alternative futures based on compelling images of the future and forecasts the impacts of each.
4. Creates an operational (policies) framework within which short-, medium-, and long-term implementing instruments (plans and programs ranging from 1 to 25 years) might be prepared through the political process.

Recognizing the inevitability of rapid change in all of the urban sectors, a sound city planning operation would have to provide for periodic revisions in all of these features.

BOLSTERING THE PLANNING PROCESS

If the best features of both the open-options and end-state approaches are to be realized, substantial improvements would be needed in the key phases of the planning process; in reality, the implementation of the logic of the new paradigm of urban planning.

A useful starting point is to view the substantive matters (the environmental, economic, social, and political/governmental subjects) in the same framework as its key processes (the establishment of goals, the development of implementing plans and programs). Each of the processes must encompass the various substantive sectors, so that, for example, goals are needed for the environment, for the local economy, for key features of the social structure, and for services delivery and other government activities. In the same light, strategies, policies, plans, and programs are needed for each of the sectors. If there is to be an integrating element to bring together the various sectors and processes, it is to be found in the "overarching images and philosophies" that can characterize the municipal planning. An official land-use plan for the city as a whole can no longer be regarded as an appropriate integrating element. "Overarching images and philosophies" in the current stage of planning would more appropriately be such integrating ideas as a conservation ethic, the encouragement of economic growth, the reinvigoration of the neighborhoods of the city, or the provision of additional choices to residents who have few choices.

The major sectors provide the backbone or structure of the urban planning activities. Even though they are closely interrelated, urban planning cannot treat them in a unified manner through giant computer models. It is important to study the interrelations by whatever means are at hand. It would be nice if we could press a computer button and immediately learn what the impact on jobs and income of various income groups would be of certain proposed major changes in land uses, but even if we cannot, studying such probable impacts is important through whatever rough-and-ready social science tools are available to us.

Urban planning, under the new paradigm for its effective functioning, must have the capacity, the will—and the authority—to deal with all four major sectors—the economic, the social, the broad environmental, and the political/governmental—and not the environmental alone as in the past. And, equally important, the various planning processes must be adjusted to a new world of strategy-and-policies planning as a substitute for the older, more limited physical master planning.

Establishment of Goals

Planning achieves its reason for being by helping to guide current decisions, not alone on the basis of helping political leaders to reconcile and pacify the contending pressure groups, but also by increasing the possibility of defining and achieving community goals. This is the feature that gives goals their importance.

It has long been appreciated that goals form a hierarchy, with some more ultimate in nature and some more instrumental. Distinct advantages can be had in clarifying just how basic the goals should be. Such clarification can be achieved by separating goals into three divisions.

Urban system goals are concerned with the outcomes of the urban system as a whole. They have relevance for all cities and over very long periods of time; thus, they are the most general and most long lasting of all. In the American context, such urban system goals include *efficiency, equity,* and *quality of life.* They have emerged from our urban history and provide the goals umbrella for urban planning; that is, they function even without open recognition of their role. Their reconciliation and prioritization are central to most urban decisionmaking.

General plan goals are the specific high-level, operational goals established to provide guidelines for general plans. These will vary from city to city and over time as conditions change, power shifts, and ideas evolve. Examples taken from the cities studied are goals to maintain the economic importance of the downtown area, to increase low- and moderate-income housing, and to reduce air and water pollution.

Instrumental goals are all the goals not encompassed by the first two categories. They essentially comprise the means of getting at the more general goals, including such endeavors as increasing or decreasing density levels, reducing scatteration in urban settlement, constructing a rail mass transit system, or providing financing for housing improvement.

In the case of lower-order goals, particular attention has to be given to the linking of physical and nonphysical objectives. Thus, economic and social/cultural goals have to be combined with environmental goals so that the physical development of the city and region is consistent with the nonphysical goals. This calls for a merging into a single planning operation some of the approaches now central to some cities, such as Boston's economic focus in its planning and Cleveland's social approach, with the more established and more common physical/environmental approaches of other cities. For example, adjustment to the growing economic importance of the service industries and of the communication revolution by the older cities will call for substantial changes in urban physical structure (including the city's relative attraction for living and working), in cultural features (education and the arts), in institutional capacity, and in approaches to protecting the relatively disadvantaged.

The linkage of physical and nonphysical goals, where an attempt is being made to reconcile the advantages of the end-state and open-options approaches, becomes more readily achievable if physical-form goals are posed whenever possible in terms of spatial relationships rather than in terms of specific locations. For example, goals for activity centers as a class would be more open to accommodating future options and opportunities as they arise than would goals specifically for the central business district or other existing centers (for example, industrial districts). Such general goals might relate to achieving certain environmental outcomes; achieving certain standards of mobility and parking; and achieving certain desirable relationships of work places and residences in and around the activity centers. In this way, the flexibility needed to provide for new human needs and new opportunities in the future can be retained.

The goals of urban planning must reflect the will of the people living and working within a given municipality. Important efforts have been attempted in various cities in involving community residents in goal-setting. There are several comments to be made about such efforts against the background of the principles discussed earlier. They should logically be carried out on a periodic basis, possibly every ten years. Members of the community should be conscious of the urban changes underway and professional planners must openly face the changing values of the community. The differences as well as the commonalities among the various income, ethnic, and age groups in the community must be a matter of conscious planning concern. Newer methods of dialogue will have to be employed in order to involve certain of these groups, including TV, classroom projects, computer gaming, and other methods. Also, this suggests that city planning has to be able to deal with a variety of goals for different neighborhoods, different lifestyles, and with different ways of viewing the community, the city, and the region.

To ensure that the municipalwide and regionwide factors are fully considered in goals efforts, care must be taken that organizations and interest groups reflecting such considerations be involved in the effort. Since expert knowledge about these broad matters, such as economic development, transportation and communications, pollution, energy conservation, is needed, use can be made of the Delphi method in the formulation of goals. This would help ensure that certain factors that are important in goal-setting, such as changing technology and population structures, were brought to bear on the goals effort. Such a combined use of both community-based nonexpert and expert opinion is needed not only in goal-setting, but in the creation of plans for the future and of instrumentalities for the execution of plans. This combination is essential to all facets of urban planning.

"Strategies-and-Policies" General Plans

For many years, urban planning has been moving in the direction of replacing the traditional mapped land-use general plan as the main tool for guiding municipal decisionmaking with a policies-or-strategy general plan. Such a shift is at the very center of a new paradigm for urban planning. The transition is by no means complete, however. The logic of guiding decisions of a developmental nature through policy planning has not yet been fully absorbed in the field of planning or by political officials.

One problem stems from the adherence by many practicing planners to certain beliefs about city development, such as the overriding desirability of separating the major urban functions, the desirability of maintaining the dominance of the downtown area, and the desirability of rail mass transit over other modes. Some of these beliefs—particularly the separation of land uses—have essentially given urban planning in certain places its very reason for being. But actually these are assumptions, mainly of an instrumental nature, and while they may well be the correct ones in certain municipalities at a given period of time, they are not ideal under *all* circumstances. They are matters to be decided by various kinds of calculations and continual testing of community preferences. For example, mixed land uses may well become a necessity in energy-shortfall situations.

These considerations argue for the advantages of working within a more general framework, a strategy-and-policies framework. The evolution of a developmental strategy, by its very nature, demands great clarity in defining the more ultimate goals that the community wants to achieve. And such clarity in goals is particularly important if advantage is to be taken of working through several possible alternative routes to achieving goals before specific policies, programs, and other tools of implementation are finally decided upon.

Strategies within the general plan could be expected to cover each of the major sectors. For example, in the economic realm, the relative emphasis to be given to the service industries as compared to manufacturing, and the emphasis to be given to strengthening the downtown as compared to other activity centers. In the social realm, the intensity of municipal efforts at improving the various neighborhoods (those in the poorest condition, those on the decline but with some strength, or those already making some efforts at self-improvement). In the physical/environmental realm, the balance of employment, housing, cultural, and other activities to be encouraged in the various kinds of activity centers. In the governmental realm, ways of strengthening the capacity of the municipal and regional governments to adequately perform the anticipated tasks of the next decades. These are only examples; the actual subjects covered within a given strategies-and-policies general plan would, of course, be geared to the special conditions, problems, and possibilities of that municipality.

Planners need to be genuinely creative in designing approaches to achieving community goals. No matter how much information is available for analytical purposes, no matter how much effective input there may be from other governmental departments and from the community, there still remains the need for a creative general plan design which provides the community and governmental officials with an understanding of where choices lie as they move into the future. The task is particularly demanding when alternative futures are considered—as they should be—since it takes great skill to make strategy-and-policy alternatives manageable and effective in decisionmaking.

The alternative futures approach permits a much more effective balancing of present values and needs as against future values and needs than does the traditional single intuitive conception of the best path to the future. The latter approach has permitted planners to hold on to values and ideas inherited from the past, which are of doubtful applicability to the present, much less the future. The alternative futures approach is needed to make planners themselves, as well as municipal politicians and the general public, more future oriented.

Use can be made of scenarios to make the alternative futures approach manageable. As a general principle, the most politically compelling scenarios are those focused on values rather than on technical considerations. Decisionmakers are likely to choose mixes rather than pure total sets (such as a pure "resources conservation" scenario or a pure "growth" scenario) to accommodate the people mixes that make up the municipality. Effectively designed packages of goals and strategies sharpen implications and permit choices reflective of different preferences and values. The scenarios should seek to ease the process of arriving at effective trade-offs.

The Art of Creating Policies, Plans, and Programs

Policies are the link between goals and general strategies on the one side and specific implementing plans and programs on the other. They express commitment to a course of action to meet the goals. The policies section of a general plan should ideally propose a specific legislative agenda for action. It should also present an agenda for administrative regulations and other forms of guidance to administrative bodies.

The policies section of the general plan, as well as policies recommended by the planning department in between general plan revisions, should be the product of choices among alternative paths. Even after specific strategies for achieving goals are chosen, there is normally a range of policy options along the pathway suggested by the strategies. A strategy that calls for "revitalizing declining parts of existing urban development" can be met by policies that call for emphasizing either private or governmental development (or certain combinations of both) and which require subsidies or strongly enforced regulations. The most attractive of the possibilities have to be evaluated and tested for responses through detailed interactions with builders, developers, various governmental officials, and a cross-section of citizens in various affected neighborhoods.

Land-use policies can set general standards to guide development by private interests, thus giving the developer choices among the geographic areas in which development may take place. This can be a substitute for specific land-use designations on the city map, or broad designations may be made and the standards might apply within the designated areas. This approach provides more choices and more ways in which trade-offs can be considered. If it is appropriate to go beyond mapped land-use designations in designing policies in the realm of land use, it is even more so when an urban planning operation considers how to carry out strategies in the economic, social, and political/governmental realms. To put everything into a land-use framework is to put the cart before the horse. Land-use designations and changes in land uses should appear when those are significant elements in realizing the goals that have been set for the city.

Planning through land-use maps has certain important advantages, however. It permits a comprehensive view of the whole municipality through a single lens. It not only permits comprehensiveness but consistency as well. Unfortunately it is also unidimensional when a multidimensional view is needed. It does not cover all the important sectors and all the important levers (other than land-use plans) that need to be used in achieving municipal goals. The other approach of a general plan that does not provide for coverage along any consistent and comprehensive lines also has its disadvantages. For it would then be hard to have a systemic view along any dimension; only a miscellany of plans, programs, and other implementating tools.

The best approach is to evolve a specially designated **implementation agenda,** which would contain the official land-use map and plan but would also contain certain other accounts and plans directed at carrying out the strategies and policies for urban development established by the municipal government. There are four such accounts and plans that can provide a municipalwide framework for urban planning appropriate to the needs of city government in the decades ahead. These are based on the major resources of a municipality as the appropriate foundation for planning.

1. *An asset account and plan* which would provide total coverage of the municipal plant in addition to providing the same advantages for the third dimension of the municipality as land-use offers on the ground.

2. A *land-use/natural resources account and plan* which would contain the present types of land-use record-keeping and plans but would be expanded to cover air and water also—including all natural amenity resources. Air and water carrying capacity as well as land capacity would be considered, as would use characteristics in all of them, thus, permitting demand/supply kinds of analyses.

3. A *manpower account and plan,* which would be comprehensive in terms of the human resources of the city, could be expected to focus on skills needed to provide for the present jobs and anticipated employment, for the necessary skills training, and for the expansion of employment within the city as a whole and within its various subareas, again, permitting demand/supply analyses.

4. *An investment plan and a fiscal plan,* which would encompass the other three and cover all public services and revenues, as well as public and private investments. A long-range fiscal plan, with five-year segments, would permit analyses of financial problems, including projected shortfalls. The availability of this kind of information would give the planning operation significant advantages over the normal budgetary operation by enabling it to relate projections to ongoing and proposed developments within the municipality.

These types of accounts and plans would provide urban planning with powerful tools of implementation. They are needed not only because they provide base information, but because they provide necessary frameworks for the establishment of concrete plans and programs to achieve the goals of the municipality.

The development of plans and programs for various elements, such as housing, transportation, land use, urban design, and safety, and for various neighborhoods of the city has been a valuable step forward in city planning. Most noticeable among the still missing features is the frequent lack of implementing levers other than land-use plans, subdivision controls, zoning, and building controls. Here the four sets of accounts and plans can be particularly useful. By subsuming the elements under the four sets of accounts and plans (for example, in matrix form), a checklist for comprehensive coverage could be provided. It would then become evident as to which features of which elements are actually provided for, and which are simply part of a wish list. Urban planning urgently needs this kind of reality structure, rather than the present mixed bag of plan specificity and wishful thinking. In the case of the individual neighborhoods of the city, specific time-related plans for infrastructure and other capital assets of the community, for land use, for manpower training and employment, for public and private investments, and for the financing of public services and facilities are needed to help mitigate the difficult neighborhood problems of the present and to provide significant improvements in the future.

Organizational and Operational Considerations

Given its developmental focus, urban planning should provide an important hinge function—that is, relate the governmental to the nongovernmental private development activities. Planners must seek to involve all the major institutions as well as the citizenry in the various phases of planning and development. What is particularly important is that city planning should seek to give private and public institutions, as well as individuals and families, a useful foundation for their own plans. Planning can do this by spelling out the implications of the municipality's plans in terms that are meaningful to different groups in the city, including both the anticipated opportunities and the kinds of uncertainties that are seen ahead. Citizen participation can have little meaning unless, at every stage in the planning and decision process, the implications of broad planning goals and strategies and specific plans and programs are translated into terms that are real to the various groups in the municipality.

The more firmly established the goals and planning strategy in a city, the more flexible and open can the execution phase be. Under such circumstances, substantial scope can be found for incremental, ad hoc private activities. Where development is to be encouraged, planning directives can provide outcome standards only (that is, standards dealing with the desired end results). Private developmental proposals could be analyzed by a centralized permit office in terms of the likelihood of achieving desired results. The highest quality proposals could then be chosen, with the first test of quality being adherence to the objectives of the plan. In many cases, such an approach would be more effective than trying to specify land uses controlled by detailed zoning.

Incentives to induce private actions must be carefully chosen, in line with available municipal resources. Tax exemptions, mortgage and other forms of insurance, the use of public powers, such as eminent domain, tax-increment financing, attractive leasing arrangements, reducing and untangling governmental regulations, and similar approaches can often provide strong leverages on private actions yet employ far less public resources than direct subsidies and public investments.

If planning directives are to provide a useful foundation for private actions, municipal government actions and expenditures must first be brought into the service of the city's goals and planning strategy. Developmental strategies require not only appropriately designed policies, plans, and programs by the planning department, but a coordinated set of actions on the part of many of the municipal departments, including those responsible for streets, highways, parking, economic development, community development, urban renewal, police, and often others. The capital program and budget ought to provide for the required facilities for the planned development, while the operating budget ought to provide for the necessary public services, if the desired private activities are to be forthcoming.

The central planning operation in many cities tends to be removed from the other parts of municipal administration. This is due in no small part to the fact that the planning department generally fails to translate its plans and program proposals into terms that are operationally meaningful for other municipal agencies. Plans that focus on relatively abstract provisions for land uses cannot accomplish this. Only plans designed in terms of people and resources (particularly fiscal resources), places, and along clearly delineated time dimensions can serve as a bridge to other political and administrative operations. Moreover, effective city planning does not depend on the quality of the central planning operation alone. It depends in large measure on the caliber of the planning carried out by the operating agencies—particularly those with developmental and financial responsibilities. Only a strongly linked set of planning operations, interrelating the work of the major operating agencies with that of the central planning agency, can hope to meet the demands of the rapid changes underway in American cities.

It is even more important to bring city planning significantly into the political arena. The mayor and the members of the city council cannot be expected to express much interest in abstract issues (such as conservation or general housing improvement), but these have real counterparts in terms of jobs, income, housing availability and costs, neighborhood services, taxes, and all the other questions that are the bread-and-butter of debates in the city council and decisions in the office of the mayor or city manager. Not only must the plans and programs of the planning agency and of the various municipal departments be translated into such real terms, but the idea of popular participation in planning should be interpreted to include the involvement in planning of a wide variety of communicators including poets, fiction writers, artists, media people, and social scientists. The many different areas of knowledge and talent need to be brought to bear on the great problems of urban planning and development.

The individual municipality, as part of a vast interdependent national system of cities, has just so much control over its future development. To optimize its chances of achieving its goals, it must fully recognize that implementation happens in an intergovernmental framework. Therefore, (1) it needs good current information on what is happening "out there" and what others are planning, (2) it needs to join forces with other cities to negotiate shifts in responsibility for public services among the various levels of government and to influence federal and state policies and expenditures, and (3) its development strategy should be designed so that progress can be made in desired directions in spite of the ups and downs of federal and state funding. Today, federal and state policies are designed with little regard for what is contained in local plans—and for good reason. With few exceptions, such city plans do not show exactly what kinds of federal and state policies and programs would be most helpful or harmful to the city's overall urban strategy. City plans should be an important means of communication with the higher levels of government and a challenge to those governments to join forces to help in achieving the goals of the individual municipalities.

Some Open Questions and a Final Note

The new paradigm for urban planning with which this volume has been concerned, consolidating the various lessons that can be learned from theory and actual practice, must still look to the effectiveness of implementation as the measure of success. Only when plans and programs are actually carried through, and the outcomes closely approximate those desired, can the whole planning operation be thought to be worthwhile. Many forces essentially outside the orbit of planning come into play. The nature of local politics and local leadership have a great deal to do with the outcomes as does the thrust of the local economy. The organization of municipal government—including that of the planning operation itself—is also significant, and mostly outside the power of planning. And the leadership and funding provided by the national government have a most powerful impact, no matter how the municipality may try to insulate itself from the worst effects of the federal government's generally erratic behavior. All these are important, and all these require careful study—in another context.

But urban planning has its own policy and power space, stemming from the broad recognition that people live in crowded, interdependent communities and that planning needs forethought to solve the most pressing problems and to create desirable environments in the face of rapid and bewildering changes. In its own orbit, city planning should be doing all it can to become a useful instrumentality in realizing the best aspects of both urban continuity and change. This calls for new approaches and new skills essentially directed at learning how to be in league with the future.

References

ADELSON, MARVIN
    1966. *Educational Ends and Innovational Means*. Los Angeles: Institute of Government and Public Affairs, University of California.

ALEXANDER, CHRISTOPHER
    1969. "Major Changes in Environmental Form Required by Social and Psychological Demands." *Ekistics* 28:165 (August):78–85.

ASCHER, WILLIAM
    1978. *Forecasting: An Appraisal for Policy-Makers and Planners*. Baltimore: Johns Hopkins Press.

ATLANTA REGIONAL COMMISSION
    1974. *The Atlanta Region: Framework for the Future*. Second interim status report, December.
    1976. *Regional Development Plan*.

AYRES, ROBERT U.
    1969. *Technological Forecasting and Long-Range Planning*. New York: McGraw-Hill.

BARLOON, MARVIN J.
    1965. "The Interrelationship of the Changing Structure of American Transportation and Changes in Industrial Location." *Land Economics* 41:2 (May):169–79.

BELL, DANIEL
    1966. "Twelve Modes of Prediction—A Preliminary Sorting of Approaches in the Social Sciences." *Daedalus* Vol. 95, No. 4 (Fall):845–80.
    1967. "The Year 2000—The Trajectory of an Idea." *Daedalus,* Vol. 96, No. 3 (Summer):639–51.

1973. *The Coming of Post-Industrial Society*. New York: Basic Books.

BELL, WENDELL

1974. "Social Science: The Future as a Missing Variable," in *Learning for Tomorrow*. New York: Random House, pp. 75–102.

BELL, WENDELL, and MAU, JAMES A., eds.

1971. *The Sociology of the Future: Theory, Cases and Annotated Bibliography*. New York: Russell Sage Foundation.

BIRCH, DAVID L.

1977. *The Community Analysis Model: An Overview*. Vol. 1. Cambridge, Mass.: Joint Center for Urban Studies of MIT and Harvard.

BLOHM, HANS, and STEINBUCH, KARL, eds.

1973. *Technological Forecasting in Practice*. Trans. Frederick and Cristine Crowley. Lexington, Mass: Lexington Books.

BOCK, EDWIN A.

1979. "Governmental Problems Arising from the Use and Abuse of the Future—The Last Colonialism?" in Dwight Waldo, ed., *Temporal Dimensions of Development Administration*. Durham, N.C.: Duke University Press, pp. 264–97.

BOLAN, RICHARD S.

1973. "Community Decision Behavior: The Culture of Planning," in Andreas Faludi, ed. *A Reader in Planning Theory*. Oxford, England: Pergamon Press.

BOLAN, RICHARD S., and NUTALL, RONALD L.

1975. *Urban Planning and Politics*. Lexington, Mass.: D.C. Heath.

BOSTON REDEVELOPMENT AUTHORITY

1977a. *Boston's Neighborhood Development Profile: Forging New Strategies for Public Investment and Development Program Design*. May.

1977b. *Boston in Perspective*. June.

1977c. *Why Boston?* July.

1977d. *Boston: State of the City Economy*. October.

1978a. *Boston's Economic Recovery*. April.

1978b. *The 1977 Recovery of Boston Employment*. September.

1979. *A Decade of Development*. May.

BOYCE, DAVID E.; DAY, NORMAN D.; and MCDONALD, CHRIS
1970. *Metropolitan Plan Making:* Philadelphia: Regional Science Research Institute.

BRANCH, MELVILLE C.
1974. *Planning Urban Environment.* Stroudsburg, Pa.: Dowden, Hutchinson & Ross.
1975. *Urban Planning Theory.* Stroudsburg, Pa.: Dowden, Hutchinson & Ross.

BROCKHAUS, WILLIAM L., and MICKELSEN, JOHN F.
1977. "An Analysis of Prior Delphi Applications and Some Observations on Its Future Applicability." *Technological Forecasting and Social Change* 10:1:103–10.

BURKHEAD, JESSE
1956. *Government Budgeting.* New York: Wiley.

BURNS, LELAND S., and GREBLER, LEO
1977. *The Housing of Nations.* New York: Wiley.

CAREY, JAMES W., and QUIRK, J. J.
1973. "The History of the Future," in George Gerbner, Larry P. Gross, and William H. Melody, eds. *Communications Technology and Social Policy.* New York: Wiley, pp. 485–503.

CHISHOLM, MICHAEL; FREY, ALLAN E.; and HAGGETT, PETER, editors.
1971. "Regional Forecasting: From Prologue to Epilogue," in *Regional Forecasting.* Colson Papers No. 22. Hamden, Conn.: Archon Books, pp. 453–67.

CLAWSON, MARION
1968. "Urban Renewal in 2000," *Journal of the American Institute of Planners* 34:3 (May):173–79.

CLAWSON, MARION, and HALL, PETER
1973. *Planning and Urban Growth: An Anglo-American Comparison.* Baltimore: Johns Hopkins Press.

CLEVELAND ACTION TO SUPPORT HOUSING
1977. *"Proposal to the Cleveland Foundation."* Mimeographed. June.

CLEVELAND CITY PLANNING COMMISSION
1974. *"The Policy Planning Report."* Mimeographed. January.

COLTON, KENT, and GOETZE, ROLF
1974. "Toward a Housing Policy and Program for the City of Boston." Mimeographed. Boston: BRA-MIT-Urban Dynamics Advisory Committee, Inc., January.

CONROY, MICHAEL E.
1974. *The Challenge of Urban Economic Development: An Evaluation of Policy Related Research on Alternative Goals for the Economic Structure of Cities.* Austin, Tex.: University of Texas Center for Economic Development.

COWAN, PETER
1962/63. "Studies in the Growth, Change and Aging of Buildings," *Transactions of the Bartlett Society.* 1:55–84.

COWAN, PETER, ed.
1973. *The Future of Planning.* London, England: Heinemann.

CURTIS, LYNN A.
1977. "The Politics of Consensus," *Social Policy* 7:4 (January/February):22–27.

DAHINDEN, JUSTUS
1972. *Urban Structures for the Future.* New York: Praeger Press.

DAVIDOFF, PAUL
1973. "Advocacy and Pluralism in Planning," in Andreas Faludi, ed., *A Reader in Planning Theory.* Oxford, England: Pergamon Press, pp. 277–96.

DE JOUVENEL, BERTRAND
1967. *The Art of Conjecture.* New York: Basic Books.

DEUTSCH, KARL W.
1963. *The Nerves of Government: Models of Political Communication and Control.* New York: Free Press.

DUNCAN, OTIS D.
1975. "Measuring Social Change via Replication of Surveys," in Kenneth C. Land and Seymour Spilerman, ed., *Social Indicator Models.* New York: Russell Sage Foundation.

DUNN, EDGAR S., JR.
1971. *Economic and Social Development: A Process of Social Learning.* Baltimore: Johns Hopkins Press.
1974. *Social Information Processing and Statistical Systems—Change and Reform.* New York: Wiley.

DYCKMAN, JOHN W.
1973. "What Makes Planners Plan," in Andreas Faludi, ed., *A Reader in Planning Theory.* Oxford, England: Pergamon Press, pp. 243–50.

EDDISON, TONY
1973. *Local Government Management and Corporate Planning.* Aylesbury, Bucks, England: Leonard Hill Books.

ELLMAN, TARA
1976. "Fiscal Impact Studies in a Metropolitan Context," in Paul R. Portney, ed., *Economic Issues in Metropolitan Growth.* Baltimore: Johns Hopkins Press, pp. 8–47.

ELLUL, JACQUES
1964. *The Technological Society.* New York: Random House.

ENCEL, SOLOMON; MARSTRAND, P. K.; and PAGE, W.
1975. *The Art of Anticipation.* London, England: Martin Robinson and Company.

EPLAN, LEON S.
1980. "Transit and Development in Atlanta." Report to the Subcommittee on the City, Committee on Banking, Finance and Urban Affairs, House of Representatives, 96th Congress, First Session. Washington, D.C.: U.S. Government Printing Office.

ETZIONI, AMITAI
1968. *The Active Society: A Theory of Societal and Political Processes.* New York: Free Press.
1973. "Mixed-Scanning: A 'Third' Approach to Decision-Making," in Andreas Faludi, ed., *A Reader in Planning Theory.* Oxford, England: Pergamon Press, pp. 217–29.

EVERED, ROGER DENNIS
1973. "Conceptualizing the 'Future': Implications for Strategic Management in a Turbulent Environment." (Ph.D. diss., Los Angeles: University of California at Los Angeles).

FALUDI, ANDREAS, ed.
    1973. *A Reader in Planning Theory.* Oxford, England: Pergamon Press.

FOWLES, JIB
    1976. "An Overview of Social Forecasting Procedures," *Journal of the American Institute of Planners* 42:3 (July):253–63.
    1977. "The Problem of Values in Futures Research," *Futures* 9:4 (August):303–14.

FRIEDMANN, JOHN
    1968. "An Information Model of Urbanization," *Urban Affairs Quarterly.* 4:2 (December):235–44.
    1973. *Retracking America: A Theory of Transactive Planning.* Garden City, N.Y.: Anchor Press/Doubleday.

FRIEND, J. K., and JESSOP, W. N.
    1969. *Local Government and Strategic Choice.* London, England: Tavistock.

GAKENHEIMER, RALPH A., ed.
    1965. "Process Planning: Symposium on Programming and the New Urban Planning," *Journal of the American Institute of Planners* 31:4 (November):282–338.

GANZ, ALEXANDER
    1974. *"Meeting the Needs of the City and Its People: A Long-Range Plan for Boston's Future—An Interim Report Reflecting New York and a Six-Month Public-Private Sector Dialogue."* Mimeographed. Boston: BRA-MIT-Urban Dynamics Advisory Committee.

GANZ, ALEXANDER, and O'BRIEN, THOMAS
    1973. "The City: Sandbox, Reservation, or Dynamo?" *Public Policy* 21:1 (Winter):107–23.

GAPPERT, GARY
    1973. "The Development of a Pattern Model for Social Forecasting," *Futures* 5:4 (August):367–82.

GARN, HARVEY A.; FLAX, M. J.; and TAYLOR, J. B.
    1975. *Models for Indicator Development: A Framework for Policy Analysis.* Washington, D.C.: Urban Institute.

GILMORE, DONALD R.
    1960. *Developing the "Little" Economies.* Supplementary Paper No. 10. New York: Committee for Economic Development.

GOETZE, ROLF; COLTON, K. W.; and O'DONNELL, V. F.
    1977. *Stabilizing Neighborhoods: A Fresh Approach to Housing Dynamics and Perceptions.* Boston, Mass.: Public Systems Evaluation, Inc.

GOLDBERG, LOUIS
    1960. *Concepts of Depreciation.* Sydney, Australia: Law Book Company.

GOODMAN, WILLIAM I., and FREUND, ERIC C., eds.
    1968. *Principles and Practice of Urban Planning.* Washington, D.C.: International City Managers' Association.

GORDON, T. J., and HAYWARD, H.
    1968. "Initial Experiments with the Cross Impact Matrix Method of Forecasting," *Futures* 1:2 (November):100–16.

GRAY, PAUL, and HELMER, OLAF
    1974. "*Summary Report: California Futures Study—Analysis of Impacts for Transportation Planning.*" Mimeographed. Sacramento: Division of Transportation Planning, Department of Transportation, Business and Transportation Agency, California.

GREENSTON, PETER, and SNEAD, CARL E.
    1976. *A Select Review of Urban Economic Development.* Washington, D.C.: Urban Institute.

GRIGSBY, J. EUGENE; PERLOFF, HARVEY S.; and SHAPIRO, PERRY.
    1973. *Prototype State-of-the-Region Report for Los Angeles County.* Los Angeles: School of Architecture and Urban Planning, University of California at Los Angeles.

HALL, PETER
    1971. *London 2000.* London, England: Faber & Faber.

HAMER, ANDREW MARSHALL
    1973. *Industrial Exodus from Central City: Public Policy and the Comparative Costs of Location.* Lexington, Mass.: D.C. Health.

HAYDEN, DELORES
   1976. *Seven American Utopias*. Cambridge, Mass.: MIT Press.

HAYNES, FREDERICK O'R.
   1975. "Citizen Access to Government," in Harvey S. Perloff, ed., *Agenda for the New Urban Era*. Chicago, Ill.: American Society of Planning Officials, pp. 85–100.

HEILBRONER, ROBERT
   1975. "Second Thoughts on the Human Prospect," *Futures* 7:1 (February):31–41.

HELLMAN, HAL
   1970. *The City in the World of the Future*. New York: M. Evans.

HELMER, OLAF
   1977. "Problems in Futures Research: Delphi and Cross-Impact Analysis," *Futures* 9:1 (February):17–30.

HINES, THOMAS
   1974. *Daniel Burnham*. New York: Oxford University Press.

HIRSCH, WERNER Z.
   1973. *Urban Economic Analysis*. New York: McGraw-Hill, pp. 297–395.

HIRSCH, WERNER Z., and SONNENBLUM, SYDNEY
   1970. *Selecting Regional Information for Government Planning and Decision-Making*. New York: Praeger.

HOLLEB, DORIS B.
   1969. *Social and Economic Information for Urban Planning*. Chicago: University of Chicago, Center for Urban Studies.

HOWELL, ANNE V.
   1977. *Los Angeles City Government: From Pueblo to Metropolis*. Los Angeles: Department of City Planning.

HUDSON, B. M.; WACHS, M.; and SCHOFER, J. L.
   1974. "Local Impact Evaluation in the Design of Large Scale Urban Systems," *Journal of the American Institute of Planners* 40:4 (July):255–65.

IKLÉ, FRED C.
 1967. "Can Social Predictions Be Evaluated?" *Daedalus* 96:3 (Summer):733–58.
 1971. "Social Forecasting and the Problem of Changing Values," *Futures* 3:2 (June):142–50.

JACOBS, ALLAN B.
 1978. *Making City Planning Work*. Chicago: American Society of Planning Officials.

JACOBS, JANE
 1961. *The Death and Life of Great American Cities*. New York: Random House.

JANTSCH, ERICH
 1967. *Technological Forecasting in Perspective*. Paris: Organization for Economic Co-operation and Development.
 1972. *Technological Planning and Social Futures*. New York: Wiley.

JENCKS, CHARLES
 1971. *Architecture 2000*. London: Studio Vista.

KAHN, HERMAN, and WEINER, ANTHONY J.
 1967. *The Year 2000*. New York: Macmillan.

KENDRICK, JOHN W.
 1964. *Guidelines for the Improvement of Wealth Data and Estimates*. A report of the Wealth Inventory Planning Study. Washington, D.C.: George Washington University.

KLAASSEN, LEO H.
 1965. *Area Economic and Social Redevelopment: Guidelines for Programmes*. Paris: Organization for Economic Co-operation and Development.

KLAASEN, LEO H., and PAELINCK, JEAN H. P.
 1974. *Integration of Socio-Economic and Physical Planning*. Rotterdam: Rotterdam University Press.

KOVITZ, RAY
 1978. "Phoenix Moves Forward to Claim Its Place in the Sun," *Los Angeles Times*, February 12, part 9, pp. 1, 29.

KRUMHOLZ, NORMAN
  1977. "The Aging Central City: Some Modest Proposals." Akron, Ohio: University of Akron Conference on Older Metropolitan Regions, May 27.

KRUMHOLZ, NORMAN, and COGGER, JANICE
  1977. "*The Challenge to Municipal Finance at a Time of Increasingly Limited Local Revenues.*" Mimeographed. Cleveland: City Planning Commission.

KRUMHOLZ, NORMAN; COGGER, JANICE; and LINNER, JOHN
  1965. "The Cleveland Policy Planning Report," *Journal of the American Institute of Planners* 41:5 (September):298–304.
  1976. "Physical Planning in Change . . . The Role of Environmental Planning: Make No Big Plans . . . Planning in Cleveland in the 70's." Mimeographed. Rutgers, N.J.: Rutgers University Conference on "Planning: Challenge and Response," September 8 and 9.

KUHN, THOMAS S.
  1964. *The Structure of Scientific Revolutions.* Chicago: University of Chicago Press.

LEE, DOUGLAS R., JR.
  1973. "Requiem for Large-Scale Models," *Journal of the American Institute of Planners* 39:3 (May):163–78.

LEE, EVERETT S.
  1966. "A Theory of Migration," *Demography* 3:1:47–57.

LEE, ROBERT D., JR., and JOHNSON, RONALD W.
  1977. *Public Budgeting Systems.* Baltimore: University Park Press.

LEVY, FRANK S.; MELTSNER, ARNOLD J.; and WILDAVSKY, AARON
  1974. *Urban Outcomes.* Berkeley, Calif.: University of California Press.

LINSTONE, HAROLD A., and TUROFF, MURRAY
  1975. *The Delphi Method: Techniques and Applications.* Reading, Mass.: Addison-Wesley.

LONG, NORTON E.
  1975. "Another View of Responsible Planning," *Journal of the American Institute of Planners* 41:5 (September):311–16.

LOS ANGELES COMMUNITY ANALYSIS BUREAU
   1977. *An Ethnic Trend Analysis of Los Angeles County 1950–1980.* Los Angeles, Calif.: Community Development Department, December.

LOS ANGELES DEPARTMENT OF CITY PLANNING
   1967. *Population Projection Model Application.* January.
   1969a. *Hollywood Community Plan Study.* June.
   1969b. *Los Angeles Goals Council Summary Report.* November.
   1970. *Concept Los Angeles: The Concept for the Los Angeles General Plan.* January.
   1971. *A User's Manual for a Demographic Allocation Model.* July.
   1972a. *Northeast Los Angeles District: Preliminary Plan.* March.
   1972b. *Westwood Community Plan: Preliminary Plan.* March.
   1974a. *Concept Los Angeles: The Concept of the Los Angeles General Plan.* April.
   1974b. *Derivation of 1990 Projected Single Family and Multiple Dwelling Units and Persons per Occupied Dwelling Unit Factors Used in August 1974 Revision of Housing Element of the City of Los Angeles General Plan.* August.
   1974c. *Environmental Impact Report for the Northeast Los Angeles District Plan.*

LOS ANGELES DEPARTMENT OF WATER AND POWER
   1972. *Water System Proposed Capital Expenditures: Five Years Ending June 30, 1977.* April.

MARRIS, PETER
   1974. *Loss and Change.* London: Routledge & Kegan Paul.

MARTINO, JOSEPH P.
   1972a. *Technological Forecasting for Decision-Making.* New York: American Elsevier.

MARTINO, JOSEPH P., ed.
   1972b. *An Introduction to Technological Forecasting.* New York: Gordon and Breach Science Publishers.

MARTINO, JOSEPH P., and CHEN, KUEI-LIN
   1978. "Cluster Analysis of Cross-Impact Model Scenarios," *Technological Forecasting and Social Change* 12:1 (June):67–71.

MATOFF, TOM
1977. "*Five Year Plan 1977–82; Issue Paper II: Transit Planning Thought in San Francisco.*" Mimeographed. San Francisco: Municipal Railway Planning Division. June.

MENCONERI, PETER; KANE, MARTIN; and SCHWARTZ A.
1974. "*Jobs, Manpower and Education.*" Mimeographed. Boston: Boston Redevelopment Authority–MIT Urban Dynamics Advisory Committee, Inc.

MEYERSON, MARTIN
1956. "Building the Middle-Range Bridge for Comprehensive Planning," *Journal of the American Institute of Planners* 22:2 (Spring):58–64.

MICHAEL, DONALD N.
1973. *On Learning to Plan—and Planning to Learn*. San Francisco: Jossey-Bass.
1974. "Speculations of Future Planning Process Theory," in David R. Godschalk, ed., *Planning in America: Learning from Turbulence*. Washington, D.C.: American Institute of Planners, pp. 35–61.

MIER, ROBERT; VIETORISZ, THOMAS; and GIBLIN, JEAN-ELLEN
1975. "Indicators of Labor Market Functioning and Urban Social Distress," in Gary Gappert and Harold M. Rose, eds., *The Social Economy of Cities*. vol. 9. Urban Affairs Annual Reviews. Beverly Hills, Calif.: Sage Publications, pp. 361–94.

MUSGRAVE, RICHARD A.
1959. *The Theory of Public Finance*. New York: McGraw-Hill.

MUTH, RICHARD F.
1969. *Cities and Housing: The Spatial Pattern of Urban Residential Land Use*. Chicago: The University of Chicago Press.

NUTT, BEV; WALKER, BRUCE; HOLLIDAY, SUSAN; and SEARS, DAN
1976. *Obsolescence in Housing*. Lexington, Mass.: D. C. Health.

OLSON, MANCUR
1973. "Evaluating Performance in the Public Sector," in Milton Moss, ed., *The Measurement of Economic and Social Research*. New York: National Bureau of Economic Research, pp. 355–409.

OLSON, SUSAN

1973. "*Cleveland's Urban Renewal Experience: Implications for the Use of Community Development Revenue Sharing Funds.*" Mimeographed. Cleveland: Cleveland Planning Commission. December.

1974. "*Impact of New Construction on the Market for Existing Downtown Office Space: Implications for the City's Revenue Base.*" Mimeographed. Cleveland: Cleveland Planning Commission. June.

PACK, JANET ROTHENBERG

1975. "The Use of Urban Models: Report on a Survey of Planning Organizations," *Journal of the American Institute of Planners* 41:3 (May):191–99.

PARADISE VALLEY PLANNING COMMITTEE

1976. "Paradise Valley Area Plan." Mimeographed. Phoenix, Arizona. June.

PERLOFF, HARVEY S.

1957. *Education for Planning: City, State, and Regional.* Baltimore: Johns Hopkins Press.

1963. *How a Region Grows.* Supplementary Paper No. 17. New York: Committee for Economic Development.

1969. "A Framework for Dealing with the Urban Environment," in Harvey S. Perloff, ed., *The Quality of the Urban Environment*. Baltimore: Johns Hopkins Press, pp. 3–31.

1978. "The Central City in the Postindustrial Age," in Charles Leven, ed., *The Mature Metropolis*. Lexington, Mass.: Lexington Books, pp. 109–30.

PERLOFF, HARVEY S.; BERG, TOM; FOUNTAIN, ROBERT; VETTER, DAVID; and WELD, JOHN

1975. *Modernizing the Central City.* Cambridge, Mass.: Ballinger Publishers.

PERLOFF, HARVEY S., and FLAMING, DANIEL J.

1976. "Approaches to the Future in U.S. Urban Transportation Planning," *Transportation* 5:2 (June):153–73.

PERLOFF, HARVEY S., and WINGO, LOWDON

1962. "Planning and Development in Metropolitan Affairs," *Journal of the American Institute of Planners* 28:2 (May):67–90.

PHOENIX PLANNING DEPARTMENT
1971. *Central Phoenix Plan.* September.
1972. *The Comprehensive Plan 1990.* March.
1975. "*Urban Form Directions: Committee Summary Reports.*" Mimeographed. Phoenix: Urban Form Directions Committees. November.
1977. "*Urban Form Directions: Phase II.*" Mimeographed. Phoenix: Urban Form Directions Committees September.
1979a. "Urban Form Directions: Planning for Phoenix to the Year 2000 AD," Draft, March.
1979b. *Interim Plan for Phoenix to the Year 1985.* March.
1979c. *An Overall Economic Development Program for Phoenix, Annual Update.* July.

PIKIELEK, FREDERICK
1974. "*Boston's 1975-1985 Public Facilities Program and Its Role in Achieving Goals for the People of the City and Their Neighborhoods.*" Mimeographed. Boston: Boston Redevelopment Authority. June.

PITTSBURGH REGIONAL PLANNING ASSOCIATION
1963. *Region with a Future.* Economic Study of the Pittsburgh Region, Volume 3. Pittsburgh: University of Pittsburgh Press.

PLATT, JOHN
1971. "How Men Can Shape Their Future," *Futures* 3:1 (March):32–47.

POLAK, FRED
1961. *The Image of the Future: Enlightening the Past, Orienting the Present, Forecasting the Future.* 2 volumes. New York: Oceana Publications.
1973. *The Image of the Future.* trans. Elise Boulding. San Francisco: Jossey-Bass.

POLE, J. R.
1978. *The Pursuit of Equality in American History.* Berkeley, Calif.: University of California Press, 1978.

PRESCOTT, JAMES R., and LEWIS, W. CRIS
1975. *Urban-Regional Economic Growth and Policy.* Ann Arbor, Mich.: Ann Arbor Science Publishers.

PRESSMAN, JEFFREY L., and WILDAVSKY, AARON B.
1973. *Implementation.* Berkeley, Calif.: University of California Press.

PUBLIC AFFAIRS COUNCIL
   1975. *The Dynamics of Neighborhood Change.* Report prepared for the Office of Policy Development and Research. Washington, D.C.: U.S. Department of Housing and Urban Development.

PYKE, DONALD L.
   1970. "Technological Forecasting: A Framework for Consideration," *Futures.* 2:4 (December):327–31.

RABINOVITZ, FRANCINE F.
   1970. *City Politics and Planning.* New York: Atherton Press.
   1973. "Politics, Personality and Planning," in Andreas Faludi, ed., *A Reader in Planning Theory.* Oxford, England: Pergamon Press.

RHYNE, RUSSELL
   1974. "Technological Forecasting Within Alternative Whole Future Projections," *Technological Forecasting and Social Change.* 6:2 (1974):133–62.

RIECKEN, HENRY W., and BORUCH, ROBERT F.
   1974. *Social Experimentation.* New York: Academic Press.

ROSE, RICHARD
   1974. *The Management of Urban Change in Britain and Germany.* London, England: Sage.

RUNYAN, DEAN
   1977. "Tools for Community-Managed Impact Assessment," *Journal of the American Institute of Planners.* 43:2 (April):125–35.

SAN FRANCISCO DEPARTMENT OF CITY PLANNING
   1971a. *"The Comprehensive Plan: Residence."* Mimeographed. San Francisco.
   1971b. *"The Urban Design Plan for the Comprehensive Plan of San Francisco."* Mimeographed. San Francisco.
   1972. *"Transportation Element of the Comprehensive Plan of San Francisco."* Mimeographed. San Francisco.
   1973a. *"The Comprehensive Plan: Recreation and Open Space."* Mimeographed. San Francisco: July.
   1973b. *"Residence: Strategy and Programs."* Mimeographed. San Francisco: December.
   1974. *"The Comprehensive Plan: Community Safety, a Proposal for Citizen Review."* Mimeographed. San Francisco: July.

SAN FRANCISCO REDEVELOPMENT AGENCY
    1977. *"San Francisco Redevelopment Program: Summary of Project Data and Key Elements."* Mimeographed. San Francisco: January.

SARIN, RAKESH K.
    1978. "A Sequential Approach to Cross-Impact Analysis," *Futures* 10:1 (February):53–62.

SCHON, DONALD A.
    1963. *Displacement of Concepts.* London, England: Tavistock.
    1971. *Beyond the Stable State.* New York: Random House.

SCHUMAKER, E. F.
    1973. *Small Is Beautiful.* London: Blond & Briggs, Ltd.

SCHWEDER, TORE
    1971. "The Precision of Population Projections Studies by Multiple Prediction Methods," *Demography* 8:4 (November):441–50.

SCOTT, MEL
    1971. *American City Planning Since 1890.* Berkeley, Calif.: University of California Press.

SHAW, R. PAUL
    1975. *Migration Theory and Fact.* Philadelphia: Regional Science Research Institute.

SHUIT, DOUG
    1975. "Phoenix at Crossroads," *Los Angeles Times.* September 7, Part 2, pp. 1, 3.

SIEGEL, JACOB S.
    1972. "Development and Accuracy of Projections of Population and Households in the United States," *Demography* 9:1 (February):51–68.

SNYDER, JAMES C.
    1977. *Fiscal Management and Planning in Local Government.* Lexington, Mass.: D. C. Health.

SONNENBLUM, SYDNEY
    1968. "The Uses and Development of Regional Projections," in Harvey S. Perloff and Lowdon Wingo, eds. *Issues in Urban Economics.* Baltimore: Johns Hopkins Press, pp. 141–85.

SOUTHERN CALIFORNIA ASSOCIATION OF GOVERNMENTS (SCAG)
   1976. "*SCAG-76, Growth Forecast Policy.*" Mimeographed. January.

SOUTHERN CALIFORNIA RAPID TRANSIT DISTRICT
   1973. "*Rapid Transit for Los Angeles: Summary Report of Consultant's Recommendation.*" Mimeographed. July.

SOUTH PHOENIX PLANNING COMMITTEE
   1976.*Area Plan for Phoenix South of the Rio Salado.*" Mimeographed. Phoenix: May.

SPRING, JOHN J.
   1975. "Proposition J: Procedures and Funding Strategy." Memorandum to Citizens Advisory Committee, San Francisco.

STEGMAN, MICHAEL A.
   1972. *Housing Investment in the Inner City: The Dynamics of Decline.* Cambridge, Mass.: MIT Press.

STERNLIEB, GEORGE, and HUGHES, JAMES W.
   1977. "New Regions and Metropolitan Realities of America," *Journal of American Institute of Planners* 43:3 (July):227–40.

STRAUS, PETER
   1977. *Five Year Plan 1977–82; Issue Paper I: Muni Metro.* San Francisco: Municipal Railway Planning Division. May.

SUSSKIND, LAWRENCE
   1973. *Understanding Technology.* Baltimore: Johns Hopkins Press.
   1975. "Strengthening Planning and Management," in Harvey S. Perloff, ed., *Agenda for the New Urban Age.* Chicago: American Society of Planning Officials, pp. 49–68.

TABB, W. K.
   1972. "Alternative Futures and Distributional Planning," *Journal of the American Institute of Planners* 38:1 (January):25–31.

THOMPSON, WILBUR R.
   1966. "Urban Economic Development," in Werner Z. Hirsch, ed., *Regional Accounts for Policy Decisions.* Baltimore: Johns Hopkins Press, pp. 81–130.

THUROW, LESTER, and THUROW, CHARLES
    1975. "Equalizing Public Services," in Harvey S. Perloff, ed., *Agenda for the New Urban Era*. Chicago: American Society of Planning Officials, pp. 69–78.

TOFFLER, ALVIN
    1969. "Value Impact Forecaster—A Profession of the Future," in Kurt Baier and Nicholas Rescher, eds., *Values and the Future*. New York: Free Press, p. 1–30.

TUROFF, MURRAY
    1970. "The Design of a Policy Delphi," *Technological Forecasting and Social Change* 2:2:149–71.

UMPLEBY, STUART A.
    1972. "Is Greater Participation in Planning Possible and Desirable?" *Technological Forecasting and Social Change* 4:1:61–76.

VAN TIL, JOHN
    1979. "Spatial Form and Structure in a Possible Future: Some Implications of Energy Shortfall for Urban Planning," *Journal of the American Planning Association* 45:3 (July):318–29.

VANSTON, JOHN H., JR.; FRISBIE, W. PARKER; LOPREATO, SALLY COOK; and POSTON, DUDLEY L., JR.
    1977. "Alternate Scenario Planning," *Technological Forecasting and Social Change* 10:2:159–80.

VERNON, RAYMOND
    1959. *The Changing Economic Function of the Central City*. Supplementary Paper No. 6, New York: Committee for Economic Development.
    1960. *Metropolis 1985: An Interpretation of the Findings of the New York Metropolitan Region Study*. Cambridge, Mass.: Harvard University Press.

WACHS, MARTIN
    1979. *Transportation for the Elderly*. Berkeley, Calif.: University of California Press.

WALKER, ROBERT A.
    1941. *The Planning Function in Urban Government*. Chicago: University of Chicago Press.

WEBBER, MELVIN M.
    1968. *"Explorations into Urban Structure."* Mimeographed. Philadelphia: University of Pennsylvania Press.
    1971. *"On Strategies for Transport Planning."* Mimeographed. Berkeley, Calif.: Institute of Urban and Regional Development, University of California.
    1973. *"On the Technics and Politics of Transport Planning."* Mimeographed. Berkeley, Calif.: Institute of Urban and Regional Development, University of California.
    1976. "The BART Experience—What Have We Learned," *The Public Interest* 45 (Fall):79–108.

WEINER, NORBERT
    1961. *Cybernetics.* New York: Wiley.

WHITE, KEVIN H.
    1974. *"Boston's Tax Strategy: The Fiscal Experience of the City."* Mimeographed. Boston: Office of the Mayor. May.
    1975. *"Boston's People and Their Economy: Mayor Kevin H. White's Program: A Summary."* Mimeographed. Boston: Office of the Mayor. July.

WHITE, KELVIN H., and KENNEY, ROBERT T.
    1973. *Planning for Boston's Neighborhoods.* Boston: BRA-MIT-Urban Dynamics Advisory Committee, Inc.

WILCOX, LESLIE D.; BROOKS, RALPH M.; BEAL, GEORGE M.; and KLONGLAN, GERALD E.
    1972. *Social Indicators and Societal Monitoring: An Annotated Bibliography.* San Francisco: Jossey-Bass.

WINGO, LOWDEN, ed.
    1963. *Cities and Space.* Baltimore: Johns Hopkins Press.

WINGO, LOWDON, and EVANS, ALAN, eds.
    1977. *Public Economics and the Quality of Life.* Baltimore: Johns Hopkins Press.

WOLF, PETER
    1974. *The Future of the City.* New York: Whitney Library of Design.

WOLFE, HARRY B.

1967. "Models for Condition Aging of Residential Structures," *Journal of the American Institute of Planners* 33:3 (May):192–96.

WRIGHT, DOUGLAS G.

1973. *"Comparative Analysis of Housing Programs."* Mimeographed. Cleveland: City Planning Commission. June.

Index

Advocacy planning, 54-55, 111-12, 224
Amenities, 17, 121, 245, 247, 259
Assets account and plan, 247, 251, 252, 294
Asset accounting, 114, 131-32, 133-43, 152, 157, 249-50, 279-80
Asset management, 125-26, 152
Assets, preservation of, 12, 229
Atlanta
    background, 73-74
    ethnic community in, 73
    regional planning in, 20, 73-80, 84-85, 172, 271, 273
    transporation in, 73, 76-77
Atlanta Regional Commission, 74

Bay Area Rapid Transit (BART), 35, 40-41
Boston
    attempts by, to learn from past, 152
    background, 43-44
    development of downtown, 45, 48-49
    economic focus of, 20, 43-51, 227-28, 248
    neighborhood revitalization in, 45, 48, 49-50, 51
    population structure of, 43-44, 47-48
    planning approach of, 45-50, 82, 84-85, 86, 173, 187, 209, 216, 272, 289
    urban renewal in, 44
Boston Plan, 50
Boston Redevelopment Authority, 44-45, 264
Brainstorming, 192, 193, 284
Britain, urban planning in, 109-10
Budget planning, 87
Buffalo, New York, 271
Bureau of Social Science Research, 196
Burnham, Daniel, 6

Capital, endurance of, 123
Capital maintenance, 145-53
Capital programming/budgeting, 9, 132, 139, 145-53, 157, 208-9, 210, 279-80
Centers concept (Los Angeles), 25, 26-27, 31, 32
Central Arizona Project, 65-66
Chicago, 6, 22, 104
Cincinnati, Ohio, 152
Cities
    and decisions of the future, 174
    decline of central, 9, 13, 16
    development of, 221-22, 271-72
    fiscal pressures on, 18-19
    need of, for information, 171

older, 173
problems of, 3, 16
process of change in, 11
Citizens, participation of, in urban planning, 28, 36, 69-70, 79, 112-13, 255, 276, 295, 297
City council, role of, in urban planning, 22-23, 105
City planning; *see* Urban planning
City planning agencies/departments, role of, 3, 7-8, 36, 256-57
Cleveland
  background of, 53-54, 56
  block grants in, 62
  dependency of, on federal government, 55, 59, 63-64, 115
  ethnic makeup of, 53-54
  housing in, 59-60, 61
  income policy in, 58-62
  population in, 53
  revitalization in, 54, 55, 59, 61
  urban planning in, 20, 53-64, 82, 111-12, 172, 209, 216, 224, 225, 227, 228, 271, 272, 289
  urban renewal in, 53, 62
Common good, promotion of, 107-8
Communication(s), in urban planning, 16, 107, 259-60
Community development departments, role of, in urban planning, 23-24, 32, 264
Community groups, involvement of, in urban planning, 112-13, 121-22
Community-managed impact assessment, 194
Conference of Mayors, 262, 265
Conservation, as inheritance issue, 130-32
Construction (new), effect of government decisions on, 145-53
Contextual information, 171-72
Contingency planning, 8, 87
Corporate planning, 263
Cost/benefit analysis, 56-57, 61, 86, 131, 191, 192, 193, 194, 197, 202-3, 223, 229, 241, 250, 284, 285
Cost/effectiveness analysis, 193, 194, 197, 284, 285
Cost/revenue analysis, 86
Creative learning, 95
Cross-impact analysis, 192, 194, 197
Cybernetic model, 102-3, 107, 108, 157, 161, 162, 275

Dallas, Texas, 152, 230, 271
Decision framework, 161
Decision theory, 200-5
Delphi technique, 193, 194, 195-97, 232, 284, 285, 290
Department of Water and Power (Los Angeles), 21-22, 31
Depreciation, in asset accounting, 137
Detroit, Michigan, 271, 272
Downtown, strengthening of, 45, 48-49, 82, 123, 140, 239
Downzoning, 224

Eagelton Foundation Program, 265
Economic elements, as subject in

urban planning, 88, 215, 216, 217-18, 235-36
Economy, changing role of urban, 15-17
Efficiency, as urban-system goal, 129, 221-24, 231
Elements, development of plans and programs for, 250-52, 295
End-state approach to future, 182-84, 283
   in combination with open-options approach, 186-87, 215, 228, 253, 290
Energy, need to consider in urban planning, 17-18, 143, 234-35, 239
Energy Policy Project, 240
Environment, consideration of, in urban planning, 26, 38-39, 82, 88, 105, 215, 216, 217-18, 226, 236-37,
Environmental impact reports (EIR), 26, 30, 42, 86, 191
Equity, as urban-system goal, 129, 224-25, 231
Extrapolation of trends, 191, 192

Family Assistance Plan, 59
Feasability, 207, 248
Federal government
   and municipal development strategy, 260-62
   role of, in urban planning, 7-8, 9-10, 23-24, 50, 55, 59, 63-64, 97-99, 112, 115, 168, 267
   use of grants, 10, 170, 172, 224
Federally Assisted Code Enforcement (FACE) program, 37
Feedback, need for, 86-87, 103-4
Fiscal-impact analysis, 259
Fiscal planning, 157, 248-50, 280
Fixed-asset accounting, 133-34
Forecasting
   accuracy of, 199-205, 285
   approaches to, in time-conscious planning, 189-98
   different techniques in, 114, 191-98, 284-85
   need for, 284-86
   problems with, 87-88
   and statements about future, 189-91
   time horizon in, 207-12, 286-87
Frankfort, urban planning in, 6
Functional obsolescence, 137-39
Future, 4-5
   alternatives to, 84-85, 238-42, 292
   end-state approach to, 182-84
   future aspects of, 120, 181-212, 277-78, 283-87
   images of, 101-5, 107, 116, 119, 157, 161, 274-75
   open-options approach to, 182-83, 184-85
   past aspects of, 119, 151-53, 277-80
   present aspects of, 119-20, 157-59, 277-78, 280-83
   and the time horizon, 87-88, 227
Futurecasting, 187

Gaming, 192, 193, 284
General plan, 8-10, 24-26, 45,

109-10, 130-31, 150, 152
General-plan goals, 220, 289
Gentrification, 13, 130
Glendale, Arizona, 65
Goal-achievement matrices, 86
Goals
    combination of nonphysical with physical, 227-30
    definition of, 219
    establishment of, 215, 216, 217-18, 219-32, 288-91
    as feature of urban planning, 36-42, 45, 83-84
    hierarchy and variety of, 219-21
Goals council/committee, 25, 104
Governmental/administrative structure, in urban planning, 215, 216, 217-18, 237
Grantsmanship, 112, 115
Growth management, 126

Historic districts, 130, 131
Hollywood, California, 28-29
Housing, as issue in urban planning, 82, 126-28, 135, 141-42, 160-61, 251
Housing and urban renewal, as inheritance issue, 126-29, 131-32
Houston, Texas, 271

Impact analysis, 86, 191
Implementation
    development of plans and programs for, 215, 216, 217, 243-52
    and organization of planning, 263-65
    and the recruitment and education of planners, 265-69
    requirements of, 253-62
    weaknesses in, 86-87
Implementation agenda, 246-50, 294
Incentives, use of, 134, 256-57, 296
Income, relationship of, to welfare, 165, 168
Income policy, in Cleveland, 58-62
Income redistribution, 82
Information
    about the future, 182
    availability of, for equity analysis, 225
    in time-conscious planning, 162
    in time-oriented planning, 163-77
    need for, in planning, 129, 139, 217-18, 250
    reverse flow of, 171-72
Information system, elements of, 163-71
Infrastructure, role of, in community goals, 152
Inheritance
    as aspect of urban planning, 123-32
    as component in future, 119, 157, 278-79
    planning approaches to question of, 139-43
In-migration, 18
Input-output analysis, 192, 194
Instrumental goals, 220, 289
Intuitive judgment, 193
Investment, focus on, in planning,

Index

86, 140
Investment leveraging, 46, 48
Investment plans, 248-50, 251, 252, 294

Jobs and economic development, 82

Kuhn, Thomas, 4n, 96

Land banking, 61
Land-use controls, and the natural environment, 170
Land-use maps, use of, in planning, 246-47, 293-94
Land use/natural resources account and plan, 251, 252, 294
Land-use plans, as implementing lever, 295
Land-use policies, use of, to set standards, 245
Land uses
  forecasts of, 87
  as issue in planning, 82
Learning, role of, in urban planning, 95-99, 103-4, 112, 161
Liabilities, as counterpoint to assets, 142
Lifetime-earning-power index, 168
Linear programming, 193
Lobbying, 59
Los Angeles
  background, 21-24
  and the centers concept, 25, 26-27, 31, 32, 83
  city government of, 22-24
  citywide plan of, 25-26, 27-28, 209
  community plans in, 26, 209
  concept Los Angeles, 25, 26-27, 83
  coordination of land-use with physical development in, 22-24
  current decisions about capital in, 146-50
  ethnic makeup of, 22, 30
  focus of urban planning in, 21-33, 230, 231, 254, 271, 273
  goal formation in, 83, 230
  general plan format, 24-26, 32-33
  and issue of physical degeneration, 137
  physical size of, 22
  plans of operating agencies, 23, 30-32
  population of, 21
  and subcity community development corporations, 264
  transportation in, 25, 29

Man-machine game, 193
Manpower account and plan, 247-48, 251, 252, 294
Manufacturing and process industries, 15-16
Mapped land-use plans, 177, 233-25
Massachusetts Law 121A, 45
Master plan
  as appropriately named, 7
  basis for, 151
  development of, 6, 7, 114, 191
  evolution away from, 8, 91-92, 183

focus of, 159
learning from experience with, 151-53
make-no-little-plans slogan of, 14
physical, 275, 283
versus policy planning approach, 10, 84-85, 218
weaknesses of, 4, 10, 87-88
Mayor, planning role of, 105
Mesa, Arizona, 65
Mixed-scanning approach to urban planning, 109, 110, 275
Model cities program, 175, 256
Modernization, as term, 129
Morphological analysis, 192, 193, 284
Muni (Municipal Railway), use of, in San Francisco, 41
Municipal data base, need for, 174
Municipal developmental strategy, 260-62
Municipal Finance Officers Association, 134
Municipality-within-a-region, 160, 163, 169, 171, 231, 281
Municipal planning, 18-19, 257-60, 260-62, 276-77, 297
Municipal policies plan, 10
Mutual learning, 276

National Alternative Inner City Futures Project, 196
National Committee on Governmental Accounting, 134
National League of Cities, 262, 265
National Planning Association's Metropolitan Area Projections, 171

National Resources Planning Board, 8
Natural resources, 17-18, 105, 170, 182
Neighborhoods
  defense of character of, 12
  development of plans and programs for, 250-52
  halt decline of, 140
  importance of, in urban planning, 39-40, 49-50, 111, 113-14, 259
  improvement of, 121-22
Network analysis, 193
New Haven, Connecticut, 263
New-towns-in-town, 128, 175, 256
New York City, 35, 134, 152, 223, 230, 263, 279
Northeast Los Angeles, 30

Oakland, California, 147
Obsolescence, of buildings, 135-39, 141
Open-options approach to future, 182-83, 184-85, 283-84
  combination of, with end-state approach, 186-87, 215, 228, 253, 290
Open space, as planning element, 38-39
Operational convenience, 207-8, 286
Operation research/systems analysis, 193
Out-migration, 18

Paradigm, development of new, 4, 157-62, 163, 176-77, 217,

Index

263
Paradigm change, 96
Parkinson's Law, 108
Past, as component in future, 119, 151-53, 277-80
Philadelphia, 8-10, 130-31, 263
Phoenix, 67, 70
   background, 65-66
   city government of, 66
   ethnic composition of, 65
   planning approach of, 20, 65-71, 83, 86, 273
   population of, 65, 66
   transportation in, 70-71
Phoenix Concept Plan 2000, 67-71, 83-84
Physical obsolescence, 135-37
Pittsburgh, 271
Planners: *see* Urban planners
Planning-approach to urban planning, 123-26, 139-43
Planning-oriented reporting, and asset accounting, 139-43
Planning-process considerations, 215-18
Policy analysis, 10, 114, 174, 176
Policy planning, 10, 84-85, 88, 233-35
Political/territorial municipality, 160-62
Pollution, effect of, on urban life, 17, 54
Population forecasting, 87, 171, 190, 191, 199, 210, 285-86
Population structure, 17, 170
Preservation, focus on, 20, 35-42, 130-32
PPBS (Planning, Programming, Budgeting System), 193
Present, as aspect of future, 119-20, 157-59, 277-78, 280-83
Property tax, 39, 45, 47
Property values, protection of, 12, 13
Public facility, capacity of, 202
Public housing projects, 37, 158-59
Public works programs, 7-8

Quality of life, as urban system goal, 129, 225-26, 231-32

Redevelopment authority, 37, 44-45, 264
Rejection-of-the-past phenomenon, 4
Regional planning, in Atlanta, 20, 73-80, 84-85, 172, 271, 273
Research and development (R&D), role of, in urban planning, 12, 185, 284
Resources, human, use of, in urban planning, 217
Revenue sharing, 112

St. Louis, Missouri, 271
San Francisco
   background of, 35-36
   city government in, 35-36
   concern for environment in, 38-40
   concern for water in, 41-42
   ethnic makeup of, 35
   goals, planning elements, and action agencies in, 36-42
   neighborhood planning in, 39-40

planning focus of, 20, 35-42, 84, 130-31, 273
pride of citizens in, 35
size of, 3
transportation in, 35, 40-41
San Francisco Planning and Urban Renewal Association (SPUR), 39
Scenario-writing, 192, 193, 194, 197, 239-40, 284, 292
Scottsdale, Arizona, 65
Seattle, Washington, 104, 230
Self-determination, as dimension in urban planning, 108
Self-directing systems, 161
Service industries, 16-17, 227-28
in Los Angeles, 26
Significant Ecological Areas (SEAs), 245
Simulation modeling, 192, 194
Social elements, and urban planning, 88, 215, 216, 217-18, 236
Social impact studies, 86
Social mobility, 170
Societal guidance, 108, 275-76
Societal learning, 95-99, 103-4, 115-16, 157, 211, 255, 274
Southern California Association of Governments, 204
Southern California Rapid Transit District (SCRTD), 31-32, 149
Strategies-and-policies general plans, 291-92
as alternatives to future, 238-42
art of creating, 243-52
development of, 215, 216, 217, 218, 233-42

subjects of, 235-38
Structural degeneration, 136
Subject matter, as feature of urban planning, 82-83

Tempe, Arizona, 65
Time, as three-fold present, 157-59
Time horizons, development of, appropriate, 207-12, 227, 286-87
Transactive planning, 112, 161
Transportation, as issue in urban planning, 25, 29, 31-32, 35, 40-41, 60-61, 70-71, 73, 76-77, 82, 113, 141
Trend extrapolation, 194

Urban conservation, 130
Urban development, 8, 15-19
Urban economic development, 172
Urban Institute, 171
Urban planning
in actual practice, 272-73
application of societal learning theory to, 95-99, 103-4
approach of, to inheritance, 139-43
blostering process of, 287-98
convergence of continuity and change in, 120-22
as decisionmaking tool, 20
definition of, 91
existence of generally accepted standards for, 81
flexibility of, 97
and the future, 4, 6-7, 11-15, 87-88, 181
goals of, 83-84

hinge function of, 253-55
history of, in U.S., 4-11
judging quality of, 81-82
long-range hopes for, 14-15
need of, to determine appropriate sources of knowledge and political power, 111-16
neighborhood planning in, 111
organization of, 263-65, 295-97
process considerations of, 215-18
purpose of, 3, 7, 14
role of expert in, 114-15
role of federal government in, 7-8
scope of incremental activities in, 255-57
shift to new paradigm in, 10, 91-93, 159-60, 176-77, 263, 273, 287-88
subject matter of, 82
time dimension of, 51, 87-88, 125, 133, 162, 163-77, 189-98, 274-77
top-down versus bottom-up, 111
tools and execution of, 84-87
transactive planning as, 112
use of advocacy planning in, 111
use of accounts and plans in, 246-50
use of land-use maps in, 246-47
value of planning-oriented approach in, 123-26, 134
Walker concept of, 263
weaknesses of, 115

Urban planner
coalition of, with social reformers, 6
education and recruitment of, 165-69
lack of foresight in early, 7
need for creativity in, 292
role of, 105, 114
Urban renewal, 5-6, 129n, 134, 256
Urban stabilization of decline, 273
Urban system
comprehension of, 160-62
conception of, as basis for paradigm, 160
improvements in, 172-74
information needed for, 163-77
opportunities and possibilities for, 175-76
special problems and difficulties of, 174-75
Urban system analysis, 114
Urban system goals, 220, 221-26, 289
Urban transformation, 15-19, 173, 174, 182, 212, 235, 271-72
Urban village, 67-71, 84

Walker concept of planning, 263
Welfare, 169-71
Work force, changing structure of, 15-17
Zoning, 6, 12, 13, 113, 185, 224, 295